I dedicate this book to Christine and to God, my Creator

Easy party treats
for children

Janette Mocke

Published in 2012 by Struik Lifestyle
(an imprint of Random House Struik (Pty) Ltd)
Company Reg. No. 1966/003153/07
Wembley Square, Solan Street, Cape Town 8001, South Africa
PO Box 1144, Cape Town 8000, South Africa
www.randomstruik.co.za
Reprinted in 2013

Copyright © in published edition: Random House Struik (Pty) Ltd 2012
Copyright © in text: Janette Mocke 2012
Copyright © in photographs: Random House Struik (Pty) Ltd 2012

ISBN 978 177007 994 6

All rights reserved. No part of this publication may be reproduced, stored in a retrieval system or transmitted, in any form or by any means, electronic, digital, mechanical, photocopying, recording or otherwise, without the prior written permission of the publishers and the copyright owner(s).

Publisher: Linda de Villiers
Managing editor: Cecilia Barfield
Editor: Gill Gordon
Design manager: Beverley Dodd
Designers: Monique Oberholzer, Helen Henn
Photographer: Ryno
Stylist: Brita du Plessis
Proofreader: Glynne Newlands

Reproduction by Hirt & Carter Cape (Pty) Ltd
Printing and binding by Times Offset (M) Sdn Bhd, Malaysia

Also available in Afrikaans as *Maklike Soet Happies*
ISBN 978 177007 995 3

All the party treats in this book were made by Janette Mocke
www.supacakes.co.za

Introduction 5

Basic recipes 6

Vehicles, planes and trains 14

Cars, aeroplanes and boats are simple to prepare using sweets and a few biscuits.

Love treats 24

Chocolate, chocolate, chocolate! Perfect for teens, or for the special people in your life.

Princesses and tea parties 32

Cute ideas for the princess party every little girl dreams of.

Animals 46

From frogs and snails to beetles and butterflies; a range of amazing animals to eat!

Little figures 60

Thread assorted sweets onto a skewer to create a cast of wonderful characters.

Aliens and creepy crawlies 70

Robots, aliens and creepy critters make up these interesting snacks.

Cone figures 78

Quick easy figures using ice-cream cones and sweets.

Marshmallows 92

Marshmallow kebabs, marshmallow and jelly bean animals, and a few other ideas.

Marie biscuits 104

Just look at what can be done with a Marie biscuit!

Rice Krispies 122

Crunchy treats made from this popular cereal.

Miscellaneous 132

Suitable for a variety of party themes.

Index 142

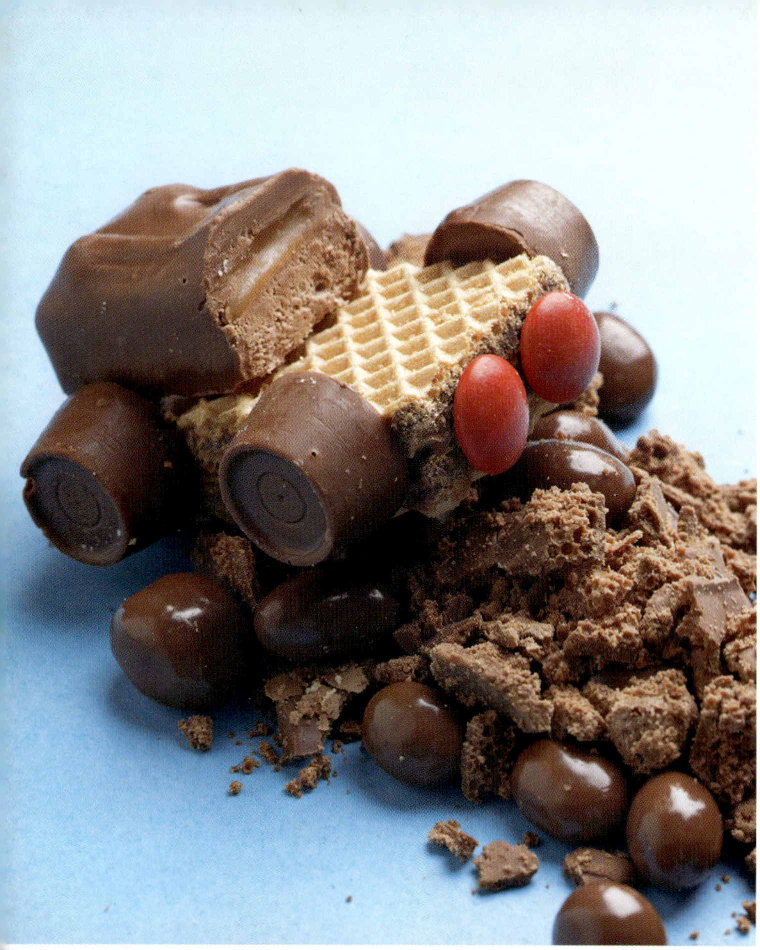
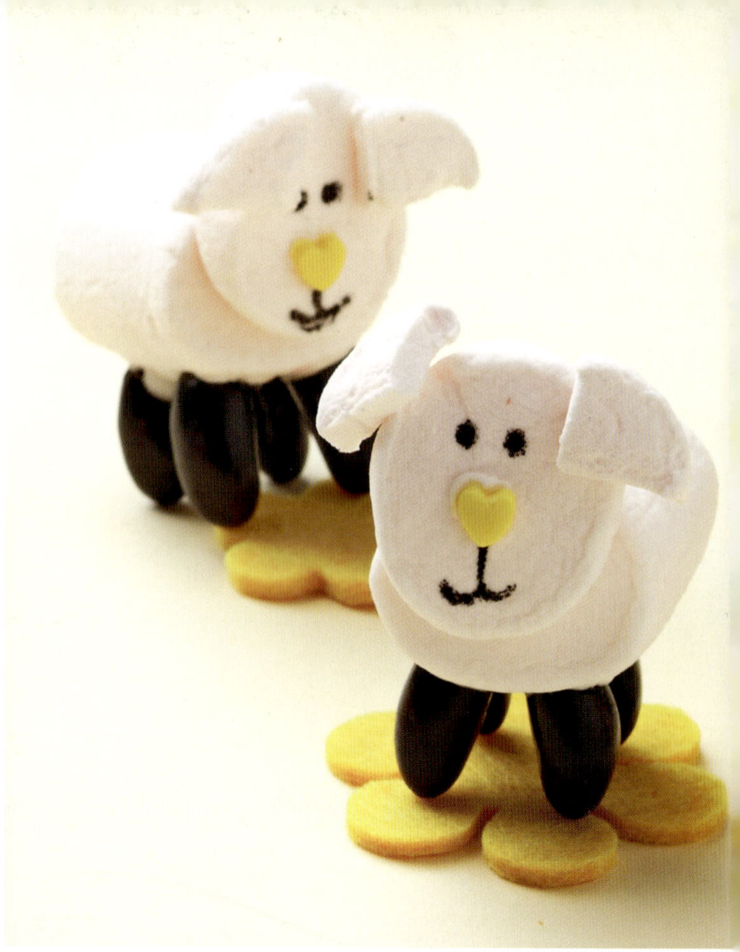
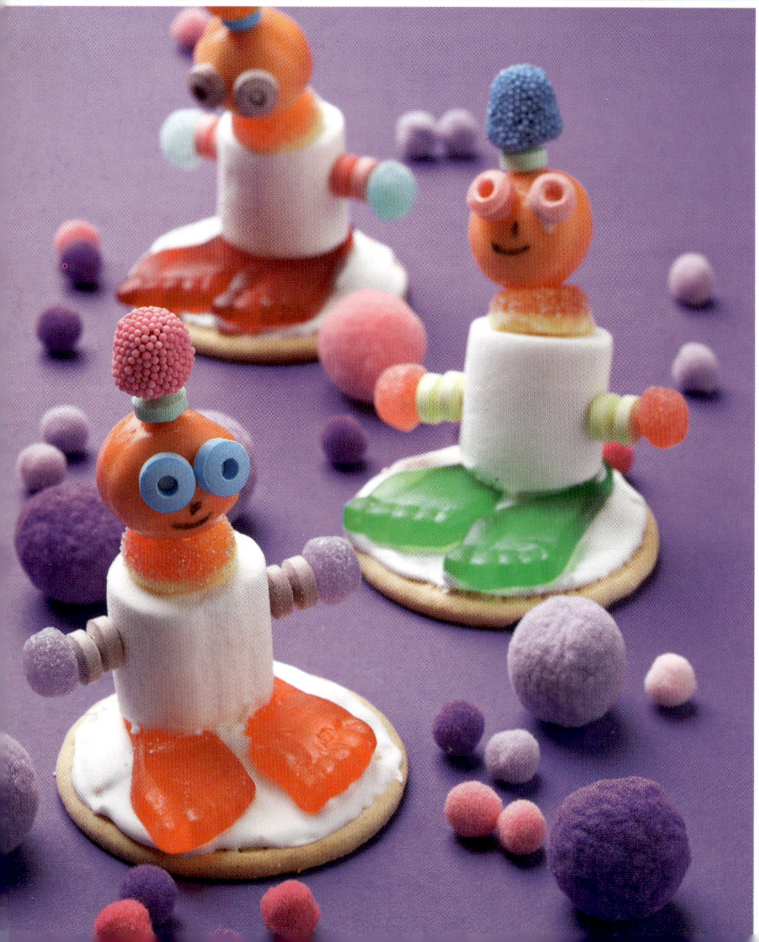
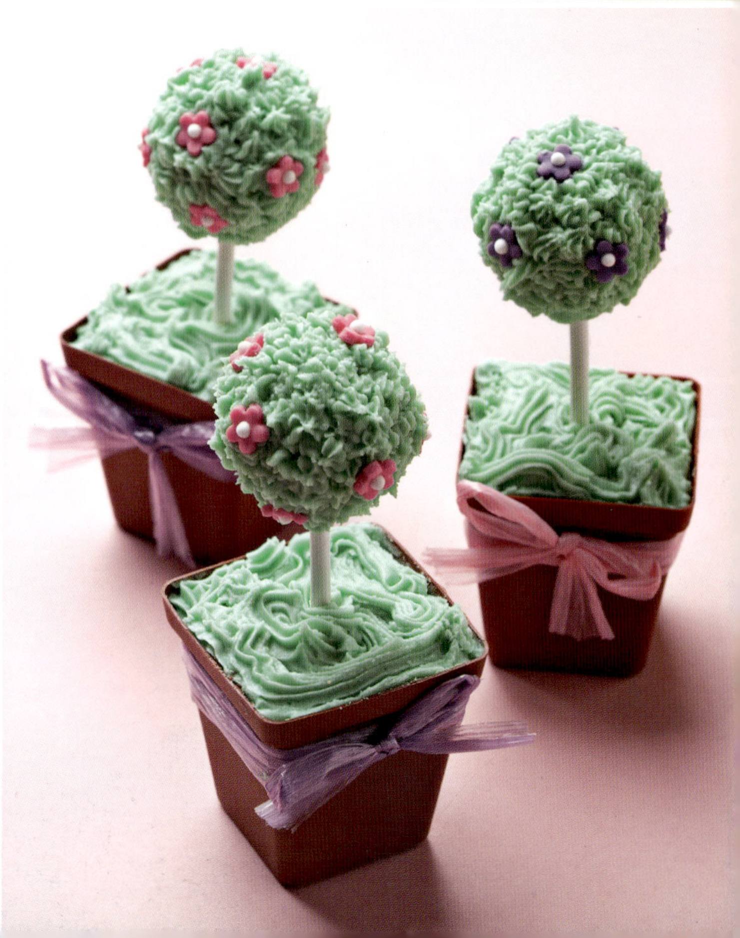

Introduction

Do you want to turn your child's party into an exciting event that will be the topic of playground conversation for a long time to come? Do you find that school holidays are often too long and your kids run out of things to do? Or are you looking for something to get your creative juices flowing? *Easy Party Treats for Children* is the solution!

First, you need to choose a theme. There are so many to choose from; I've chosen princesses, aliens, creepy crawlies, and vehicles. Once you've decided on a theme, turn to the applicable chapter to find out how to make a variety of treats to suit your theme. In addition, there are chapters featuring treats made from readily available ingredients, such as ice-cream cones, marshmallows, Rice Krispies and Marie biscuits, that can be adapted to suit any theme.

All children love sweet treats, especially at parties and, with *Easy party treats for children*, you'll find that preparing for a party is a breeze. It doesn't matter if you are a mother, father, grandmother, grandfather, aunt, uncle or teacher – you will find something to use in this book. And, what's more, even the kids will want to join in and help make the treats!

Enjoy!
Janette Mocke

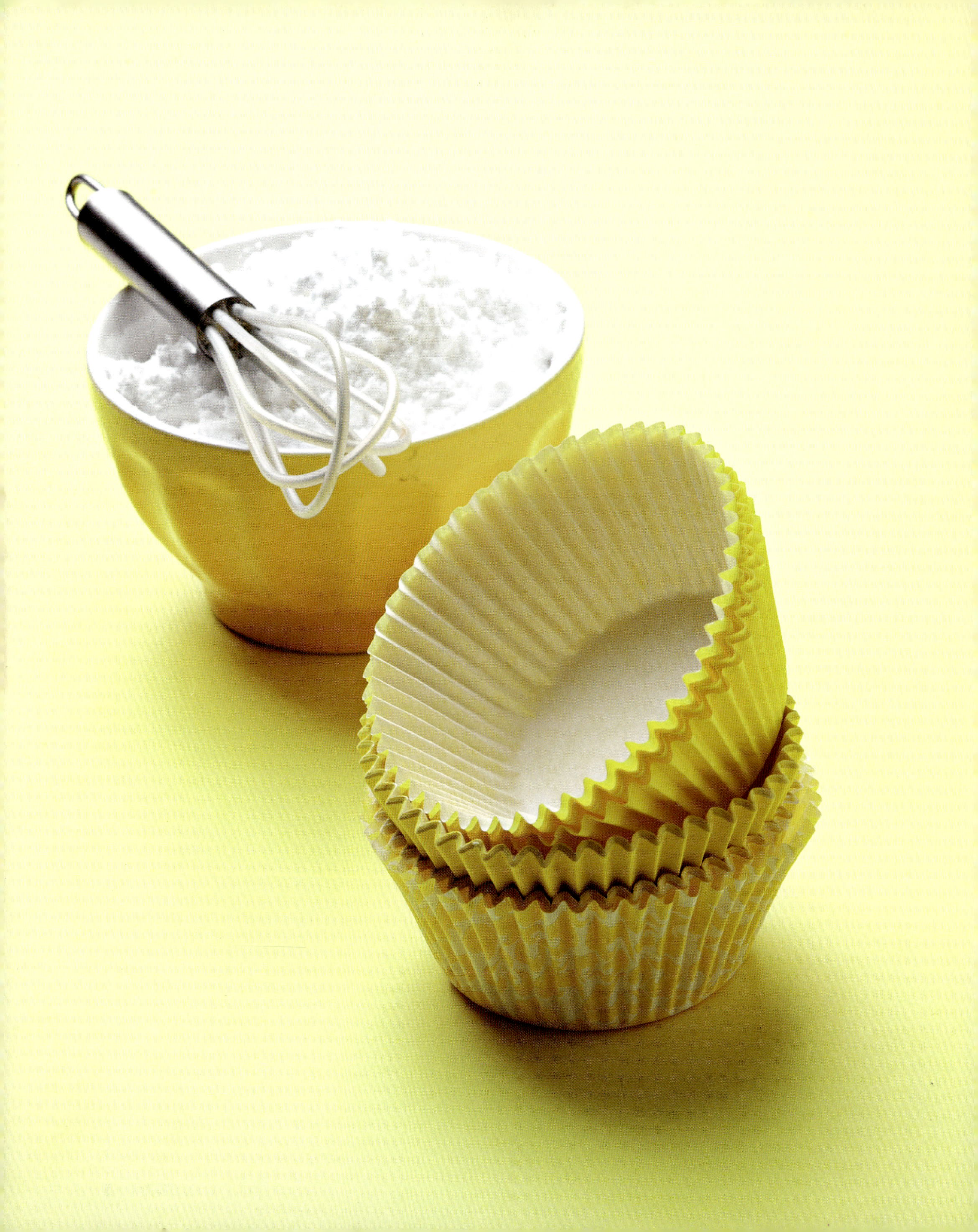

Basic recipes

Butter icing

500g icing sugar, sifted
100g butter or block margarine, at room temperature
30ml hot water
2.5ml vanilla essence
food colouring (optional)

Cream the icing sugar and butter (or margarine) together.
Gradually add the hot water and mix to a smooth consistency (do not overmix, or the icing will become runny). Mix in the vanilla essence.

To colour ready-mixed icing, use a few drops of liquid colouring or powdered food colouring, which is available from speciality baking shops.

Glacé icing

250ml icing sugar
about 30ml hot water
2ml essence of your choice
food colouring (optional)

Sift the icing sugar.
Add the remaining ingredients and mix until very smooth and runny.
Add one or two drops of colouring at a time, until the desired shade is obtained.

Royal icing

750ml icing sugar
2 extra-large egg whites
5ml lemon juice

Sift the icing sugar.
Whisk the egg whites until foamy, then add the icing sugar, one spoonful at a time.
Add the lemon juice midway and continue to add the icing sugar, while beating or whisking to the desired consistency.
Cover the icing until needed, to prevent it from drying out.

Coloured chocolate

white chocolate
powdered oil-based food colouring

Microwave the white chocolate for a few minutes, stirring often, until melted.
Carefully add the food colouring, a little at a time, mixing it in very well each time until the chocolate is the desired colour.

Tip: Powdered food colouring is available from specialist baking stores.

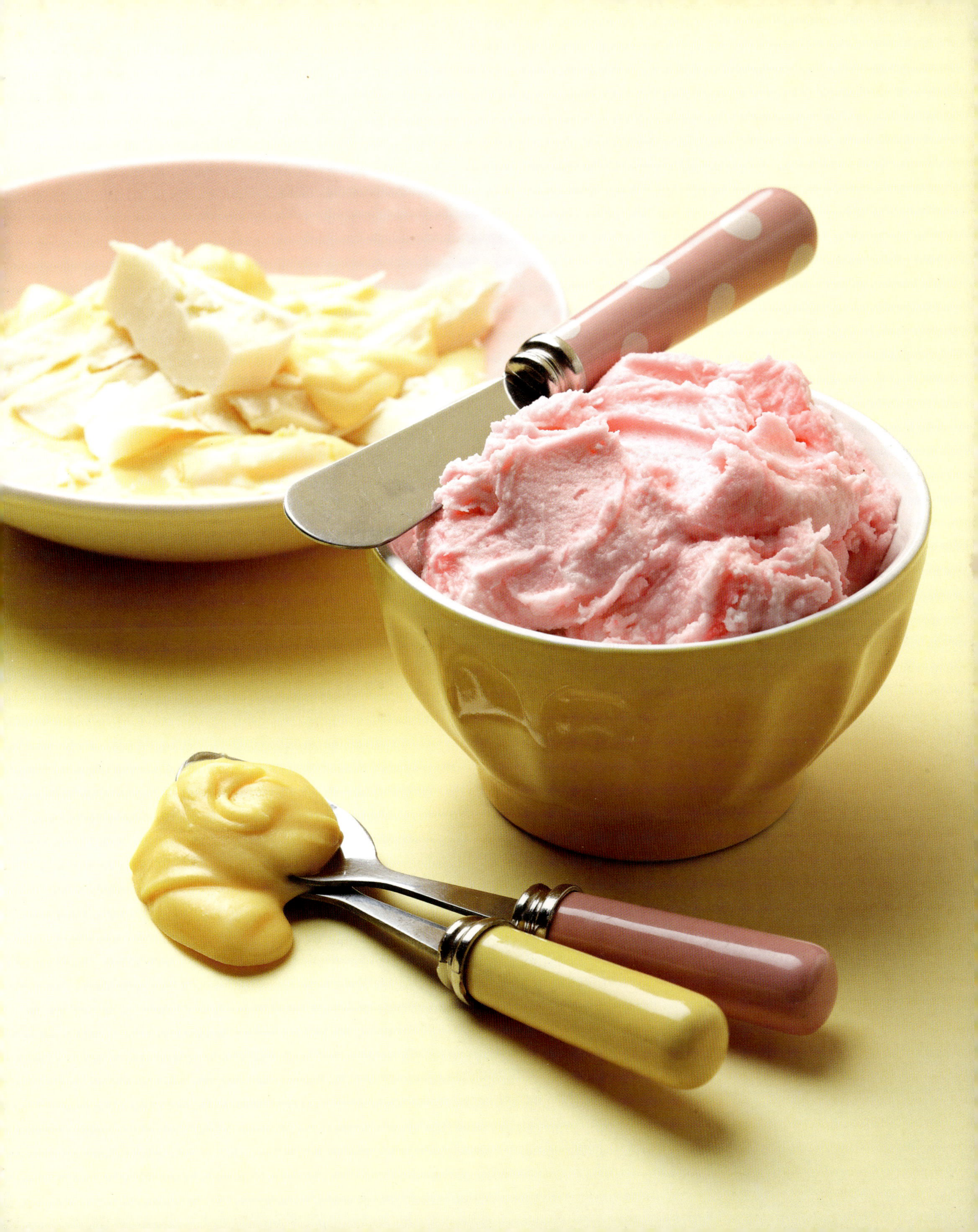

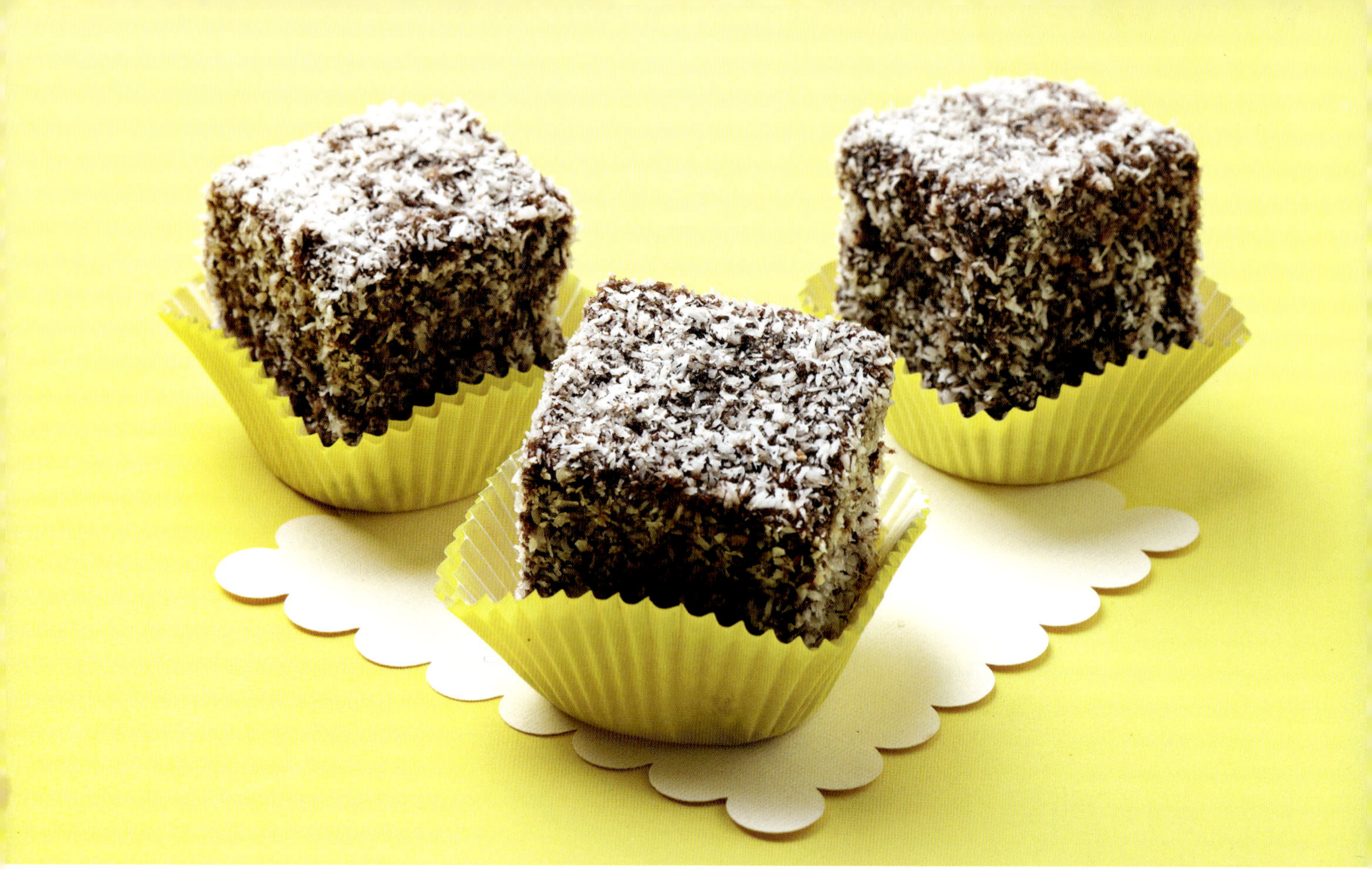

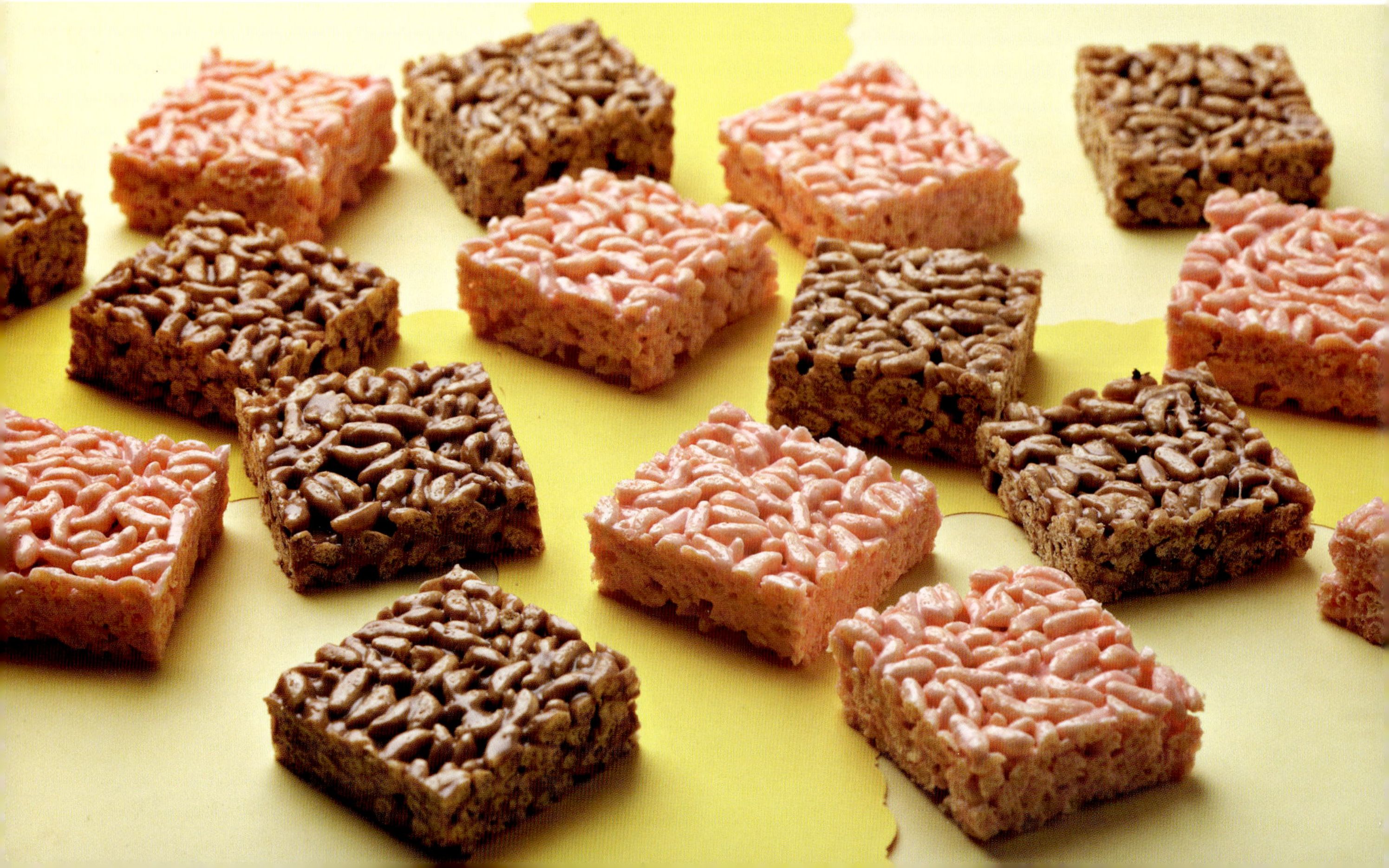

Lamingtons

4 extra large eggs
375ml castor sugar
250g butter or margarine
750ml cake flour
10ml baking powder
5ml cream of tartar
2ml salt
250ml milk
5ml vanilla essence

CHOCOLATE SAUCE
500ml sugar
125ml icing sugar
80ml cocoa
250ml water
45ml butter

200g packet desiccated coconut

Preheat the oven to 180°C.
Beat the eggs and castor sugar together.
Melt the butter and add to the mixture, beating well.

Sift the flour, baking powder, cream of tartar and salt together and fold alternately with the milk and vanilla essence into the butter mixture.
Spoon into a greased baking pan (34 x 24cm) and bake for 15–20 minutes.
Allow to cool and cut into squares.

Chocolate sauce:
Place all the ingredients into a saucepan and heat to boiling point.

Using a fork or kitchen tongs, dip squares of cake into the chocolate sauce and then roll in the coconut. Place on a wire rack until set.

Rice Krispies squares

30ml margarine
35 pink marshmallows
300ml Rice Krispies

Microwave the margarine in a large bowl for 1 minute.
Add the marshmallows and microwave for a further 3 minutes.
Add the Rice Krispies and mix well.
Press the mixture into a 20 x 20cm baking pan and allow to cool.
Cut into squares or use as required (see pages 122–131).

Chocolate Rice Krispies squares

30ml margarine
35 white marshmallows
100g milk chocolate, broken into pieces
300ml Rice Krispies

Microwave the margarine in a large bowl for 1 minute.
Add the marshmallows and milk chocolate and microwave for ± 3 minutes.
Add the Rice Krispies and mix well.
Press into a 20 x 20cm baking pan and allow to cool.
Cut into squares or use as required (see pages 122–131).

Basic butter biscuits

125g butter
125ml castor sugar
5ml vanilla essence
1 large egg, lightly beaten
500ml cake flour
60ml cornflour
5ml baking powder
pinch of salt

Preheat the oven to 180°C.

In a large bowl, cream the butter and castor sugar together until light and fluffy.
Add the vanilla essence and egg to the mixture.

Combine the dry ingredients, mix in lightly and knead to a firm dough.
Dust your working surface with flour. Roll out the dough to 4mm thick and use a cookie cutter to cut out rounds (or your chosen shapes).

Grease a baking pan, arrange the biscuits and bake for 10–12 minutes until golden brown. Let the biscuits cool completely before decorating.

Fridge brownies

250g butter or margarine, cubed
500g icing sugar
100ml cocoa powder
2 eggs, lightly beaten
Marie biscuits (2 x 200g packets)

In a large bowl, microwave the butter or margarine for ± 1½ minutes or until melted.
Sift the icing sugar and cocoa powder together and stir into the melted butter.
Fold the eggs into the mixture and microwave for ± 3 minutes.
Break the Marie biscuits into pieces and combine with the chocolate mixture.
Spoon into a 20 x 20cm baking pan and leave to cool.
Place in the fridge to set, then cut into squares or shapes, as required.

Coconut ice

1 can condensed milk
500g icing sugar
400g desiccated coconut
pink food colouring

In a bowl, combine the condensed milk, icing sugar, desiccated coconut and a drop or two of food colouring.
Press the mixture into a 20 x 20cm baking pan.
Leave to set before cutting into squares or shapes, as required.

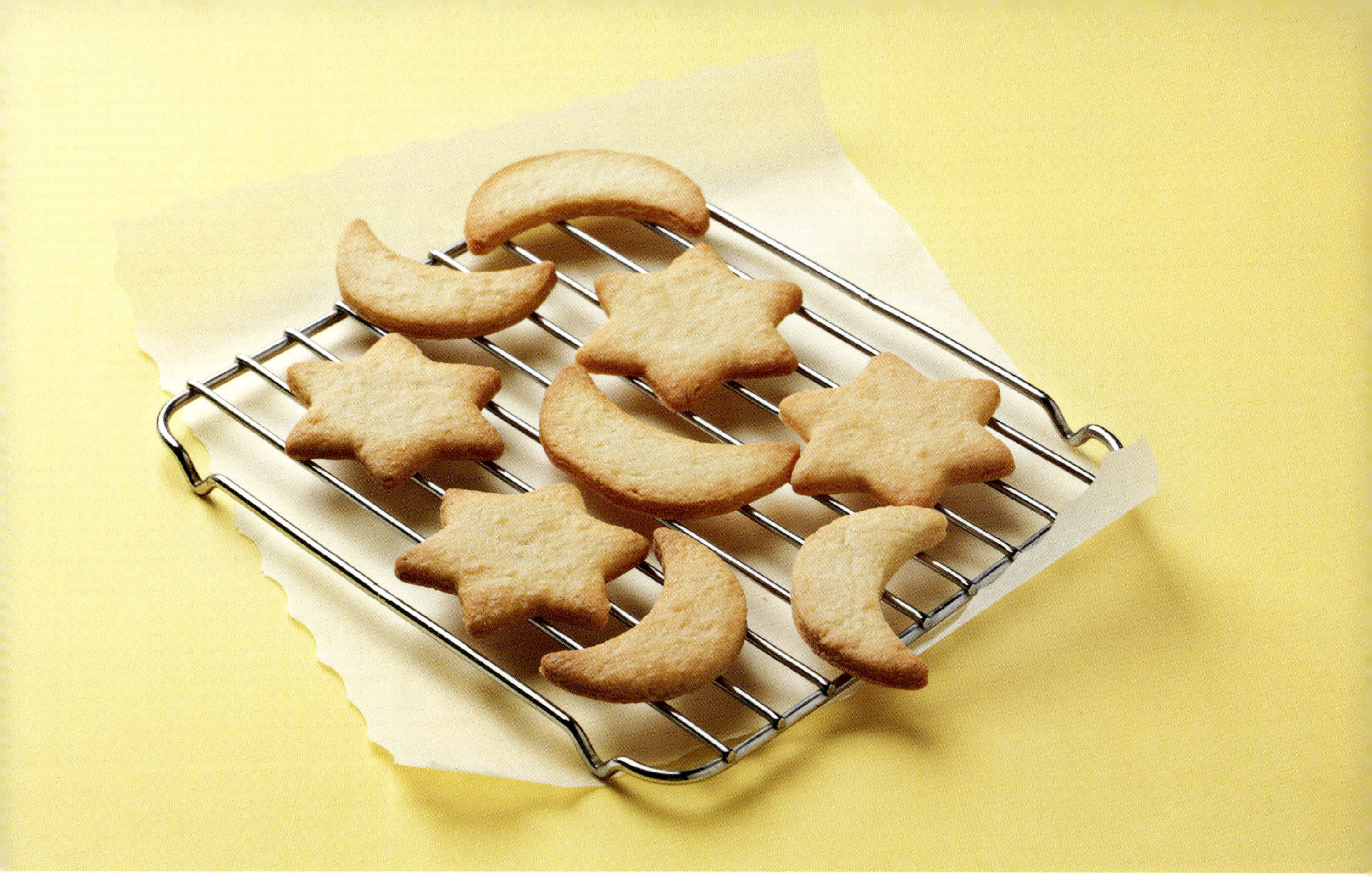

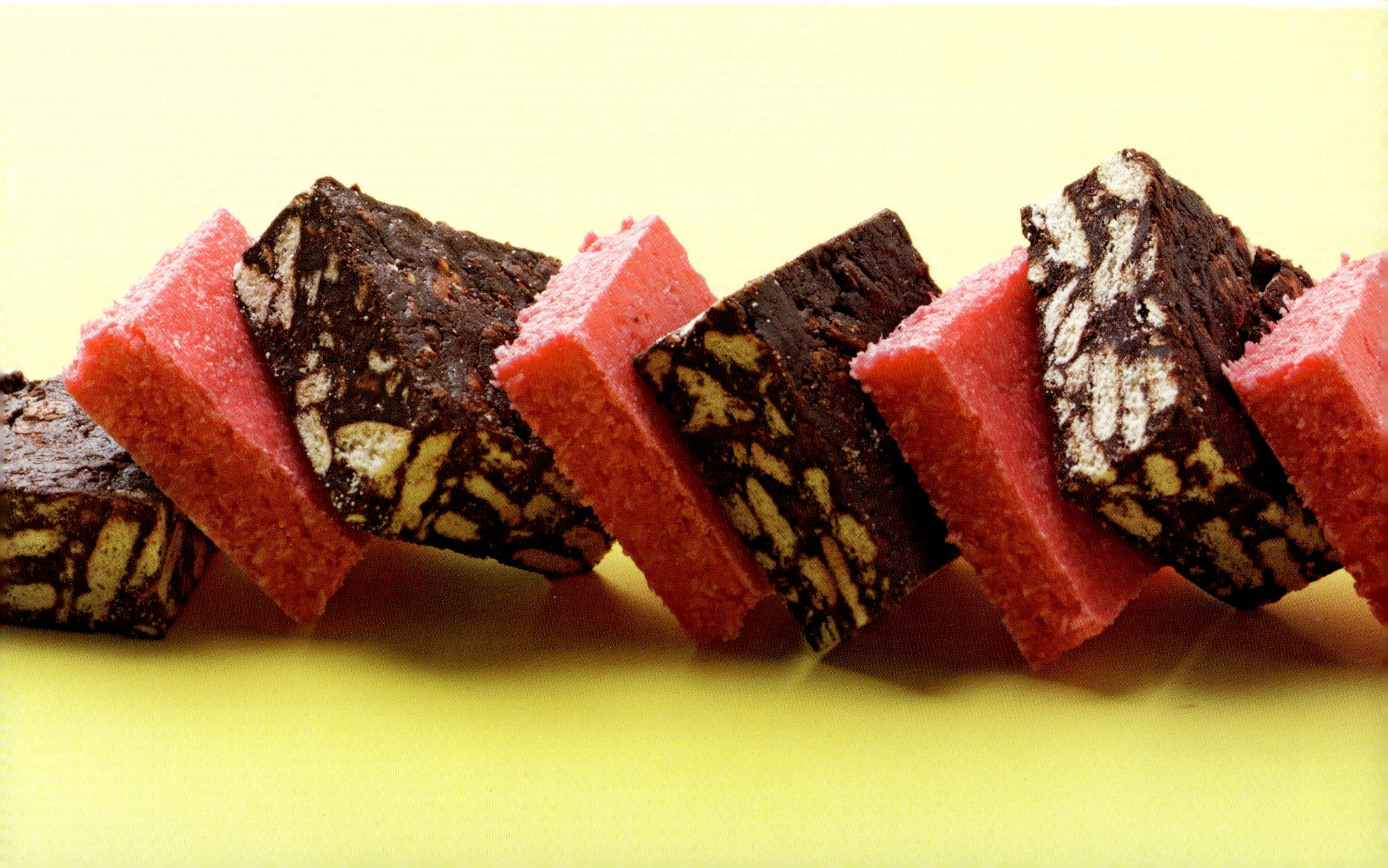

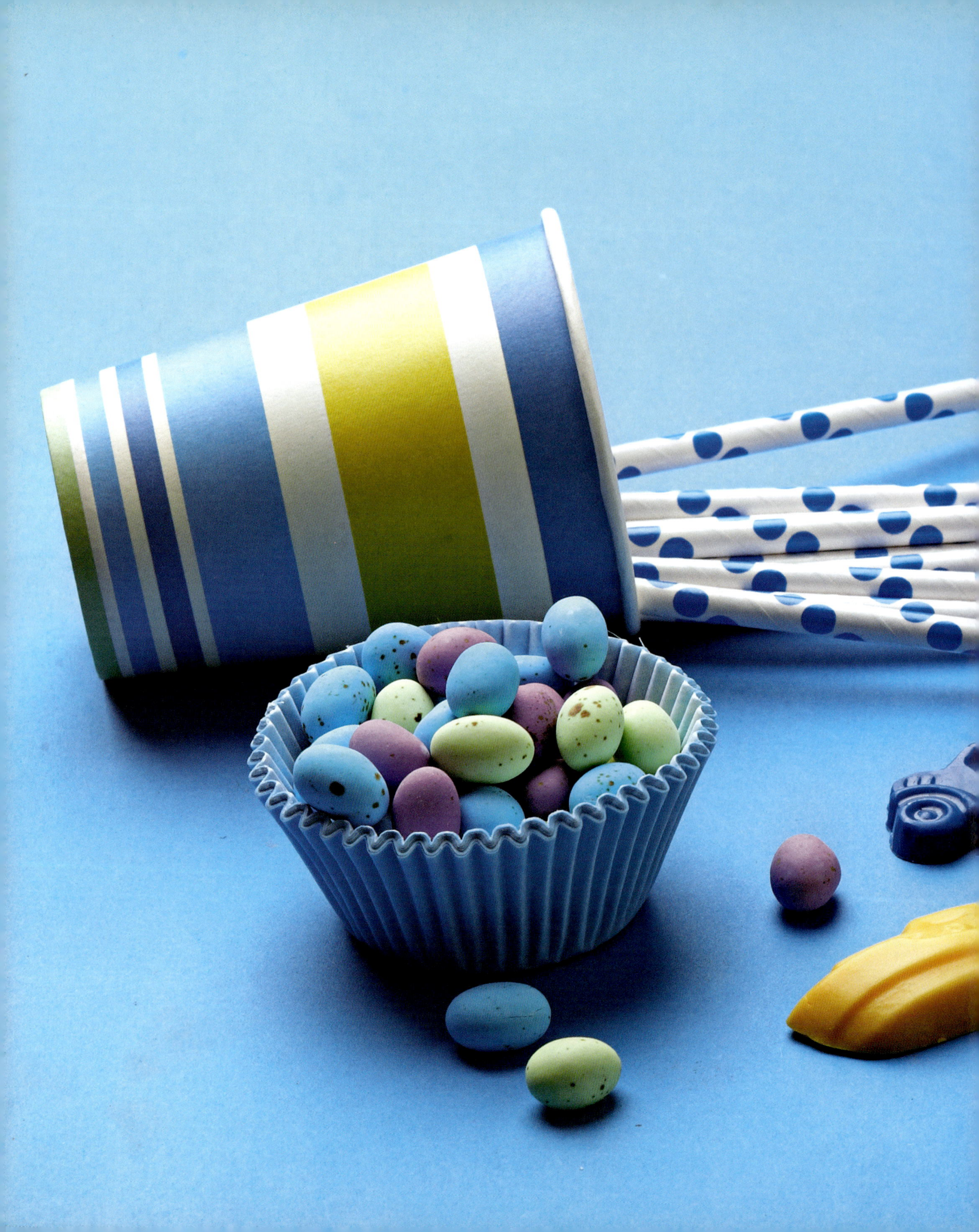

Vehicles, planes and trains

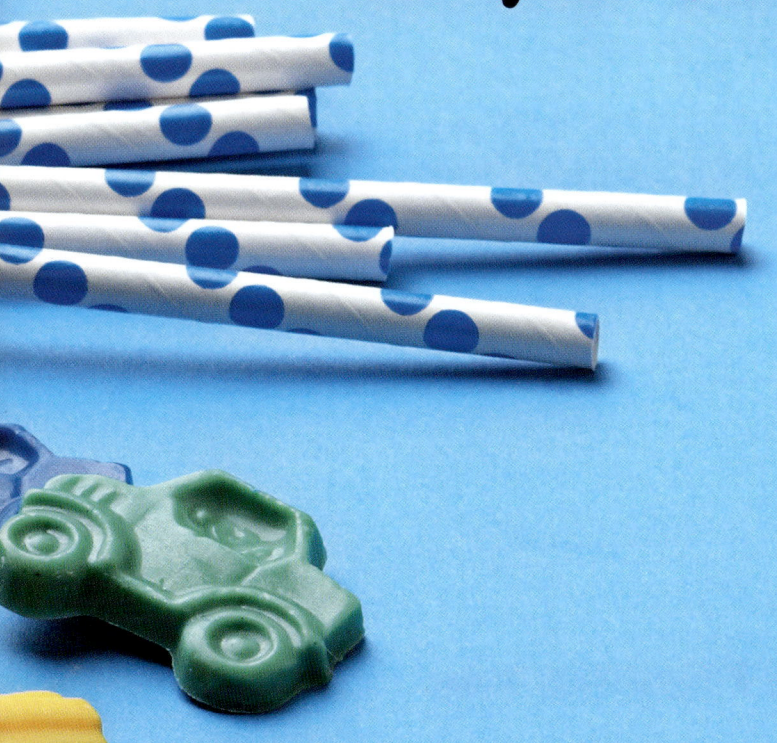

Lamington train

9 lamington squares (page 11, or store-bought)
glacé icing (page 8)
liquorice strips
round sweets for the wheels
2 sugared jelly rings
2 dome-shaped sugared jelly sweets
variety of small sweets

1 rectangular cake board

Use 3 lamington squares to form the locomotive. Use glacé icing to stick 2 lamington squares together, and stick another one on top of the back square. Place the locomotive on the cake board (use glacé icing to secure it).

Cut a square out of the top lamington, leaving a 1cm edge all round. Do the same with the remaining 6 squares, to form the carriages of the train.

Cut the liquorice strips into pieces ± 3cm long. Press one end of a piece of liquorice into the back of the lamington locomotive and press the other end into another lamington, so it appears as if the train carriage is hooked to the locomotive. Repeat with the rest of the lamingtons to form the train.

Using a little glacé icing, stick the round sweets to the lamingtons, so they resemble the wheels of the train. Stick 2 sugared jelly rings at the front of the locomotive and place 2 dome-shaped sugared jelly sweets on top of the jelly rings, to form the funnels.

Finally, place a variety of small sweets on the locomotive and carriages.

MAKES 1 TRAIN

Tractors

40 mini Marie biscuits
glacé icing (page 8)
10 small Chomps or chocolate wafer biscuits
10 Tennis biscuits
10 marshmallows
20 filled round biscuits
10 Jelly Babies
10 liquorice pieces

Using glacé icing, stick the mini Marie biscuits together in twos, and leave to set.

Stick a small Chomp in the centre of each Tennis biscuit. Then stick a marshmallow on top of one end of the Chomp.

Stick the filled round biscuits at the back of the Tennis biscuit and the mini Marie biscuits at the front, to form the wheels.

Stick a Jelly Baby 'driver' to the front of the marshmallow.

Stick a piece of liquorice at the front of the Chomp, to form the tractor's funnel.

Set aside until the icing sets.

MAKES 10

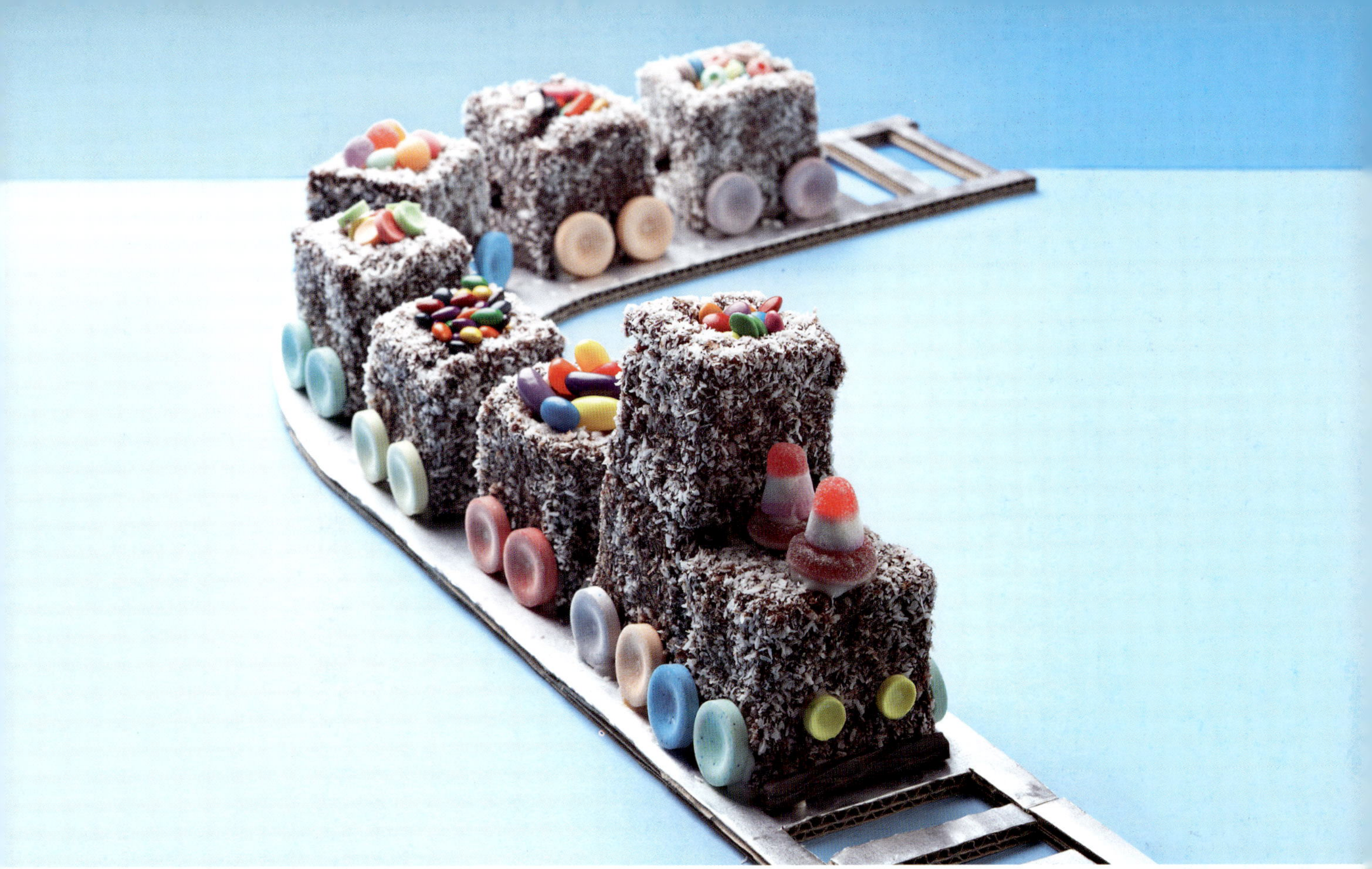

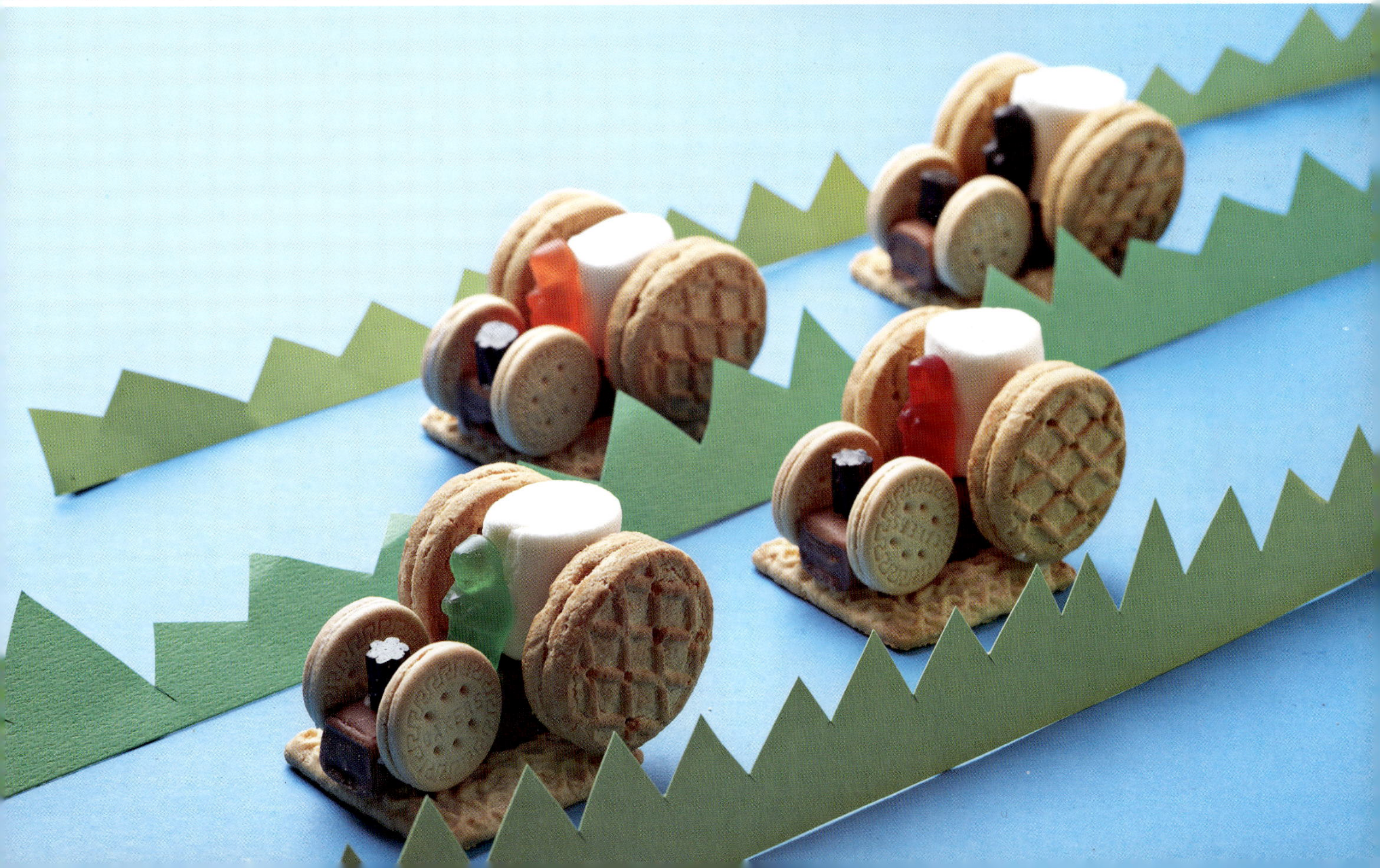

Marshmallow trains

10 rectangular wafer biscuits, cut in half
glacé icing (page 8)
10 whole wafer biscuits
20 marshmallows
30 small round flat sweets
40 round flat sweets

Using glacé icing, stick half a wafer biscuit to one end of a whole biscuit.
Stick 1 marshmallow upright on the half biscuit, and another half biscuit on top of the marshmallow.

Stick the other marshmallow on its side at the front of the whole wafer biscuit.
Stick 2 small sweets to the front of the marshmallow, for the headlights, and 1 on top, for the funnel.

Stick 4 large round sweets to the sides of the biscuit, for the wheels.

Leave to stand until the icing sets.

MAKES 10

Sports cars

10 finger biscuits
glacé icing (page 8)
20 Smarties
20 large round sweets
10 Jelly Babies

Using small amounts of glacé icing, stick 2 Smarties to the front sides of the finger biscuit and 2 large round sweets to the back, for the front and back wheels.

Cut the Jelly Baby in half and stick the upper body on top of the finger biscuit, so it looks like the driver sitting in the open cab.

Leave to stand until the icing sets.

MAKES 10

F1 cars

10 finger biscuits
20 cocktail sticks
20 mini round Allsorts
20 large round Allsorts
5 square Allsorts
glacé icing (page 8)
5 rectangular wafer biscuits
10 Jelly Babies

Push cocktail sticks through the front and back of the finger biscuit. Skewer 2 round mini Allsorts onto the cocktail sticks at the front, and 2 large round Allsorts to the back, to form the wheels.

Cut the square Allsorts diagonally in half to form 2 triangles. Use glacé icing to stick 1 triangle to the back of the finger biscuit. Cut the wafer biscuit in half lengthwise and stick one half on top of the Allsorts triangle, to form the spoiler of the car.

Cut the Jelly Baby in half. Use glacé icing to stick the upper body to the finger biscuit, in front of the spoiler.

Leave to stand until the icing sets.

MAKES 10

VEHICLES, PLANES AND TRAINS

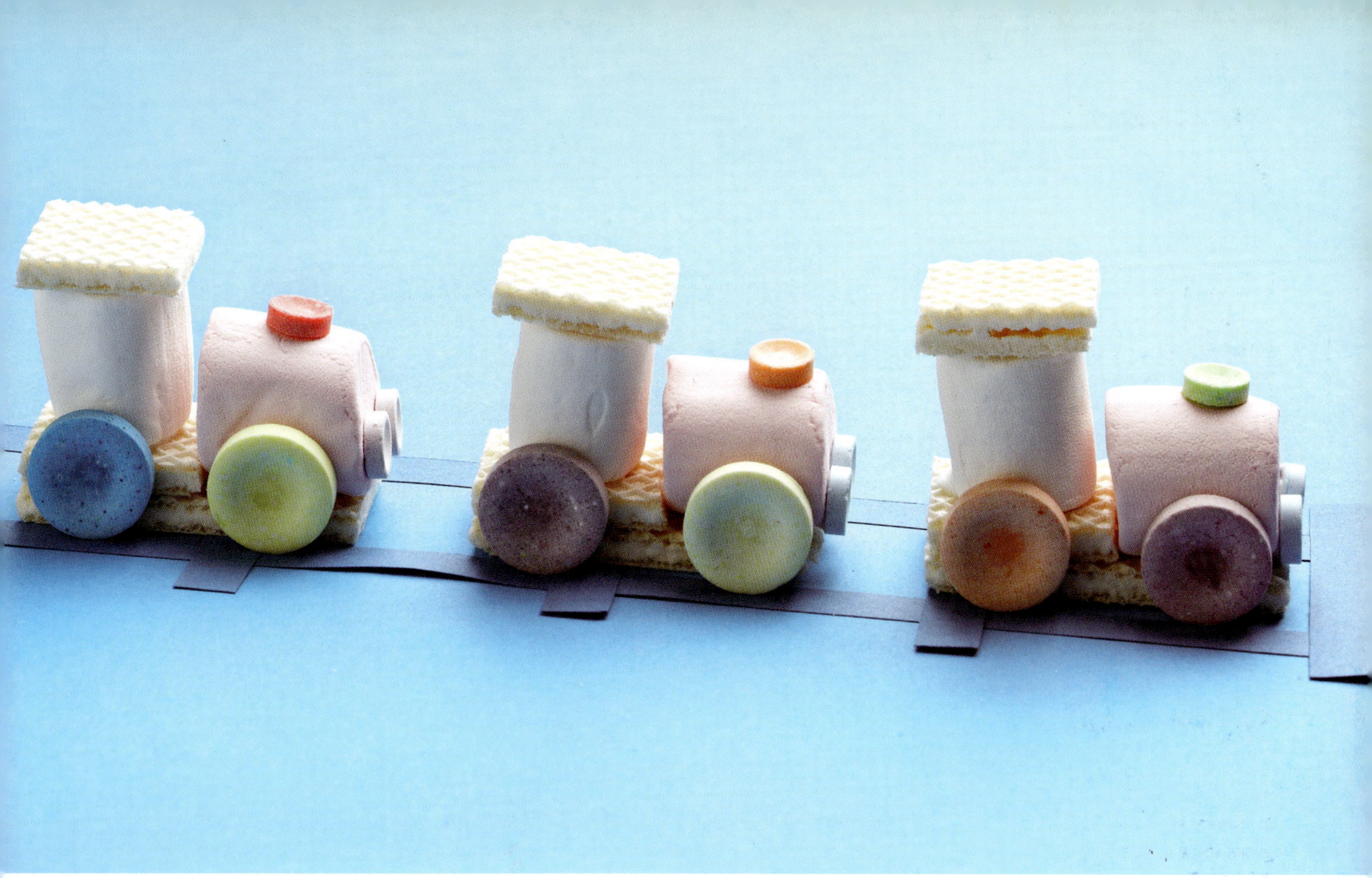

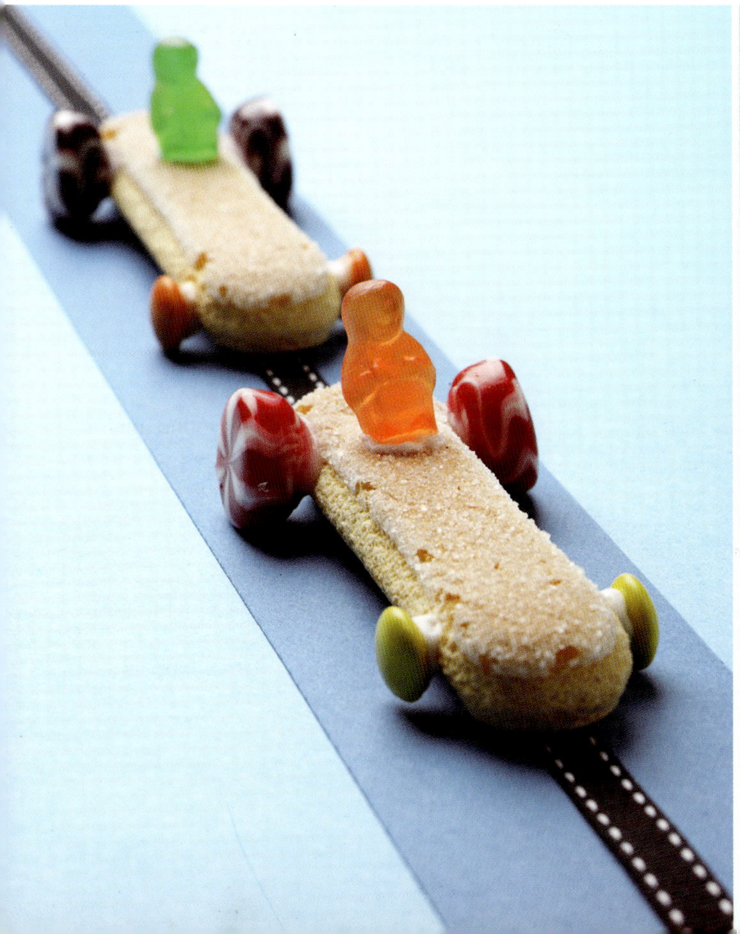

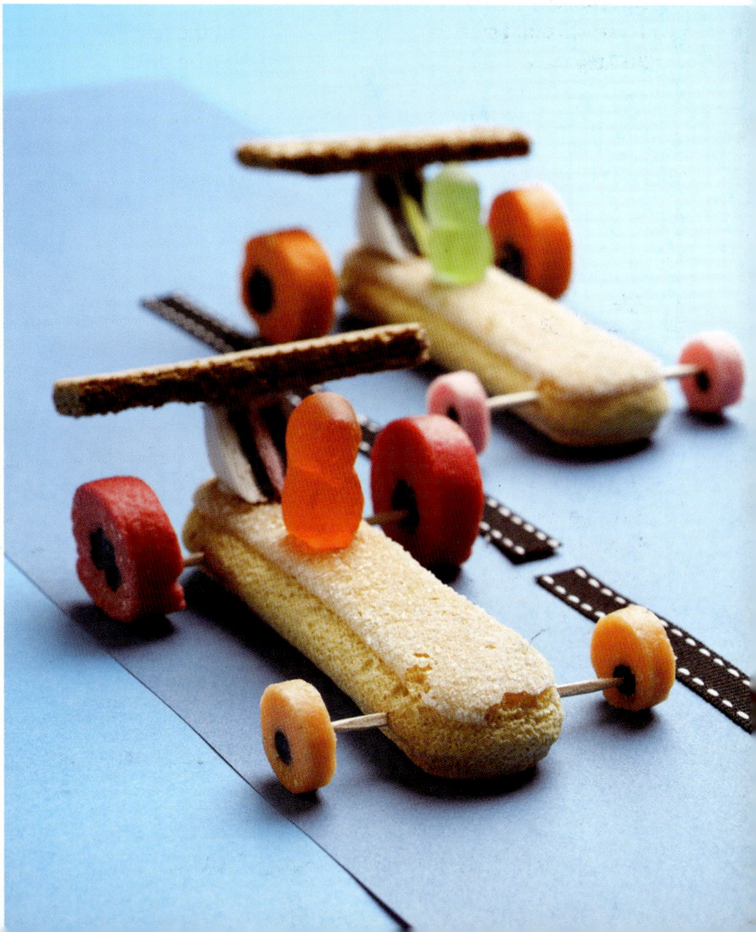

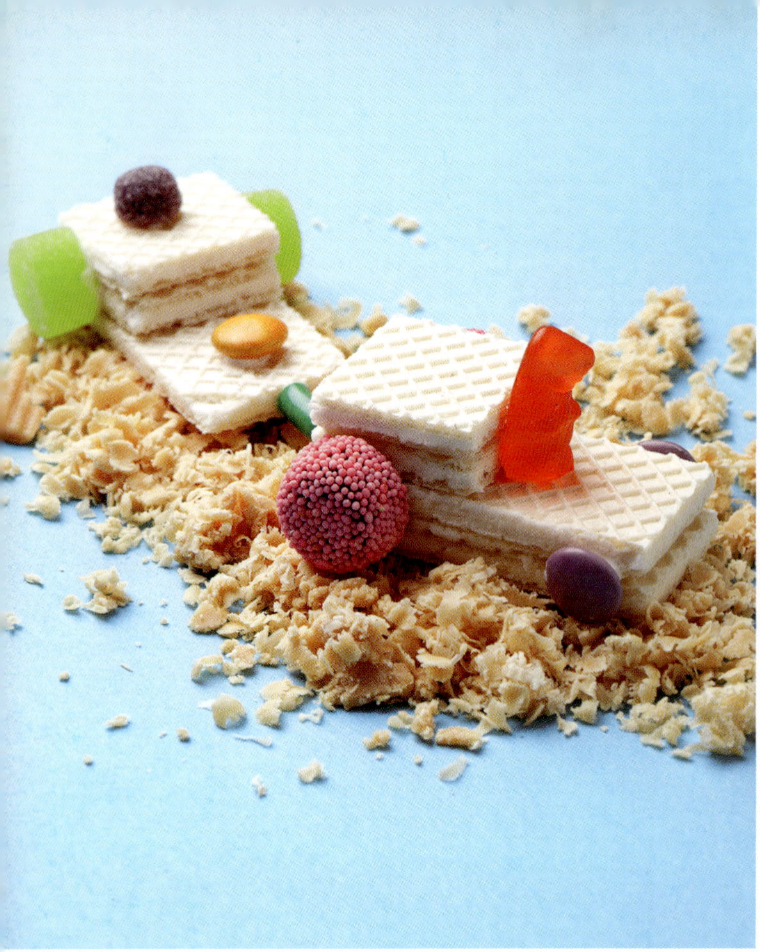
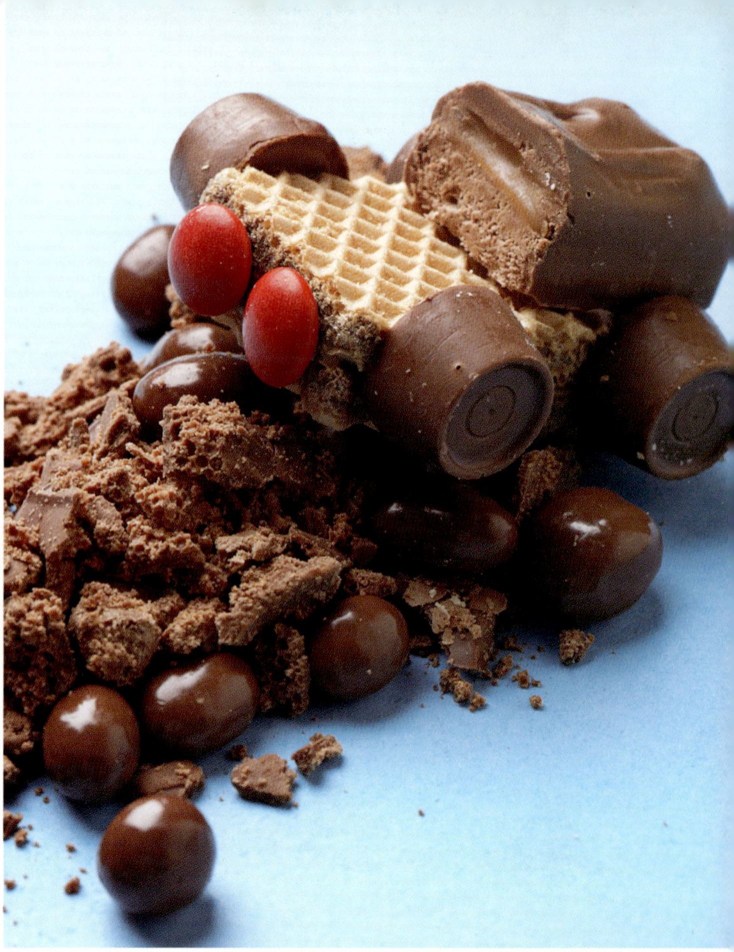
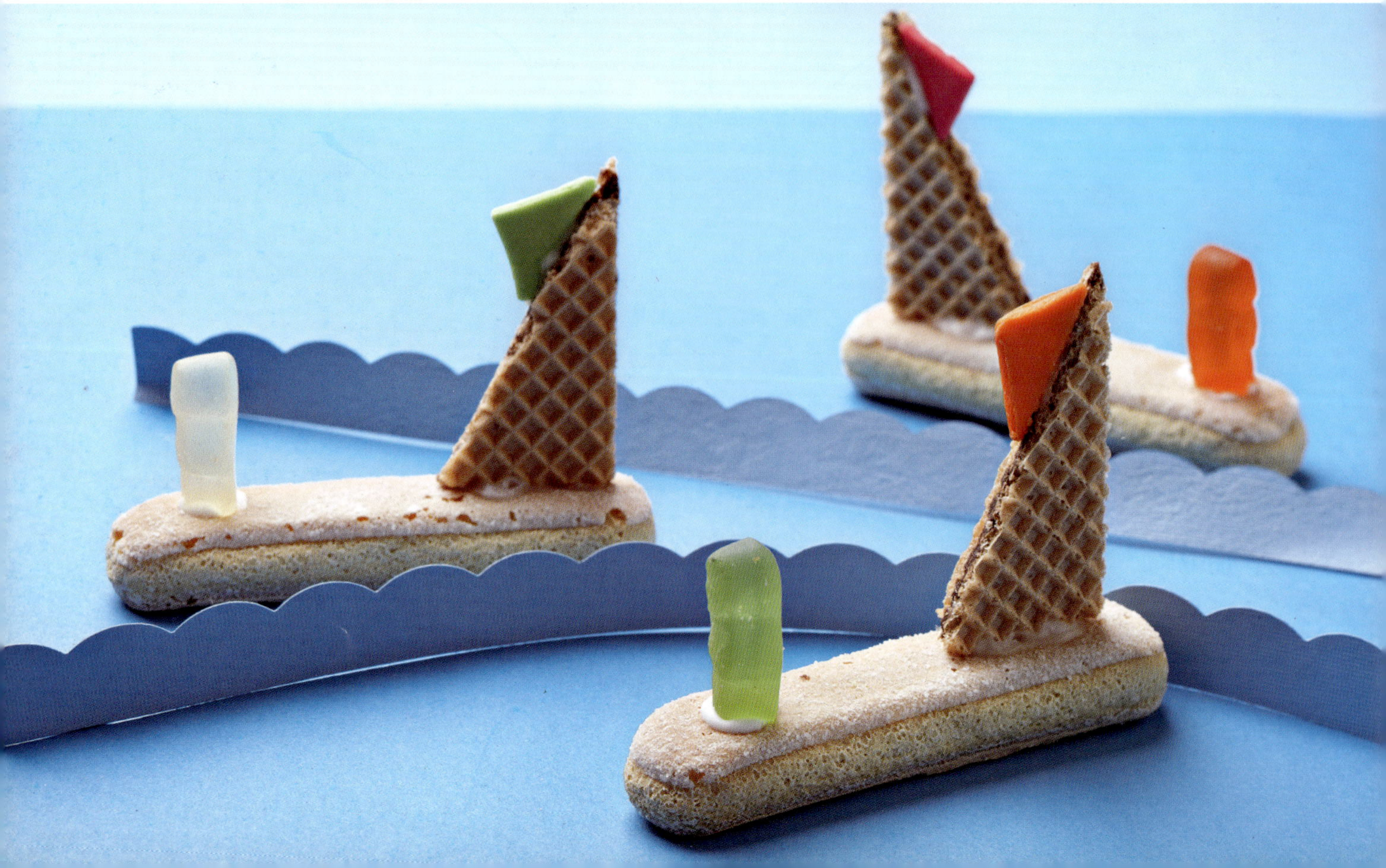

Jeep with trailer

JEEP
20 rectangular wafer biscuits
glacé icing (page 8)
10 wafer biscuits (cut in two)
20 large round sweets
20 Smarties
20 Jelly Babies
10 small ring-shaped sweets

TRAILER
10 wafer biscuits (cut in two)
glacé icing (page 8)
10 whole wafer biscuits
20 round sweets
10 Smarties
10 Jelly Tots
10 oblong liquorice sweets

For the jeep: Stack 2 whole wafer biscuits on top of each other, securing them with glacé icing. Then stack 2 half wafer biscuits on top of each other, and place them on the back of the whole biscuit, to form the cab.

For the wheels, stick 2 large round sweets to the back of the biscuit and 2 Smarties to the front, using glacé icing. Cut the Jelly Baby in half and use glacé icing to position the upper body in front of the cab. Finally, stick a small ring-shaped sweet to the back of the jeep, for the towing hook.

For the trailer: Stack 2 wafer biscuit halves on top of each other, using glacé icing, and place this on the back of the whole biscuit. Use glacé icing to attach 2 round sweets, for the wheels. Add the Smartie and Jelly Tot as shown in the picture. Cut off one end of the oblong liquorice sweet and stick the sweet to the front of the trailer.

Leave to stand until the icing sets.

MAKES 10

Chocolate 4x4

50 g plain chocolate
20 chocolate wafer biscuits
40 Rolo chocolate toffees
20 Smarties
5 mini Bar One chocolates, cut in half

Melt the chocolate in the microwave, stirring often.

Using some melted chocolate, stick 2 wafer biscuits on top of one another. Stick 4 Rolo toffees to the sides of the wafer biscuits, for the wheels, and 2 Smarties to the front, for the lights.

Stick one half of a mini Bar One on top of the wafer biscuits, to form the cab.

Leave to stand until the chocolate sets.

MAKES 10

Sailboats

5 wafer biscuits (cut in half diagonally to form 10 triangles)
glacé icing (page 8)
10 finger biscuits
10 Jelly Babies
square Allsorts

Using glacé icing, stick 1 wafer biscuit triangle to one end of the finger biscuit, with the straight edge at the back, to form the mast and sail. Cut the Jelly Baby in half and stick the top half at the other end of the finger biscuit.

Separate the square Allsorts into layers. Cut the outer coloured layers into triangles, and use glacé icing to stick 1 triangle to the top of the wafer biscuit, for the flag.

Leave to stand until the icing sets.

MAKES 10

VEHICLES, PLANES AND TRAINS

Aeroplanes

10 rectangular wafer biscuits
glacé icing (page 8)
30 Smarties
10 finger biscuits
10 sugared jelly rings

Cut 5 of the wafer biscuits in half and cut the halves into triangles. Cut the other 5 wafer biscuits lengthwise in two. Using glacé icing, stick 3 Smarties on top of each long half. When the Smarties are secure, stick one long half on top of each finger biscuit, about one-third from the front, to form the wings.

Stick 1 triangular wafer biscuit at the other end of the finger biscuit, to form the tail of the plane.

Stick a sugared jelly ring to the front of the finger biscuit, to form the propeller. Leave to stand until the icing sets.

MAKES 10

Helicopters

10 edible cupcake cases
butter icing (page 8)
10 Marie biscuits
cake beads
10 Jelly Babies
25 rectangular wafer biscuits
± 60 Smarties

Using kitchen scissors, cut away about one quarter of the cupcake case. Fill an icing bag with butter icing and pipe a semicircle onto the Marie biscuit, then set the cupcake case on top (positioning the open side of the cupcake case where there is no icing). Press cake beads into the edges of the icing, for decoration.

Cut the Jelly Baby in half and use a little butter icing to stick the upper body to the Marie biscuit, inside the cupcake case opening.

Cut 2 wafer biscuits in half lengthwise. Stick 2 halves across each other on top of the cupcake case, to form the rotors. Stick the other 2 halves, on their sides, to the base of the Marie biscuit, to form the skids.

Cut 1 wafer biscuit in half diagonally and stick 1 triangle to the cupcake case to form the tail of the helicopter. Stick Smarties to the tail and the rotors as shown, for decoration. Leave to stand until the icing sets.

MAKES 10

Other ideas

- Look for sweets and chocolates shaped like trains, planes, cars or ships, or make your own by melting coloured chocolate (*see* page 8) and setting it in vehicle-shaped moulds. Use these as table decorations or offer them as extra treats.

- Pile round black sweets on top of one another, to resemble car tyres.

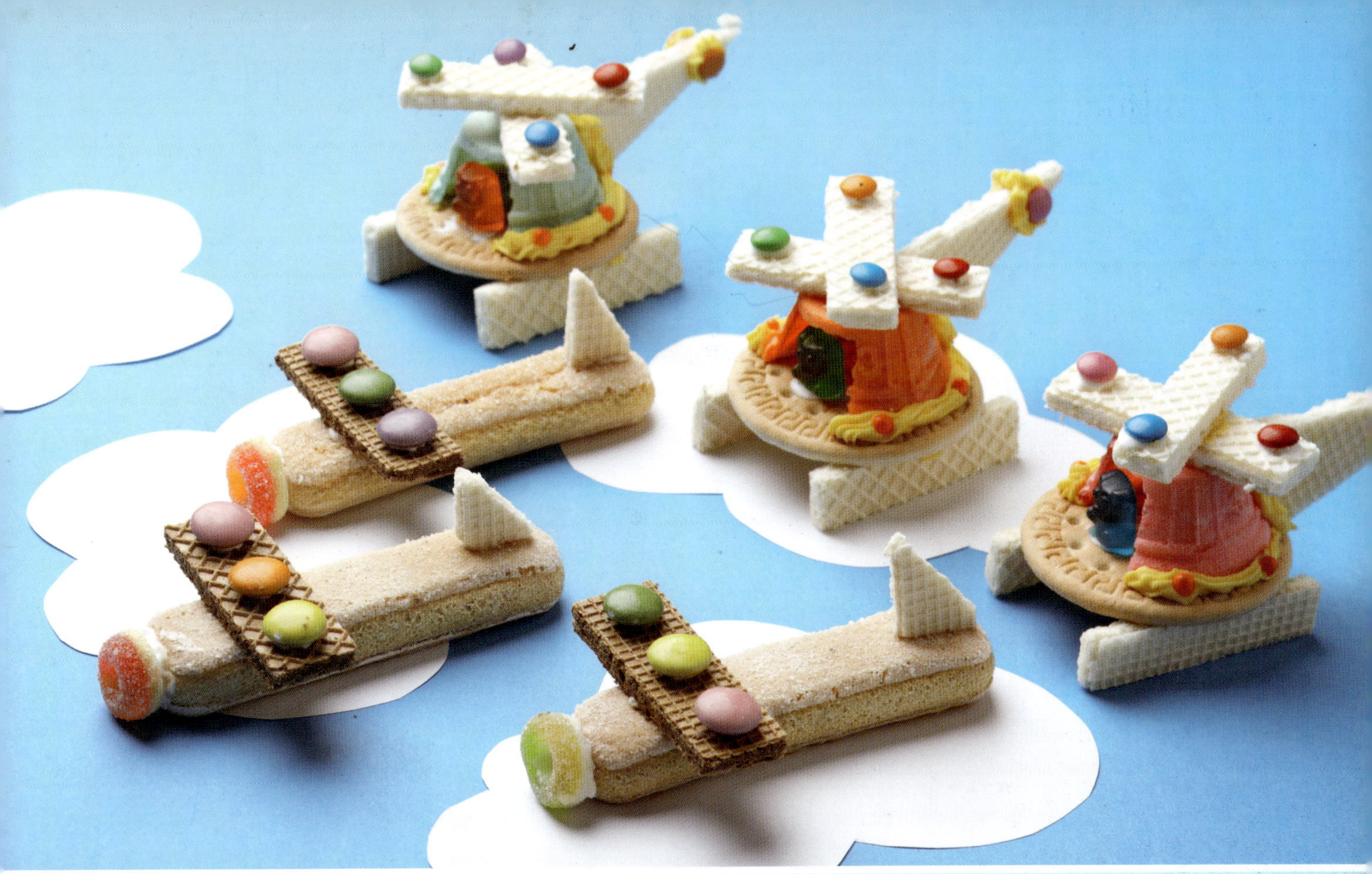

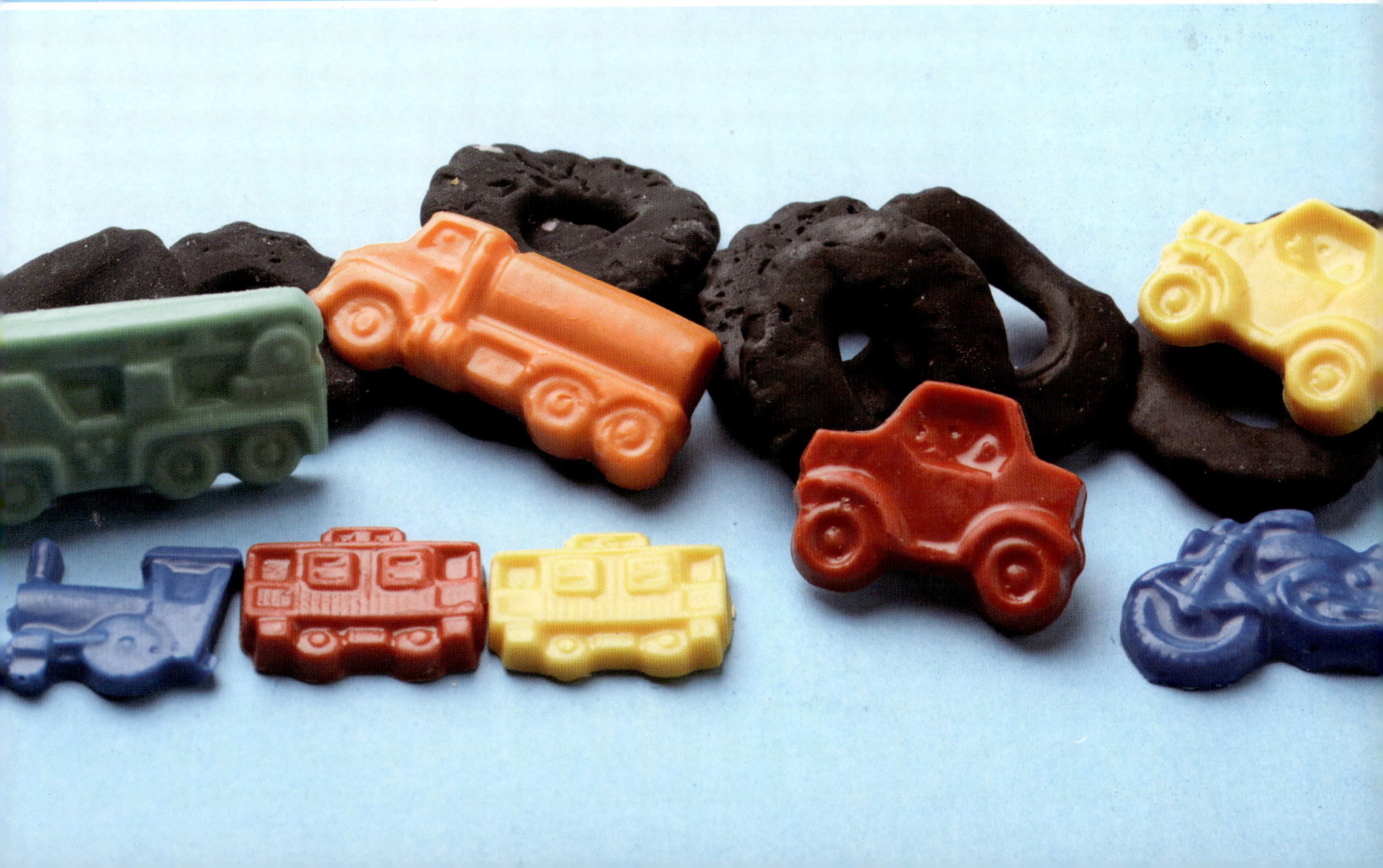

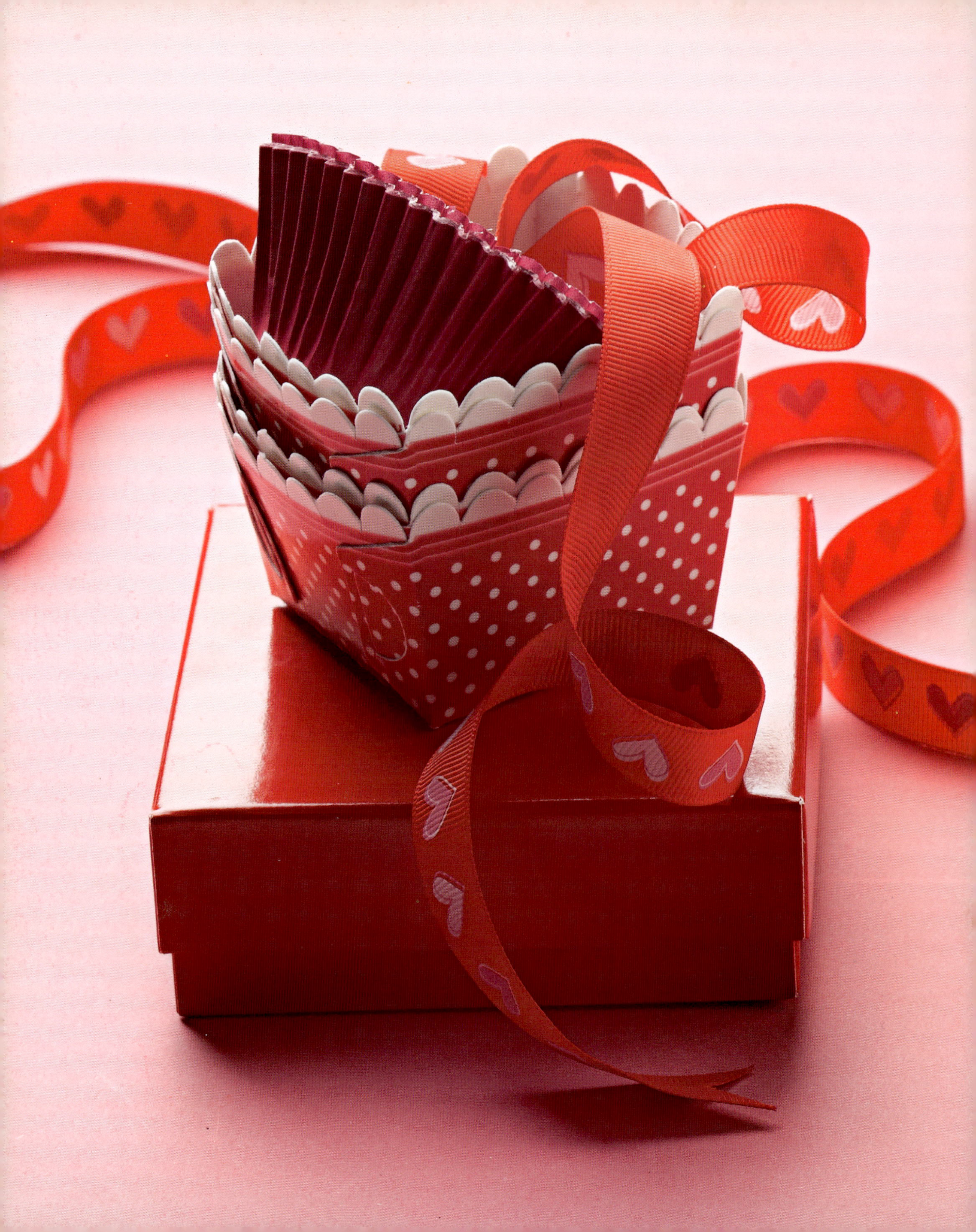

Love treats

Marshmallow surprise

red-coloured chocolate (page 8)
15 marshmallows
30 Marie biscuits
300g milk chocolate
heart-shaped cake decorations
 (cake confetti)

Melt the red-coloured chocolate, pour into animal-shaped moulds and leave in the fridge until set. Remove from the moulds and place on wax paper.

Place a marshmallow in the centre of half the Marie biscuits. Microwave them one by one for 30 seconds, or until the marshmallow puffs up. Place a second Marie biscuit on top of the puffed-up marshmallow, pressing gently until the marshmallow comes out of the sides of the biscuit. Repeat, using all the Marie biscuits, and set aside to cool.

Place a quarter of the milk chocolate in a shallow bowl and melt it in the microwave. Dip the base of each biscuit into the melted chocolate and allow to set.

Place the biscuits on a wire rack, dipped side down. Melt the remaining milk chocolate and use a spoon to drizzle it over the biscuits, making sure the top and sides are completely covered. (Put a bowl or foil-covered baking tray under the rack to catch any chocolate dripping down, as it can be used again.) Allow to set well.

Using small blobs of melted chocolate, stick the chocolate animals and cake confetti to the biscuits. Leave until set.

MAKES 15 BISCUITS

Layered chocolate fudge

pink-coloured chocolate (page 8)
decorative moulds

WHITE CHOCOLATE FUDGE LAYER
200g white chocolate
120ml condensed milk

MILK CHOCOLATE FUDGE LAYER
100g milk chocolate
60ml condensed milk

extra chocolate, for melting

Melt the pink-coloured chocolate, pour into teddy bear or heart-shaped moulds and place in the fridge until set. Remove from the moulds and store on wax paper. Line a 10 x 20cm baking pan with wax paper.

Melt the ingredients for the white chocolate fudge layer in the microwave, stirring often to prevent the chocolate from burning. Pour into the baking pan and set aside until the white chocolate fudge layer has started to set.

Repeat, using the ingredients for the milk chocolate fudge layer. Pour over the white chocolate fudge layer, and place in the fridge until completely set.

When the fudge has set, cut it into squares and remove from the baking pan.

Melt the extra chocolate in the microwave and use this to stick a coloured chocolate decoration to each fudge square. Leave to set.

MAKES 15 SQUARES

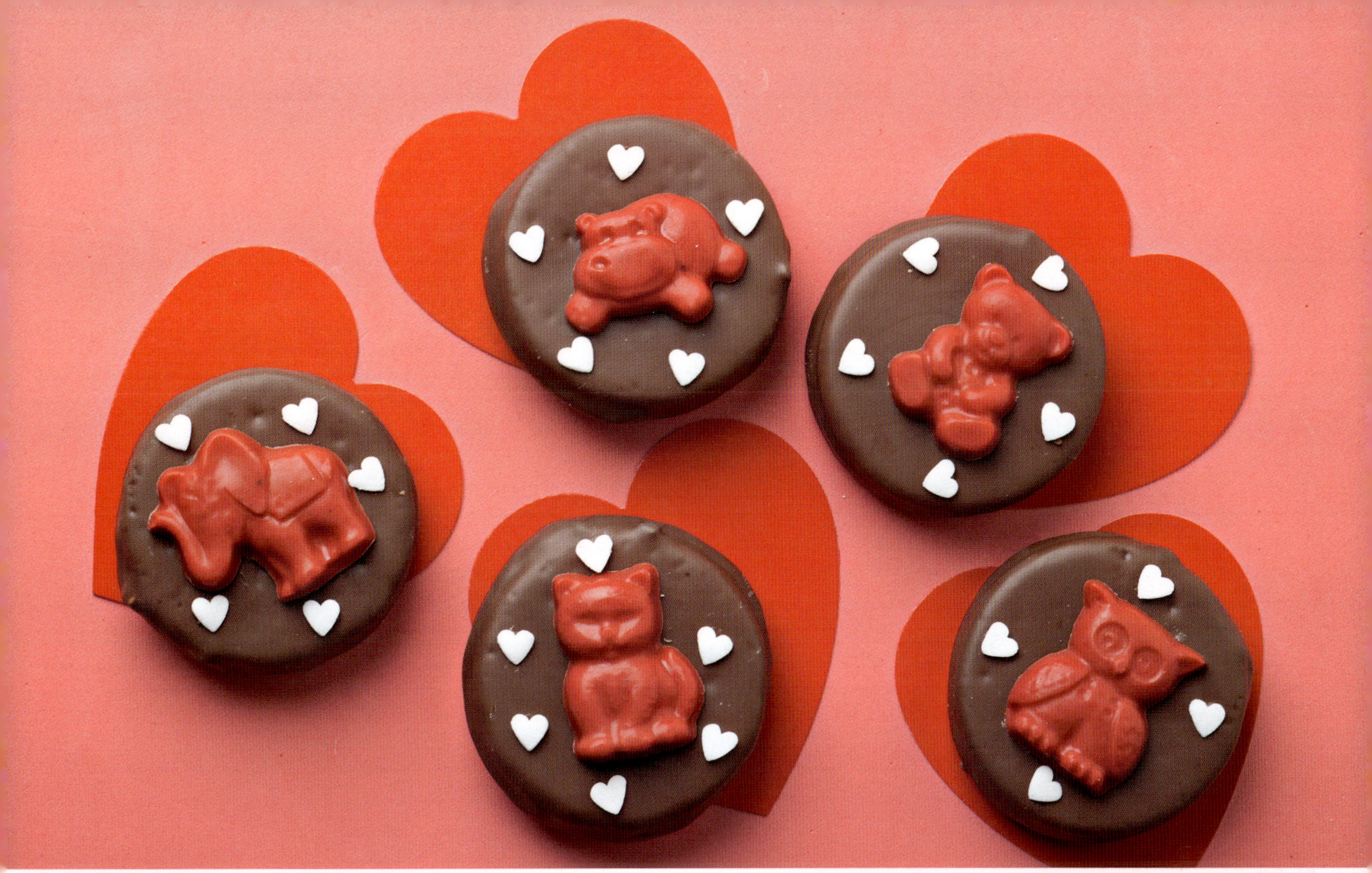

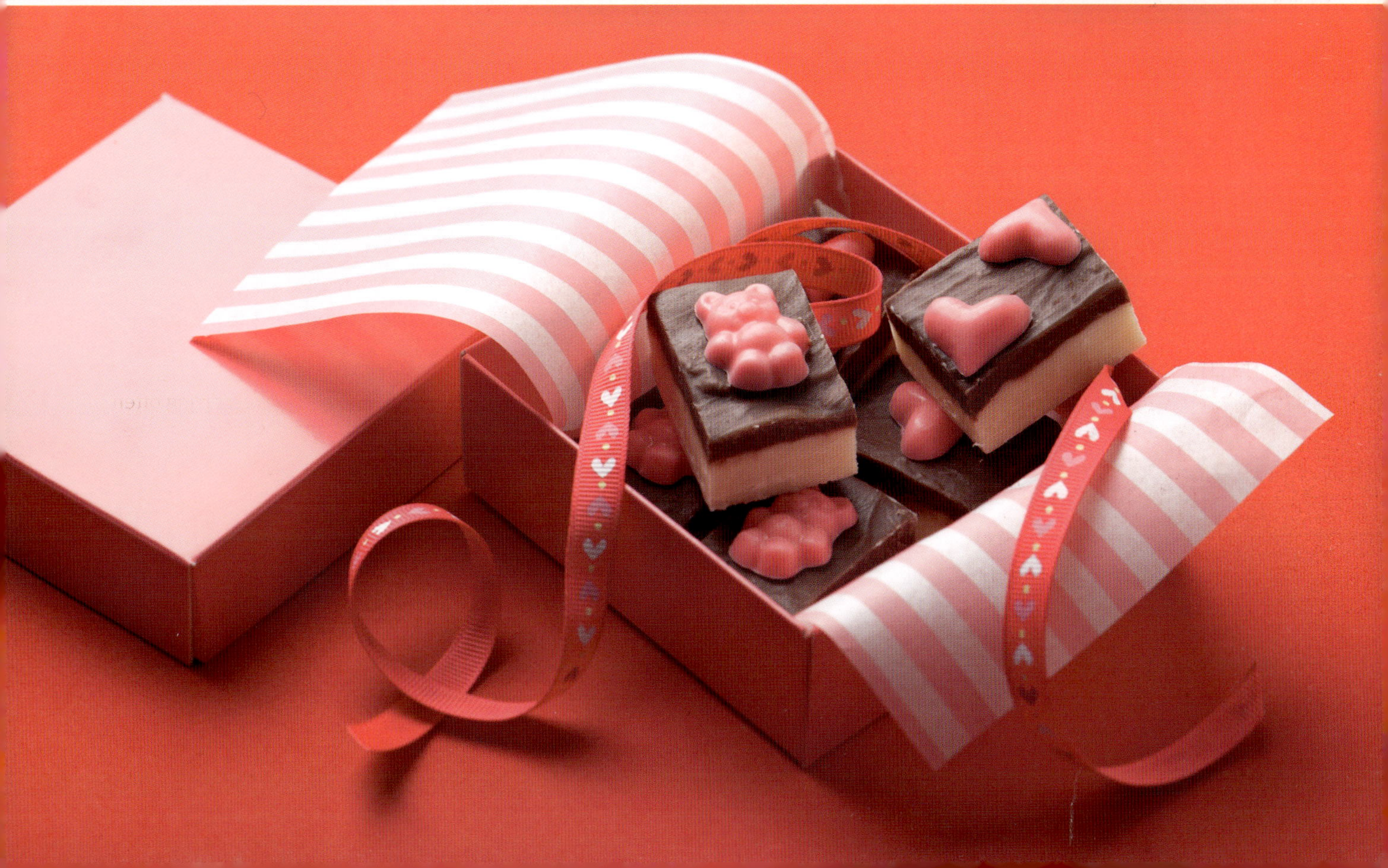

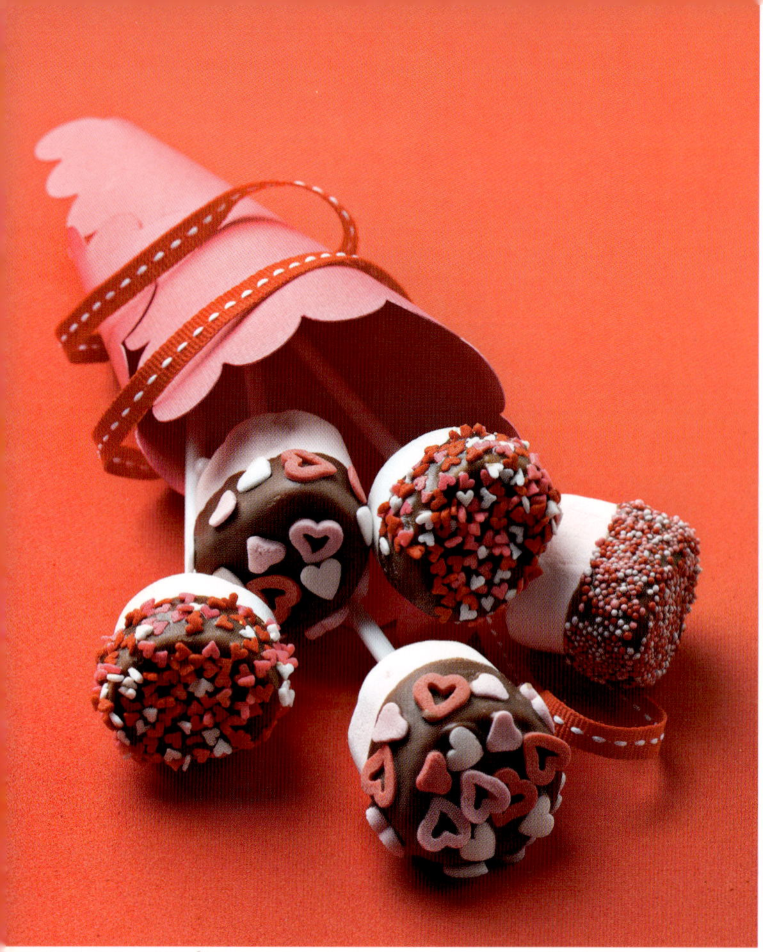
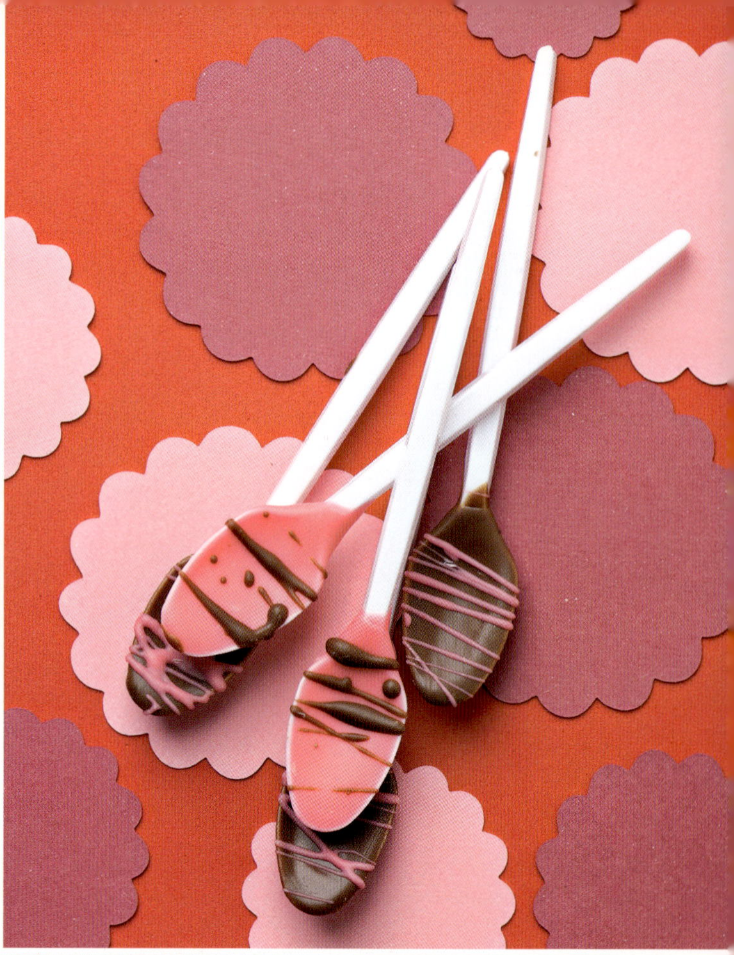
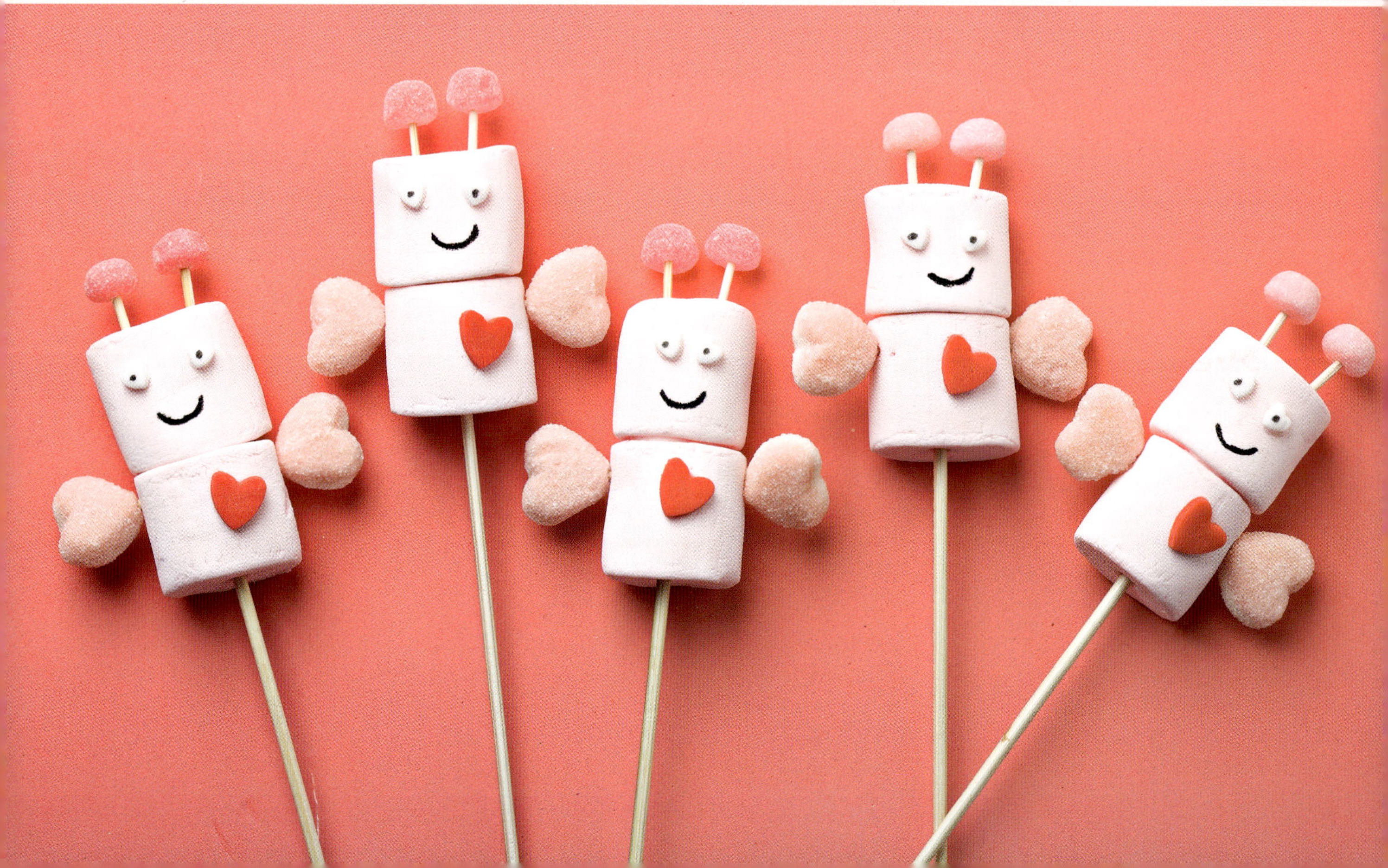

Marshmallow love lollies

10 marshmallows
10 lollipop sticks
50g milk chocolate
variety of decorations (cake confetti, coloured sugar crystals, chocolate vermicilli etc)
ribbon for decoration (optional)

Press a marshmallow onto each stick. Melt the chocolate in the microwave and dip each marshmallow into the chocolate until half-covered.

Allow most of the chocolate to drip off, then dip the lolly into the decorations.

Leave to cool, then tie small pieces of ribbon around the lollies, if preferred.

MAKES 10

Chocolate spoons

12 plastic spoons
10 g pink-coloured chocolate (page 8)
100g milk chocolate
ribbon for decoration (optional)

Wash the plastic spoons and dry them well.

In a small bowl, melt the pink chocolate in the microwave. Dip 6 spoons in the melted chocolate and place them in the fridge until set. (Retain any unused chocolate.)

Melt the milk chocolate and dip the other 6 spoons in it. Place in the fridge until set.

Place all 12 spoons on a wire rack. Melt the milk and pink chocolate again. Using opposite colours, dip a fork into the melted chocolate and drizzle across the spoons for decoration.

Leave to set, then tie a piece of ribbon around each spoon, if preferred.

MAKES 12 SPOONS

Love bugs

20 marshmallows
10 wooden skewers
20 cocktail sticks
20 heart-shaped jelly sweets
20 Jelly Tots
20 small white sugar hearts
10 larger red sugar hearts
glacé icing (page 8)

Thread 2 marshmallows onto each wooden skewer (soak them first, to make it easier).

Cut a cocktail stick in two and push it sideways through the bottom marshmallow. Press a heart-shaped sweet onto each end of the stick, to form the wings. Cut another cocktail stick in two, press it into the top marshmallow and push 2 Jelly Tots onto the tips, for the antennae.

Using a dab of glacé icing, stick 2 white sugar hearts to the top marshmallow, for the eyes, and a red heart to the bottom marshmallow. Use a pen with edible ink to draw the eyes and the mouth.

MAKES 10

LOVE TREATS

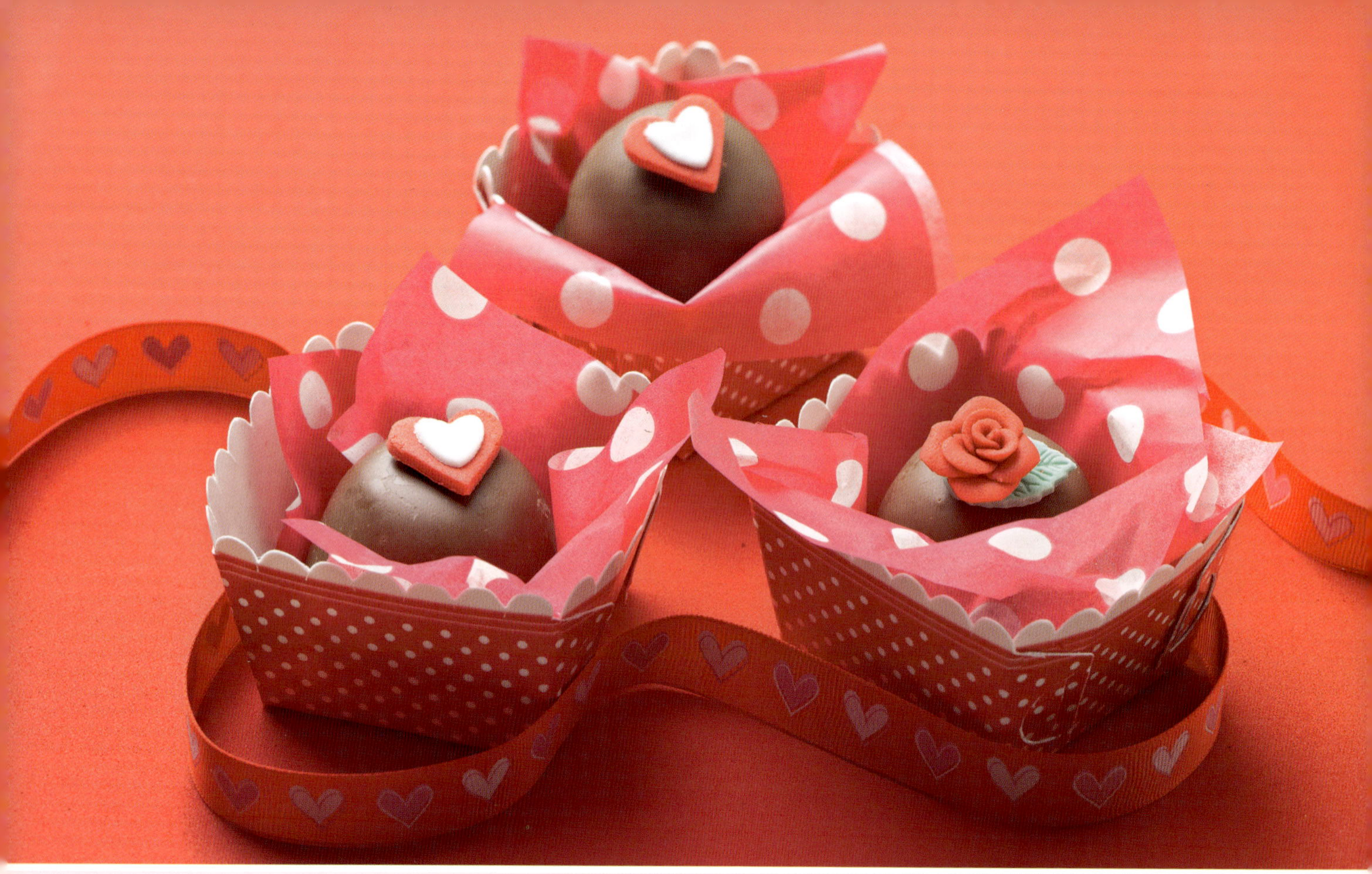

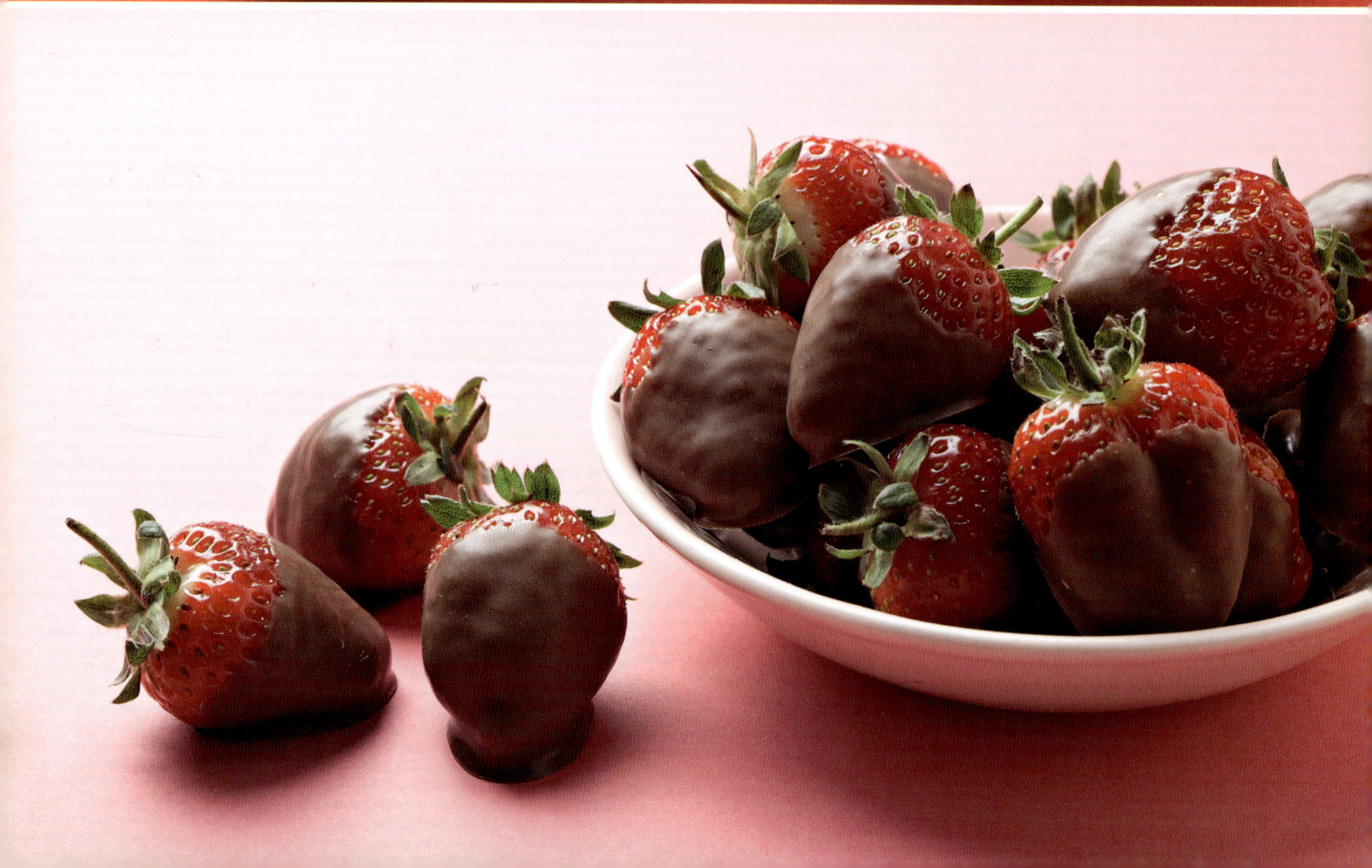

Sweetie Pie for your darling

10 Sweetie Pies
small piece of milk chocolate
sugar roses and leaves
sugar hearts, various sizes
edible glitter

Melt the chocolate in the microwave, stirring often. Use melted chocolate to stick sugar roses and hearts onto the Sweetie Pies.

Leave to stand while the chocolate sets and then sprinkle over some edible glitter.

A decorated Sweetie Pie in a lovely container makes a lovely gift for your darling.

MAKES 10

Tip: If you can't get Sweetie Pies, use a chocolate-coated biscuit or a small chocolate cupcake or muffin.

Other ideas

- Melt leftover coloured chocolate in the microwave (you can re-melt chocolate that has already been melted). Pour into moulds that suit the theme of the party and leave to set. Use these as table decorations or extra treats.

- Dip whole strawberries in melted chocolate and serve as extra treats.

- Remove Caramello bears from their packaging and place on a plate, for decoration.

- Place pink and red sweets or biscuits in pretty containers or small plates, to add to the table decorations.

LOVE TREATS

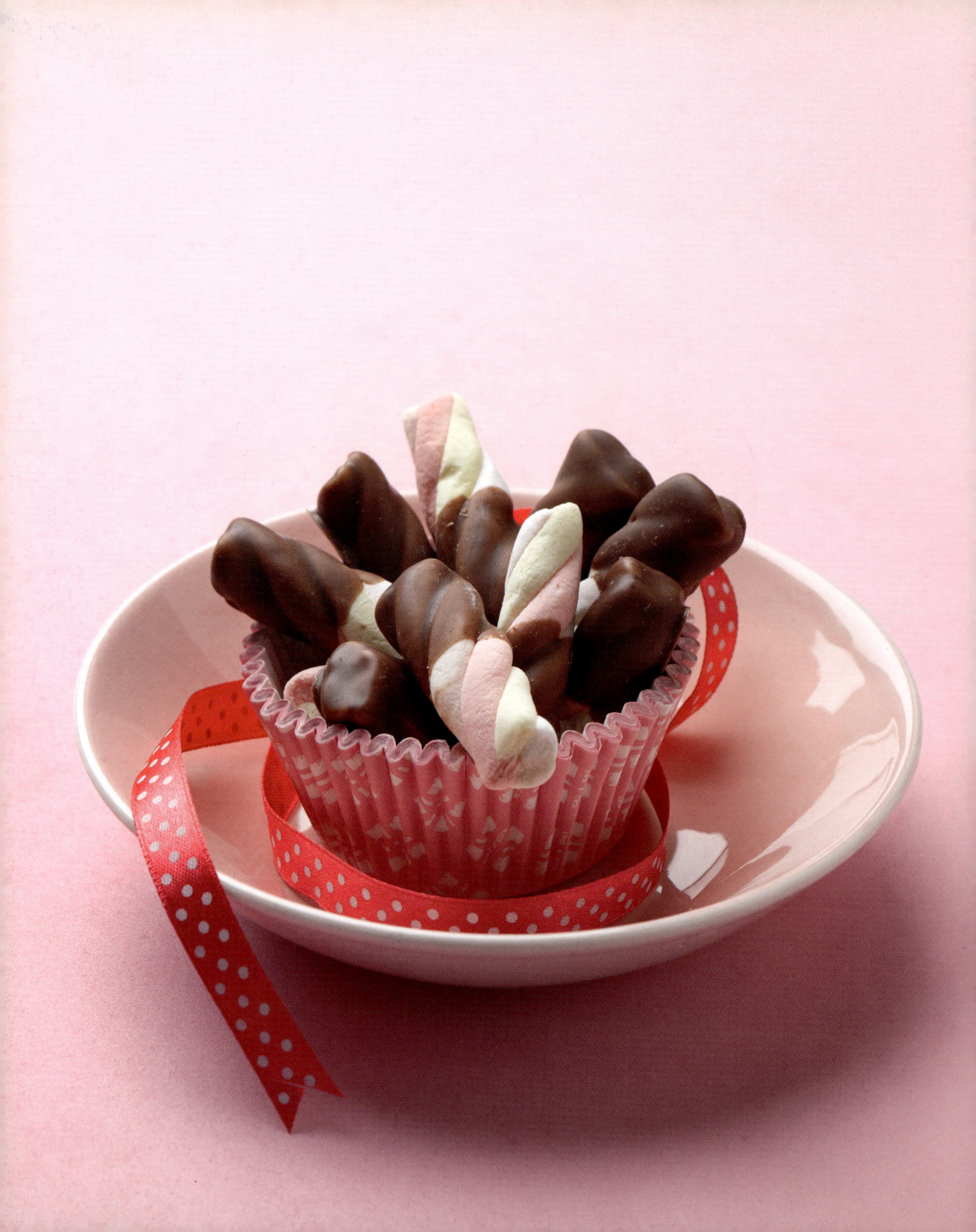

Princesses and tea parties

Forest log

cake board or large flat plate
white and brown butter icing (page 8)
2 mini caramel or jam rolls (for a big cake, use large jam rolls)
desiccated coconut
green food colouring
shop-bought fondant in white, red, black, purple, blue and yellow
variety of sugar flowers, leaves and butterflies

Use a dab of butter icing to stick 2 mini caramel or jam rolls together lengthwise on a cake board or flat plate. Cover with brown butter icing, roughening it to create the texture of bark.

Add a few drops of green food colouring to the dessicated coconut and mix in very well. Spread white butter icing over the cake board and sprinkle with the green coconut, pressing it down lightly, for the grass.

Use the fondant to make the ladybird, worm and the bees (*see* photograph), and place these on the forest log. Decorate with sugar flowers, leaves and butterflies. (*See also* pages 58–59 for ideas for mini insects and other creatures.)

MAKES 1 FOREST LOG

Princesses

10 plain cupcakes or muffins (home-made or shop-bought)
pink and white butter icing (page 8)
10 small paper plates or Marie biscuits
10 small dolls
sugar flowers
cake beads

Remove the bought cupcakes or muffins from their paper cases. Slice off the tops to make them flat, then turn the cupcakes or muffins upside down and use a little butter icing to stick them to the paper plates or Marie biscuits.

Make a hole in each cupcake and place a small doll inside.

Fill an icing bag with butter icing and, using a star-shaped nozzle, decorate the cupcake or muffin to 'dress' the princess. Finish off with sugar flowers and cake beads.

MAKES 10

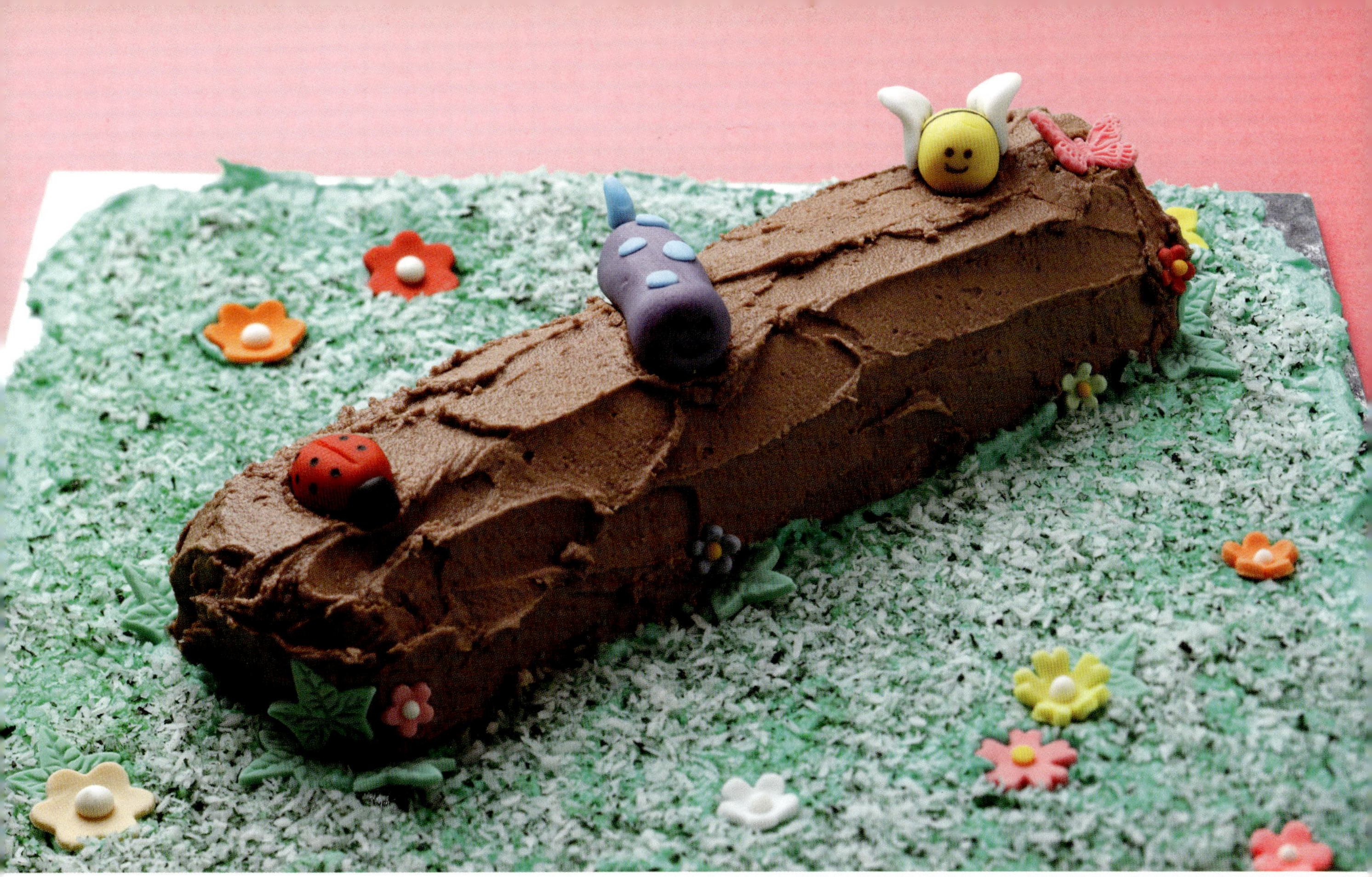

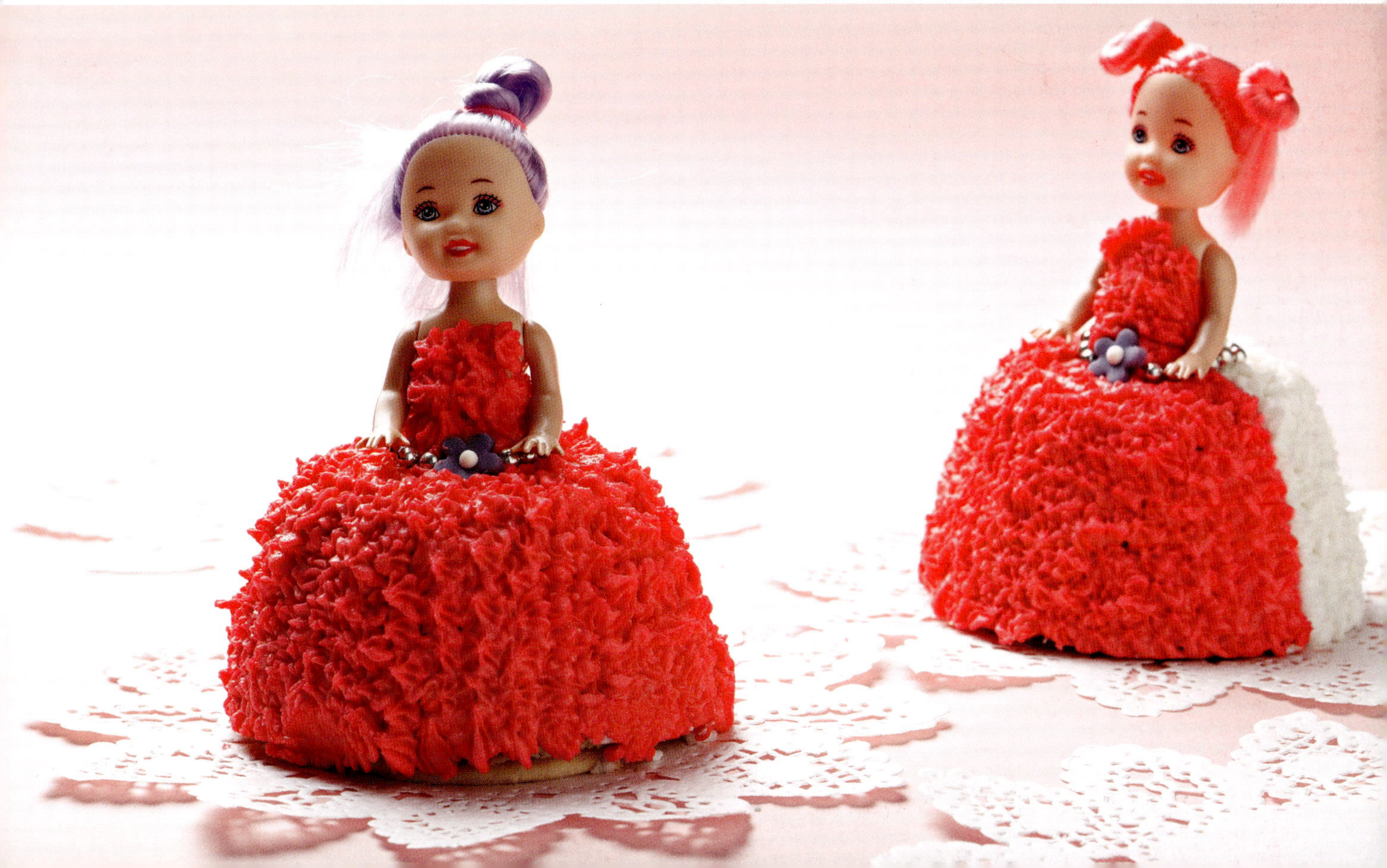

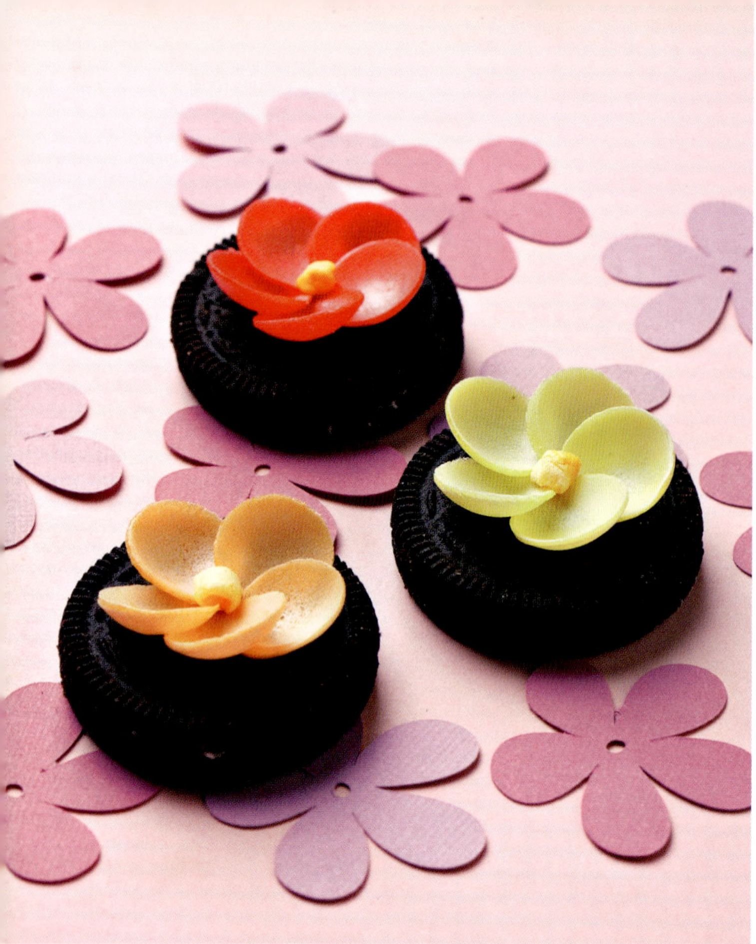
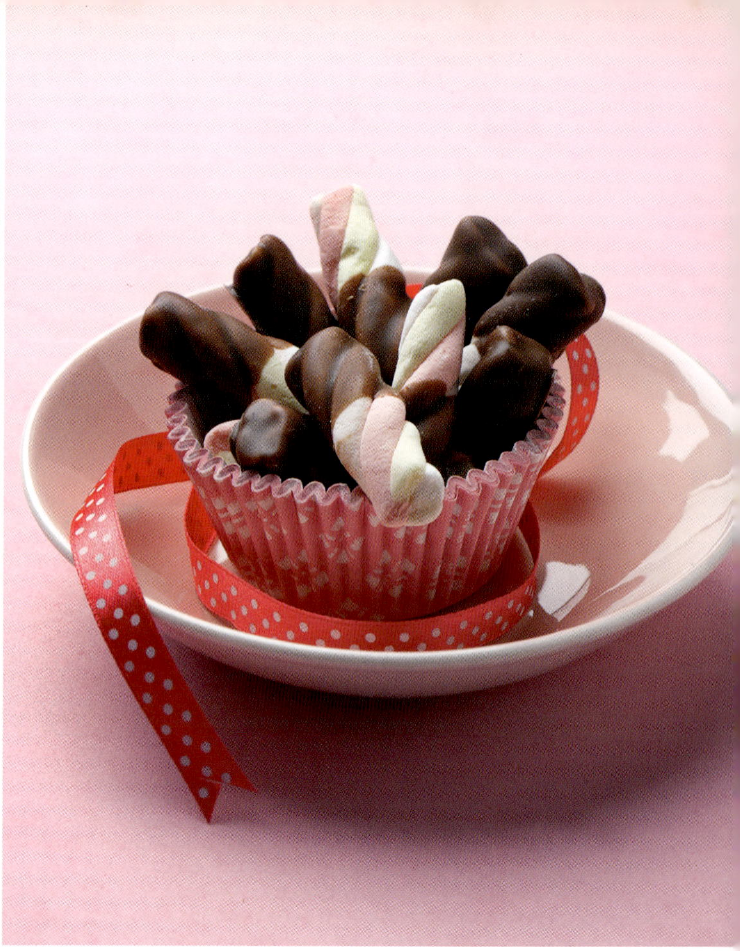
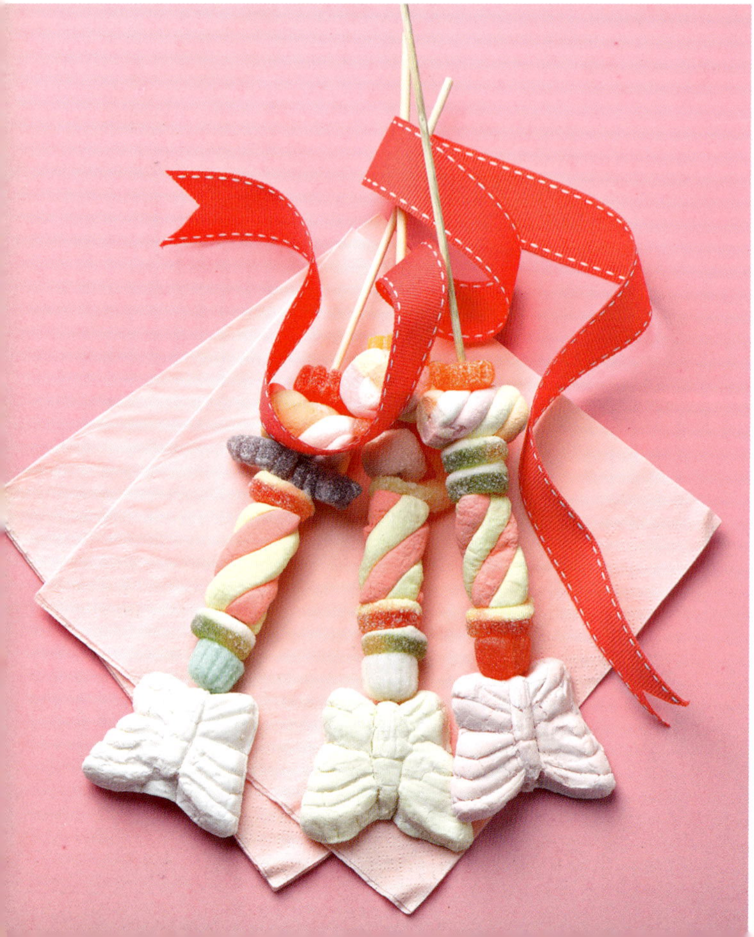
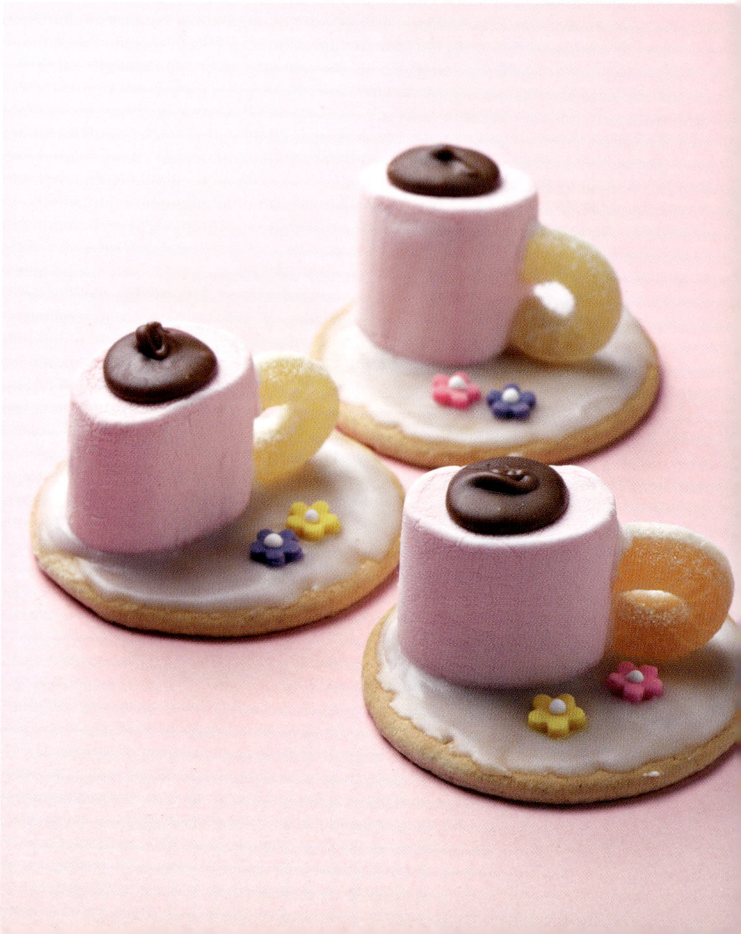

Oreo flowers

50g milk chocolate
16 Oreo biscuits (1 packet)
16 edible wafer flowers (available from specialist bakeries)

Melt the chocolate in the microwave, stirring often. Dab a blob of chocolate onto the centre of each Oreo biscuit and stick a flower on top.

Leave the chocolate to set before serving.

MAKES 16

Mini marshmallow treats

200g milk chocolate
100 mini marshmallow twists

Melt the chocolate in the microwave, stirring often. Dip one end of the marshmallows into the melted chocolate and place on wax paper to set. (If the chocolate sets too quickly, melt it again in the microwave.)

MAKES 100

Butterfly lollies

20 wooden skewers
40 twisted marshmallows
sour worms
other jelly sweets
20 marshmallow butterflies

Soak the wooden skewers in lukewarm water. This makes it easier to push them through the sticky sweets.

Push the skewers through the sweets as shown, with the marshmallow butterfly at the top. (Place a firm jelly sweet last, to prevent the other sweets from slipping down when the lollies are placed upright in a container.)

MAKES 20

Hot chocolate cups

10 Marie biscuits
glacé icing (page 8)
10 marshmallows
10 sugared jelly rings
50g milk chocolate
300ml icing sugar
20 sugar flowers

Spread glacé icing over the Marie biscuits, for the saucers. Place a marshmallow on top of each one, slightly away from the centre.

Cut off one side of a sugared jelly ring and use a dab of icing to stick it to the right-hand side of the marshmallow. Hold it in place for a few seconds, until it is secure.
Melt the chocolate in the microwave and combine with the icing sugar. Using a teaspoon, drizzle the chocolate mixture over the marshmallow.

Place 2 sugar flowers in front of the marshmallow. Leave to stand until set.

MAKES 10

PRINCESSES AND TEA PARTIES

Tea cups

glacé icing (page 8)
pink butter icing (page 8)
10 Marie biscuits
10 edible cupcake cases
10 sugared round jelly rings
30 sugar flowers
Jelly Tots

Roll out the glacé icing and cut out 10 flowers the size of the Marie biscuit. Using a small blob of butter icing, stick these to the biscuits and press flat. Using a little butter icing, stick a cupcake case to the flower.

Cut off one side of a jelly ring and use a dab of butter icing to stick this to the right-hand side of the cupcake case. Hold it in place for a few seconds until it sticks. Stick 3 sugar flowers to the front of each cup, for decoration.

Fill an icing bag with the pink butter icing and decorate the rim of the cup. Fill each cup with Jelly Tots.

MAKES 10

Baskets

glacé icing (page 8)
10 edible cupcake cases
10 round biscuits
thin liquorice strips
variety of small sweets

Using glacé icing, stick the cupcake cases to the round biscuits. For the handles, cut the liquorice strips into pieces and stick into place with glacé icing. Set aside until the icing sets, otherwise the handles will come unstuck. Fill the cupcake case with small sweets.

MAKES 10

Dipped wafers

coloured chocolate (page 8)
10 wafer biscuits
sprinkles (100's & 1000's)

Melt the chocolate in the microwave, stirring often. Dip the wafer biscuits in the melted chocolate and stand upright in a container. Just before the chocolate sets completely, sprinkle over the 100's & 1000's.

MAKES 10

Bundles of biscuits

assorted biscuits (finger biscuits, round biscuits with holes)
variety of fabric or paper ribbons, string, raffia, etc.

Tie the biscuits together in bundles of two or three. Use any biscuits, and choose ribbon colours and textures to fit your theme. This is a quick, easy treat to make.

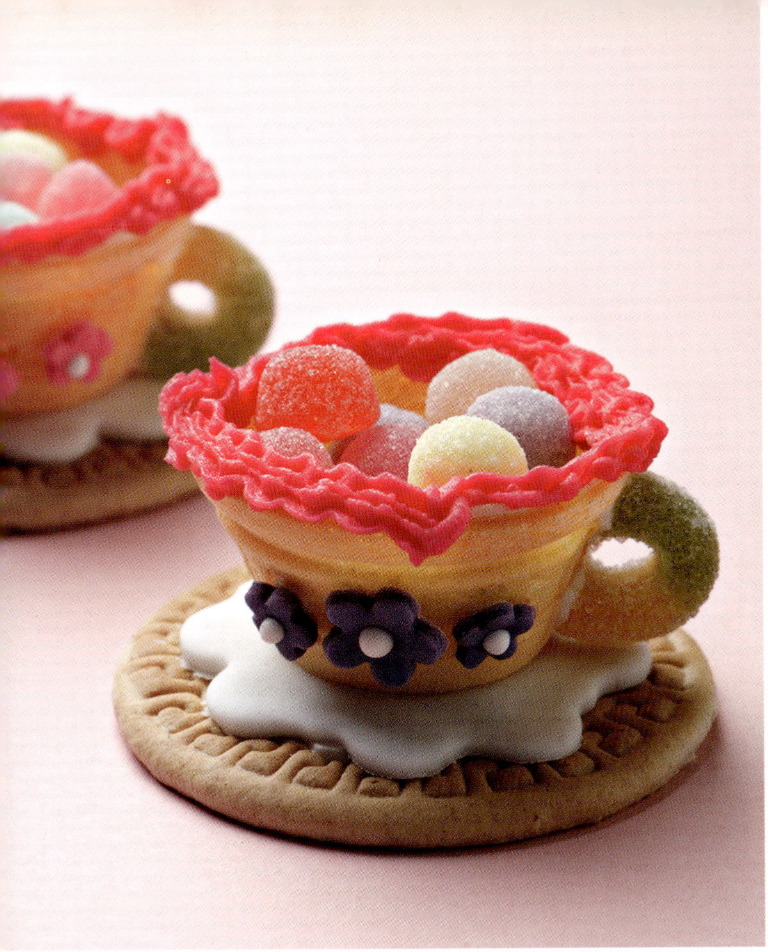
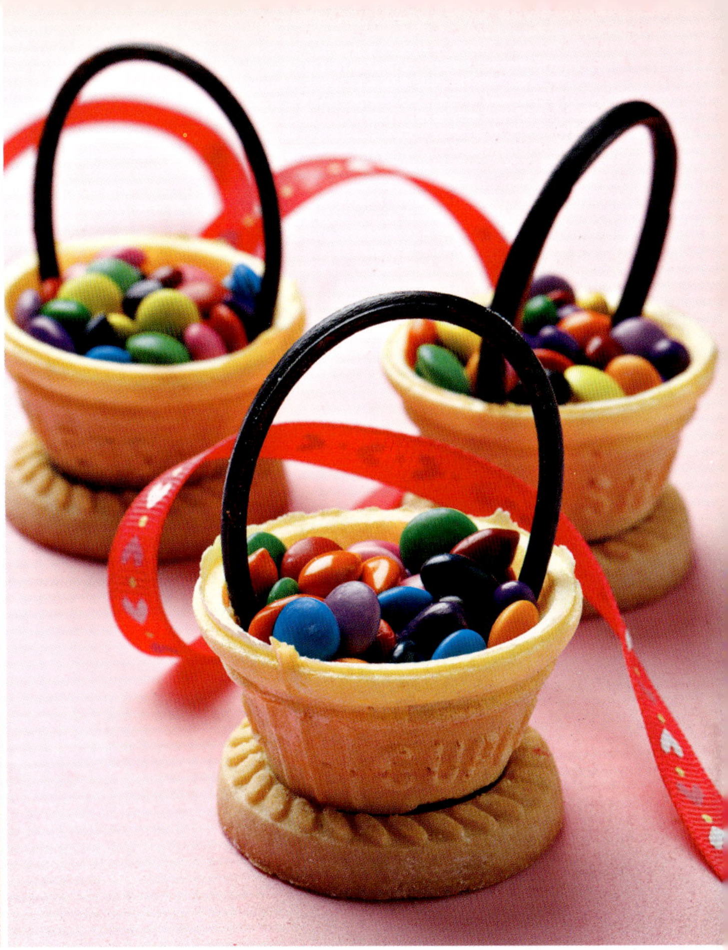
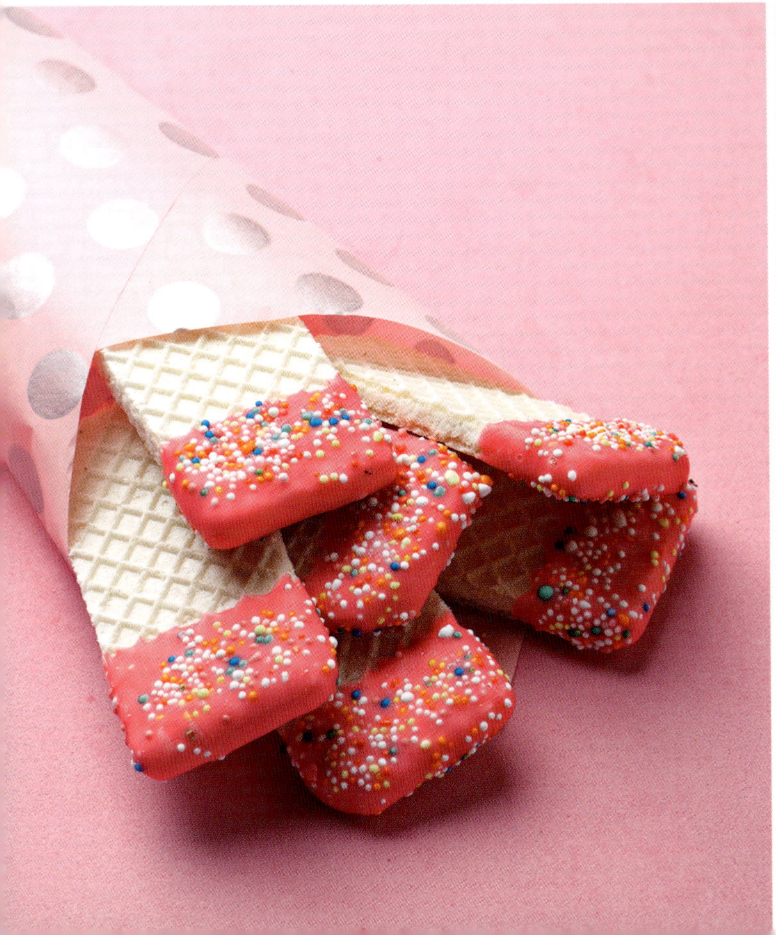
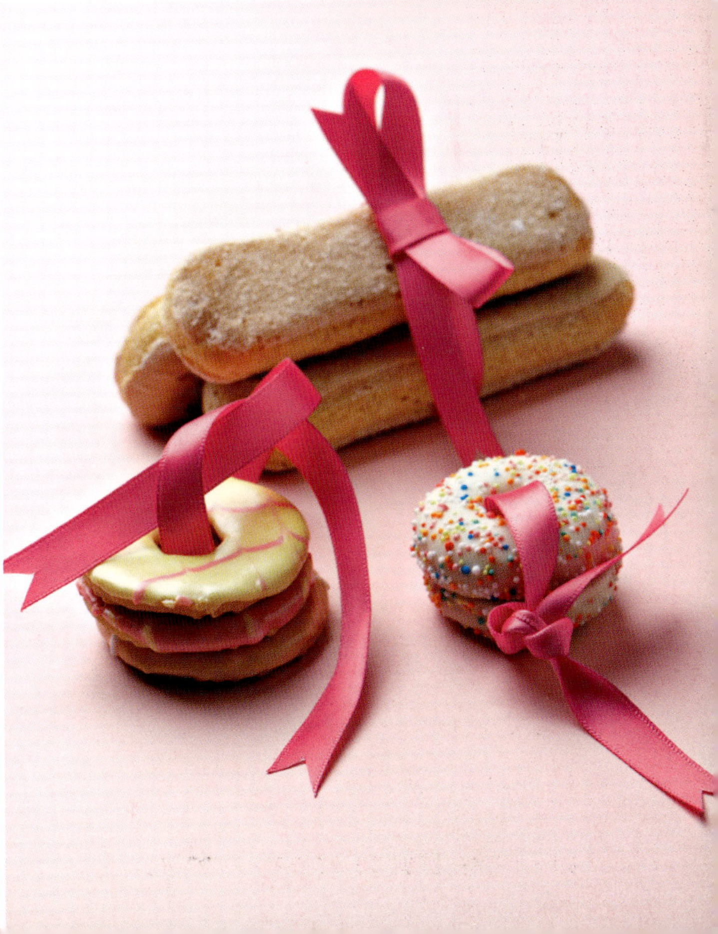

Coconut ice with a difference

one quantity of coconut ice (page 12)
glacé icing (page 8)
16 edible wafer flowers

Cut the coconut ice into 5 x 5cm squares. Using glacé icing, stick the flowers on top of the coconut ice squares. Leave to stand for the icing to set.

These coconut ice squares can be individually wrapped to make a lovely take-home gift.

Coconut ice balls

one quantity of coconut ice (page 12)
pink food colouring

Prepare the coconut ice, colouring only half the mixture pink. Instead of pressing it into the baking pan to set, make multi-coloured balls by combining 1 teaspoon of white coconut ice and 1 teaspoon of pink and rolling it into a ball, using your hands. Allow to set.

Lollipop trees

10 small plastic potplant containers
marshmallows
10 round lollipops
green butter icing (page 8)
small sugar flowers
coloured ribbon or raffia for decorating

Wash and dry the potplant containers well.
Press 3 or 4 marshmallows firmly into the container. Remove the wrapper and push the lollipop into the marshmallows so it stands firmly upright.

Fill an icing bag with green butter icing and pipe stars over the marshmallows and the lollipop. Decorate the lollipop with sugar flowers and tie some raffia or a ribbon around the container.

MAKES 10

Decorated sugar cubes

green butter icing (page 8)
40 sugar cubes
40 sugar flowers

Using the butter icing, pipe a leaf on top of each sugar cube. Stick a sugar flower to the leaf and leave to set.

MAKES 40

Sweet bracelets

Jelly Beans
small jelly rings
other jelly sweets

sterile darning or upholstery needle
thin hat elastic

Arrange the sweets as preferred, allowing 16–18 per bracelet. Thread the needle with the elastic, then wet the needle before pushing it through the Jelly Beans and sweets (this makes pushing it through easier); wipe the needle if it becomes too sticky. Knot the elastic to close the bracelet and neaten any loose ends.

Fun Sweetie Pies

yellow and pink coloured chocolate (page 8)
10 Sweetie Pies
5 sugar flowers
5 sugar butterflies
edible glitter

Melt the chocolate in the microwave, stirring often. Using a fork, trail yellow chocolate streaks over half of the Sweetie Pies and pink chocolate streaks over the other half.

While the chocolate is still soft, place a sugar flower or butterfly on top of each Sweetie Pie. (If it has already set, use small drops of melted chocolate to stick down the decorations.) Sprinkle with edible glitter. These can be wrapped to make a lovely gift.

MAKES 10

PRINCESSES AND TEA PARTIES

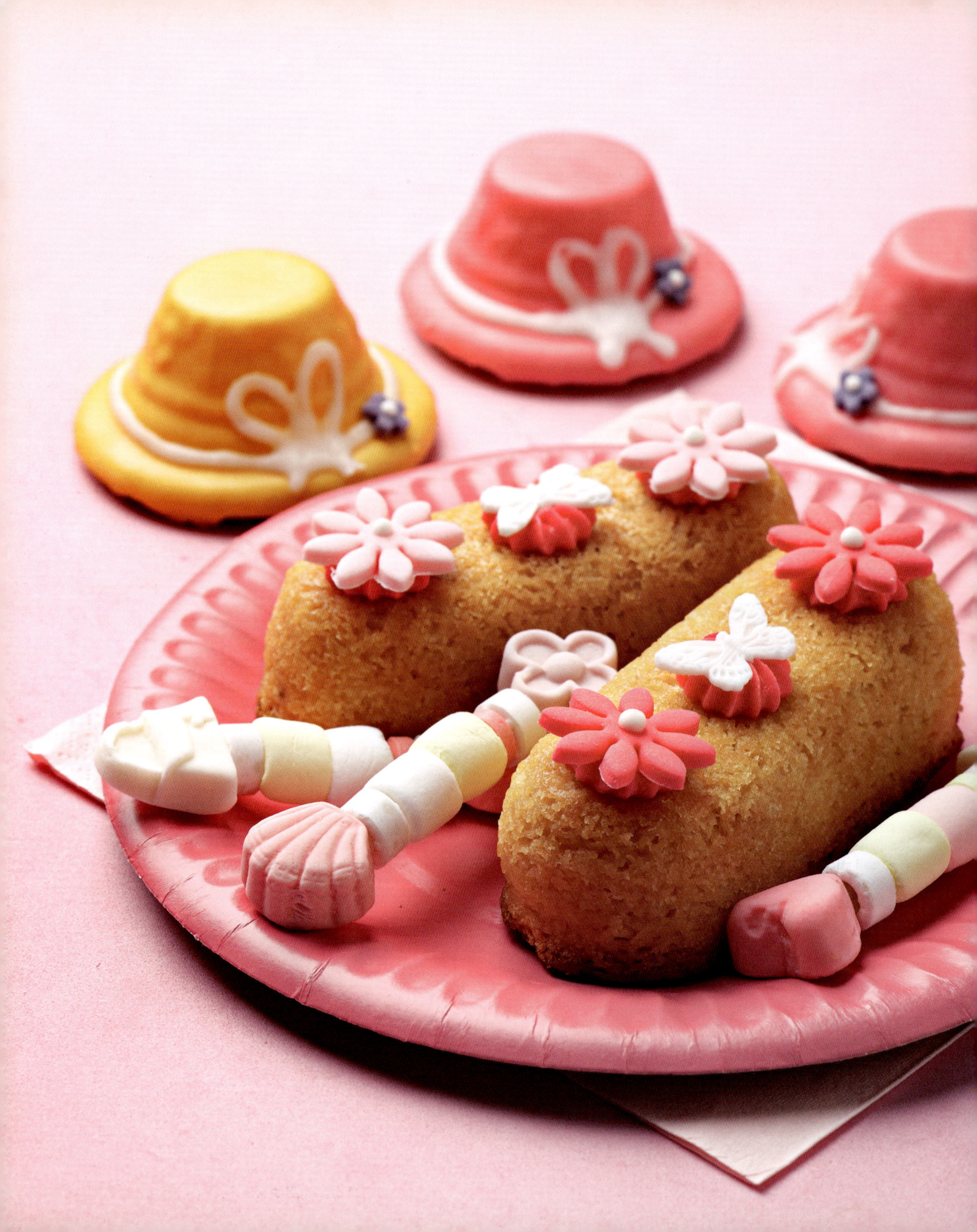

Hats

12 edible cupcake cases
chocolate, for melting
variety of small sweets
12 Marie biscuits
coloured chocolate (page 8, this quantity is enough for 4 hats, so make as much as you need of each colour)
glacé icing
sugar flowers to decorate

Trim the edible cupcake cases so they are even, with no bits are sticking out. Melt the chocolate in the microwave. Press the edge of the cupcake case into the melted chocolate. Quickly fill the case with sweets and place a Marie biscuit on top while the chocolate is still soft. Leave to stand for the chocolate to set.

Place the hats on a wire rack. Melt the coloured chocolate and slowly pour some over each hat to cover it completely. Leave to set.

Using an icing bag fitted with a thin nozzle, pipe glacé icing around the brim of the hat in the shape of a bow. Decorate with the sugar flowers while the icing is still wet. Leave to stand for the icing to set completely.

MAKES 12

Twinkies with a difference

butter icing (page 8)
10 Twinkies or mini Swiss rolls
sugar flowers and butterflies

Use a dab or two of butter icing to stick sugar flowers and butterflies onto the Twinkies. Add other decorations as preferred.

MAKES 10

Mini princess lollies

princess sweets
cocktail sticks
mini marshmallows
jelly rings or round sweets

Push a princess sweet onto one end of a cocktail stick. Add mini marshmallows and round sweets as preferred, and end with another princess sweet.

PRINCESSES AND TEA PARTIES

Daisies

1 quantity of basic butter biscuit dough (page 12)
shop-bought fondant (pink and yellow)
glacé icing (page 8)
yellow and pink sprinkles

Preheat the oven to 180°C. Roll out the dough to 5mm thick and cut out rounds. Bake for 12–15 minutes or until golden brown. Allow the biscuits to cool completely.

Roll out the fondant on a clean, smooth surface lightly dusted with cornflour (Maizena). Using a cookie cutter, cut out rounds the same size as the biscuits. Use a dab of glacé icing to stick the fondant circles onto the biscuits.

Gather the fondant and roll out again, then cut out the daisies. Place yellow daisies on the pink biscuits and pink daisies on the yellow biscuits.

Put a dab of glacé icing in the centre of each daisy and scatter sprinkles over the wet icing (use yellow sprinkles on the pink flowers and pink sprinkles on the yellow flowers). Leave to set, then shake off the excess sprinkles.

Tip: Use Marie biscuits if you don't have time to bake the biscuits.

Flower biscuits

1 quantity of basic butter biscuit dough (page 12)
white chocolate, for melting
Smarties

Preheat the oven to 180°C. Roll out the dough to 5mm thick and cut out small flower shapes. Bake for 12–15 minutes or until golden brown. Allow the biscuits to cool completely.

Melt the chocolate. Place a dab of chocolate in the centre of each biscuit and press down the Smartie. Leave to stand until the chocolate is set completely.

Tip: These small biscuits are a good way to use up leftover dough.

Other ideas

- Melt coloured chocolate (page 8), pour into flower, leaf or butterfly moulds and allow to set. Use as decorations or extra treats for the party.

- Buy ready-made sweet bracelets for extra treats or as decorations.

- Place princess sweets in transparent containers.

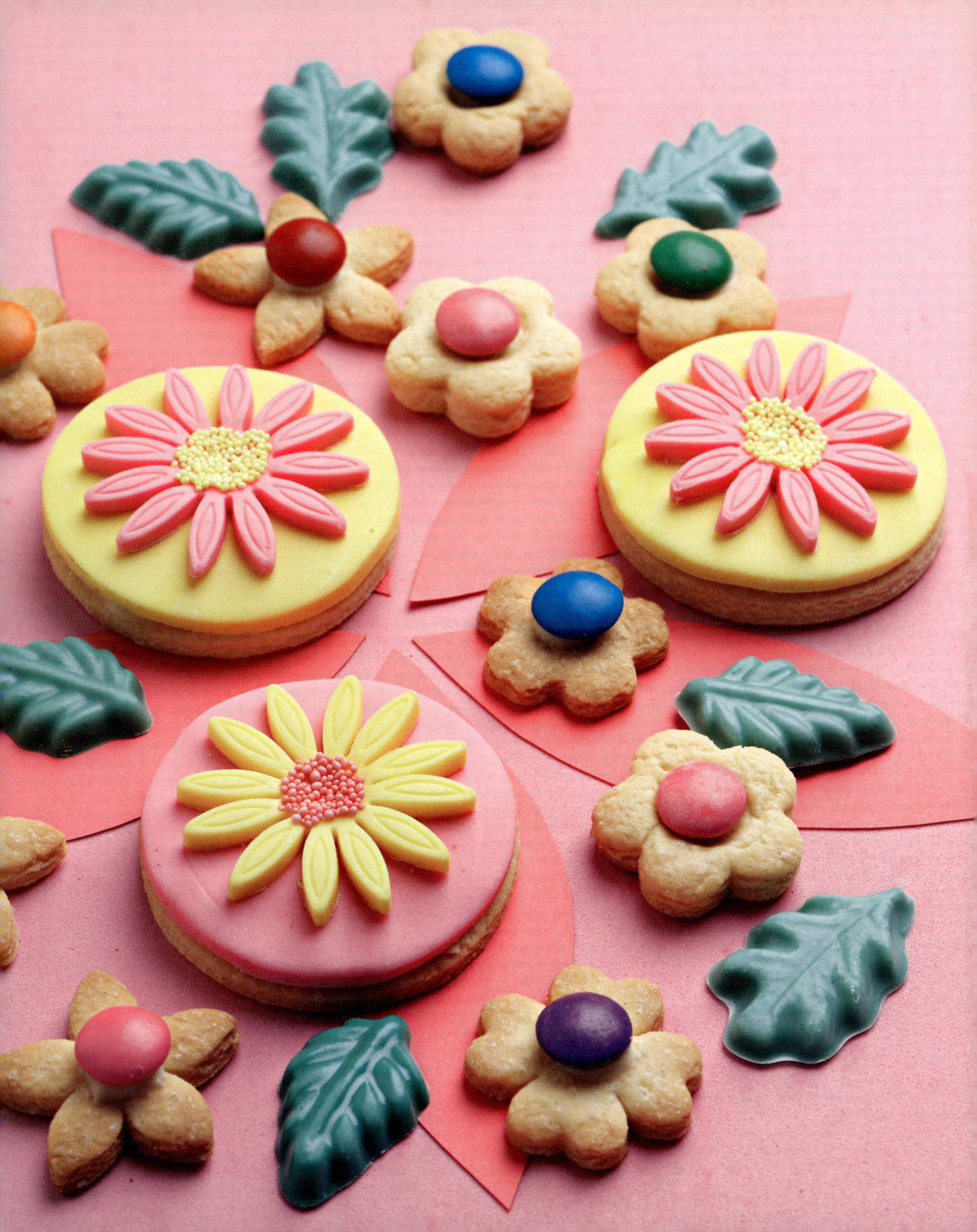

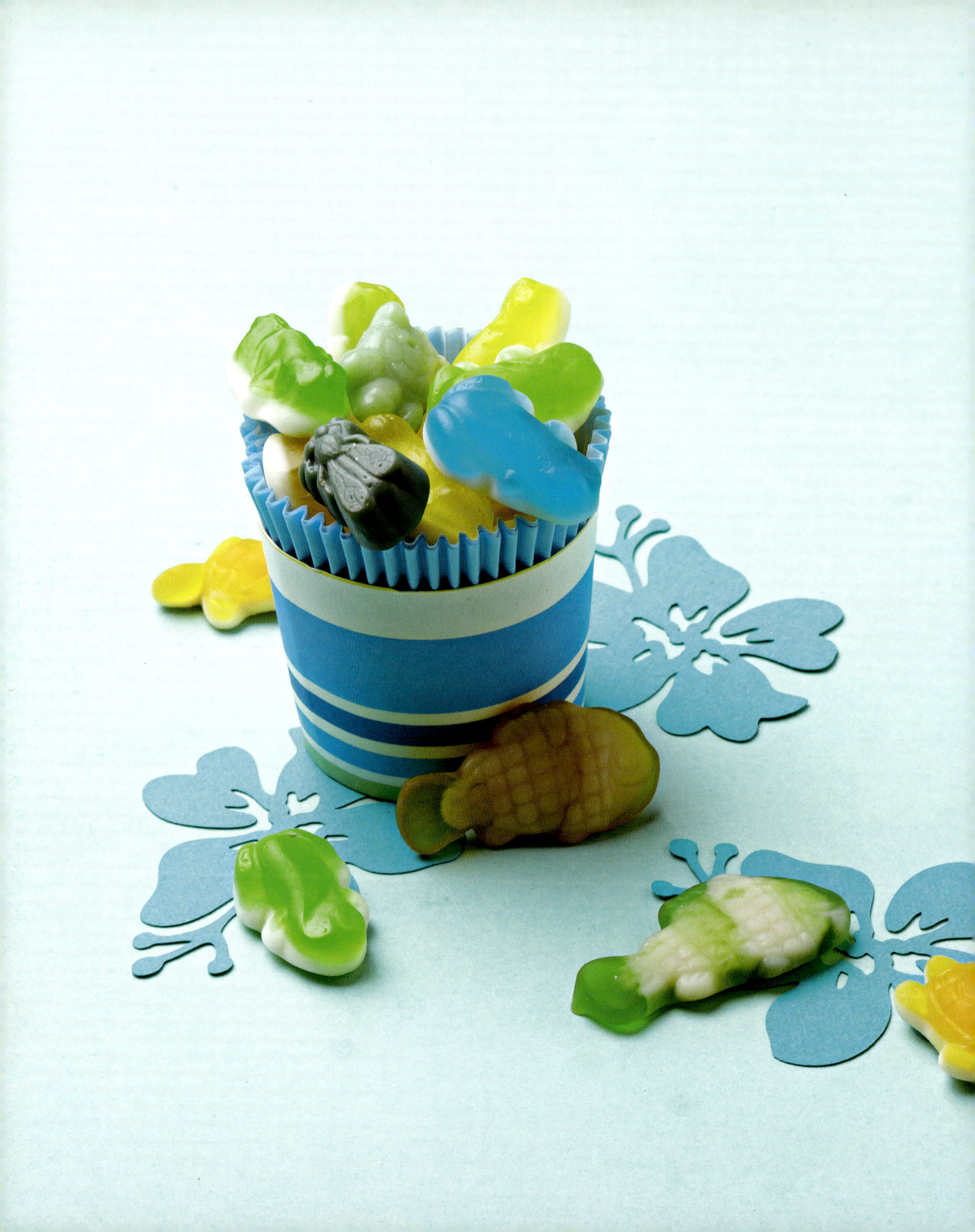

Animals

Green frogs

10 Marie biscuits
green butter icing (page 8)
20 green edible cupcake cases
20 green jelly rings
small sweets
10 pink or red sour worms
green glacé icing (page 8)
10 green Jelly Tots
20 silver sugar balls

Spread green butter icing over the Marie biscuit and place a green cupcake case on top, slightly towards the back. Cut out a section of the jelly ring. Stick 2 jelly rings into the butter icing, right up against the cupcake case, for the feet. Fill the cupcake case with small sweets.

Using glacé icing, stick the sour worm onto the cupcake case, then stick the second cupcake case, upside down, to the bottom case, to form the head (the worm helps keep the mouth open).

For the eyes, cut a Jelly Tot in half and use green glacé icing to stick the 2 halves on top of the cupcake case. Use green glacé icing to stick a silver sugar ball in front of each Jelly Tot.

MAKES 10

Swiss roll snails

5 mini Swiss rolls
50g milk chocolate
10 finger biscuits
20 orange sugar balls
20 short liquorice strips

Cut the mini Swiss rolls in two. Melt the chocolate in the microwave, stirring often. Use some melted chocolate to stick half a Swiss roll to one end of each finger biscuit, to form the shell.

Use melted chocolate to stick a small round sweet on top of each short liquorice strip and leave to set for a few seconds. Stick 2 strips onto the other end of the finger biscuit, for the feelers. Leave to set.

Dip the tip of a fork into the melted chocolate and move it quickly back and forwards over the snails, to make streaks.
(Tip: place some wax paper underneath to prevent your work surface from being covered in chocolate.)

MAKES 10

48 ANIMALS

Sweetie Pie snails

50g milk chocolate
10 Sweetie Pies
10 Chomps or chocolate wafer biscuits
20 blue sugar balls
20 short liquorice strips

Melt the chocolate in the microwave. stirring often. Using a little melted chocolate, stick the Sweetie Pie onto one end of the Chomp, to form the body. (If the chocolate sets too quickly, melt it again.)

Use a dab of melted chocolate to stick the sugar balls on top of the liquorice strips, then leave to set.

Use melted chocolate to stick the liquorice strips to the front of the Chomp, for the feelers, and leave until the chocolate sets.

MAKES 10

Marshmallow snails

glacé icing (page 8)
10 marshmallows
10 Marie biscuits
10 Jelly Babies or sour worms
short liquorice strips
icing tube or non-toxic pen

Using glacé icing, stick a marshmallow to the centre of the Marie biscuit.

Cut a Jelly Baby or sour worm in half and attach one half to the front and the other half to the back of the marshmallow, using glacé icing. Use a lot of icing, so it looks like slime.

For the feelers, cut very small pieces (± 5mm) of liquorice strip and stick 2 on top of each Jelly Baby's head, using glacé icing. Use an icing tube or non-toxic koki to draw spots on the snails.

MAKES 10

ANIMALS

Marshmallow worms

60 marshmallows
10 wooden skewers (presoaked)
glacé icing (page 8)
40 small round sweets
15 mini marshmallows
15 oblong liquorice sweets

Thread the marshmallows onto the skewers (you should get 6 marshmallows onto a skewer). Place blobs of glacé icing on top of the 4 centre marshmallows and press a round sweet on each. Put aside to set.

Use glacé icing to stick 2 mini marshmallows to the front of half the worms, for the feelers, and 1 to the back, for the tail. Do the same with the liquorice sweets for the remaining worms. (Just press them into the marshmallow; they don't need to be stuck down with glacé icing.) Use an icing pen or a non-toxic pen with edible ink to draw friendly faces on the worms.

MAKES 10

Chocolate worms

green fondant
50g milk chocolate
40 Rolo chocolate toffees
40 Smarties
10 chocolate balls
short liquorice strips
blue sugar drops
icing tube, for writing

Roll out the fondant to ± 3mm thick and cut out a leaf shape. Use a cocktail stick to draw veins on the leaf, and a small flower-shaped cookie cutter to cut out a piece, as if a bite has been taken out of it.

Melt the chocolate in the microwave, stirring often. Use drops of melted chocolate to stick 4 Rolo toffees to the leaf, as shown. Use a drop of chocolate to stick different coloured Smarties on top of the Rolos.

Cut the liquorice strips into 1cm pieces and use melted chocolate to stick 2 strips on top of the chocolate ball, for the feelers. Stick down 2 blue sugar drops, for the eyes, and draw a mouth using the tube of icing. Use a dab of chocolate to stick the head in front of the Rolos.

MAKES 10

ANIMALS

Marshmallow mice

Marie biscuits
glacé icing (page 8)
10 white marshmallows
shop-bought white fondant
10 large silver sugar balls
20 blue sugar balls
40 pink Jelly Tots
short liquorice strips

Spread glacé icing over the Marie biscuit and stick a marshmallow in the centre, slightly towards the back.

Form the head of the mouse using fondant and use glacé icing to stick this to the front of the marshmallow. Use glacé icing to attach a silver sugar ball for the nose, 2 blue sugar balls for the eyes, and 2 Jelly Tots for the ears.

Cut 2 Jelly Tots in half and use glacé icing to stick them to the Marie biscuit, for the feet. For the tail, cut the liquorice strips into short pieces (± 15–20mm) and push a piece into the back of the marshmallow.

MAKES 10

Coconut ice mice

one quantity of white coconut ice (page 12)
desiccated coconut, for coating
white chocolate, for melting
30 pink or purple Smarties
short liquorice strips

Prepare the coconut ice according to the recipe. Instead of pressing it into a baking pan, form 10 mouse shapes. Roll the shapes in coconut to coat completely, then put aside to set.

Melt the white chocolate in the microwave, stirring often. Using the melted chocolate, stick a Smartie to the front of the mouse, for a nose. Make 2 slits on the top of the head and use melted chocolate to stick 2 Smarties into the slits, for the ears.

Cut the liquorice strips into lengths: 20mm for the tail, 10–15mm for the whiskers and 5mm for the eyes. Push the liquorice pieces into the head and body to finish off the mouse.

MAKES 10

ANIMALS

Peacocks

50g milk chocolate, for melting
20 chocolate balls
10 Marie biscuits
15 orange Jelly Beans
10 black Jelly Beans
mini Jelly Beans in different colours
10 Oreos or chocolate biscuits
mini brown liquorice sweets
20 blue sugar drops

Melt the chocolate in the microwave, stirring often. Stick 2 chocolate balls together with a dab of melted chocolate, to form the body. Leave to set until the balls are firmly stuck together. Use some melted chocolate to stick the body upright in the centre of a Marie biscuit.

Cut an orange Jelly Bean in half diagonally. Use a dab of melted chocolate to stick the 2 halves to the front of the body, for the feet. Push the cut ends slightly under the chocolate ball. Cut a black Jelly Bean in half and stick one half on either side of the bottom chocolate ball, for the wings.

For the peacock's tail, use blobs of melted chocolate to stick different coloured mini Jelly Beans to the Oreo (leave a space in the centre to attach the biscuit to the body). Leave to stand until the Jelly Beans are stuck firmly to the Oreo.

Stack a few liquorice sweets behind the chocolate balls, then place the Oreo tail on top, using melted chocolate to attach it to the sweets and the chocolate balls (the sweets support the tail at the right height). Leave to stand until the chocolate sets.

For the beak, cut the tip off an orange Jelly Bean and use melted chocolate to stick it to the top chocolate ball. Finally, stick down blue sugar drops for the eyes.

MAKES 10

Tip: Mini Jelly Beans work best for the peacock's tail.

Crabs

64 jelly rings
10 Marie biscuits
glacé icing (page 8)
20 jelly orange slices
10 edible cupcake cases (cookie cups)
20 small round sweets

Cut open 60 of the jelly rings. Spread glacé icing over the Marie biscuit. Place 3 cut jelly rings along each side of the biscuit, for the legs (keep the front clear for the claws).

Trim the jelly orange slices, as shown in the picture. Cut the remaining jelly rings into 4. Using 1 piece of jelly ring and an orange slice per claw, position the 2 claws. To create the body, use a little glacé icing to stick an upturned cupcake case on top of the legs. Leave to stand until the icing sets.

Use glacé icing to stick 2 round sweets to the front of the cupcake case, for the eyes.

MAKES 10

Octopuses

10 Marie biscuits
glacé icing (page 8)
blue vermicelli or cake glitter
80 sour worms
10 large round sweets
20 sugar stars
10 sugar drops
icing tube

Spread glacé icing over the Marie biscuit, and sprinkle with blue vermicelli or cake glitter, to represent the sea.

Stick 8 sour worms around the edge of the biscuit, for the tentacles, leaving a space in the centre. Place a large round sweet in the centre, for the head (use an extra dab of glacé icing to stick it down firmly). Leave to stand until the glacé icing has set completely.

Use small drops of glacé icing to stick 2 sugar stars to the head, for the eyes, and a sugar drop for the nose. Use the icing tube to draw the mouth.

MAKES 10

ANIMALS

Turtles

10 Marie biscuits
blue butter icing (page 8)
20 green jelly slices
10 jelly rings
10 large Jelly Tots
10 jelly sweets
20 sugar balls

Spread blue butter icing over the Marie biscuit.

Cut the jelly slices lengthwise in 2 so they are flatter. Place 4 jelly slices on top of the Marie biscuit, for the flippers, as shown.

For the body, stick the jelly ring in the centre of the biscuit, so that it rests on top of the flippers. Press a large Jelly Tot into the centre of the jelly ring (use a dab of butter icing to stick it down).

For the head, stick the jelly sweet on top of the butter icing. Add sugar balls for the eyes, using a little butter icing.

MAKES 10

Mallow mermaids

10 marshmallow fish
glacé icing (page 8)
yellow butter icing (page 8)
10 flat apricot sweets
10 small star-shaped sweets
20 Jelly Tots
10 sugar balls
pink and blue icing tubes or glacé icing

Trim the head of the fish to make it flatter, but don't cut it off.

Use glacé icing to stick the apricot sweet to the head of the fish, for the mermaid's head. Put the yellow butter icing into an icing bag and use a star-shaped nozzle to pipe hair around the face. Place a small star-shaped sweet in the hair.

Use a dab of glacé icing to stick down the Jelly Tots and sugar ball, as shown in the picture. Using an icing tube or glacé icing in a piping bag, draw the mermaid's face.
Leave to stand until all the icing has set.

MAKES 10

ANIMALS

Stingrays

10 cocktail sticks
70 ring-shaped sweets
10 Jelly Tots
10 finger biscuits
10 wafer biscuits
glacé icing (page 8)
20 small round chocolate sweets
mini liquorice sweets

Thread 7 ring-shaped sweets onto a cocktail stick. Put a Jelly Tot on one end of the cocktail stick and press the other end into a finger biscuit, for the tail.

Cut a wafer biscuit in half diagonally, to form 2 triangles. Using glacé icing, stick 1 biscuit triangle on either side of the finger biscuit, with the pointed end towards the cocktail stick, for the 'wings'. Leave to set.

Using glacé icing, stick 2 round chocolate sweets to the front of the finger biscuit, for the eyes. Separate the layers of the mini liquorice sweets and cut each layer diagonally into 2 triangles. Use dabs of glacé icing to stick these to the finger biscuit, for the scales.

MAKES 10

Penguin on an igloo

white butter icing (page 8)
10 Sweetie Pies
10 Marie biscuits
shop-bought white fondant
10 shop-bought penguins

Stick a Sweetie Pie to a Marie biscuit with a dab of butter icing. With a blunt knife, cover the Sweetie Pie with butter icing. Use a cocktail stick to mark the icing so it resembles blocks of ice.

Shape some white fondant to make the igloo entrance and stick this to the front of the Sweetie Pie.

Place the penguin on top of the igloo.

MAKES 10

Tip: Cake decorating shops should stock penguins made from fondant icing. Alternatively, buy plastic penguins. If you are very creative, you can make the penguins yourself, using fondant.

ANIMALS

Buzzy bees

glacé icing (page 8)
10 Romany Creams or chocolate-filled biscuits
10 Marie biscuits
10 flat apricot sweets
20 jelly orange slices
yellow butter icing (page 8)
10 oblong liquorice sweets

Using glacé icing, stick a Romany Cream to a Marie biscuit.

Draw a face on an apricot sweet with a non-toxic pen or icing tube, and use a dab of icing to stick this in front of the Romany Cream, for the bee's head.

Cut one end off 2 jelly orange slices and use glacé icing to stick these behind the head, for the wings.

Fit an icing bag with a star-shaped nozzle and fill with yellow butter icing. Pipe 3 stripes across the body (from one side of the Marie biscuit to the other). Finish by piping a small star at the each end of the stripe, for the bee's feet.

Cut off one end of the oblong liquorice sweet and stick it at the back of the body, for the bee's sting.

MAKES 10

Speedy beetles

50g milk chocolate, for melting
10 Oreos or chocolate biscuits
20 plain pretzels
20 Smarties

Melt the chocolate in the microwave, stirring often. Using melted chocolate, stick 2 pretzels to the bottom of the Oreo so the large loops are visible, as shown. Leave until set.

Use melted chocolate to stick 2 Smarties on top of the Oreo, for the eyes.

MAKES 10

56 ANIMALS

Dragonflies

20 wafer biscuits
10 finger biscuits
glacé icing (page 8)
30 round flat sweets
20 mini marshmallows
short liquorice strips

Cut all the wafer biscuits diagonally in half. To make the wings, position 4 cut wafer biscuits in an 'X' shape (place 2 biscuits with the pointed ends touching, and 2 biscuits with the wide ends towards the centre).

Spread glacé icing on the bottom of the finger biscuit and place it over the centre of the wafer biscuits, as shown in the picture.

Using glacé icing, stick 3 round sweets to the top of the finger biscuit. Push short liquorice strips into 2 mini marshmallows and stick these to the front of the finger biscuit, for the eyes.
Leave until the glacé icing is well set.

MAKES 10

Butterflies

15 wafer biscuits
10 finger biscuits
glacé icing (page 8)
60 Smarties
20 Jelly Tots
short liquorice strips

Cut 10 wafer biscuits in half diagonally, to form triangles. Cut the other 5 wafer biscuits in half, to form 10 squares, and cut each square diagonally into 2 triangles. Using glacé icing, stick the wafer triangles to the finger biscuits as shown, for the wings. Leave to set.

Decorate the wings with Smarties (using glacé icing, place 2 Smarties where the wings meet and 1 on each wing tip, as shown).

Stick 2 Jelly Tots at the front of the finger biscuit, for the eyes. Cut the liquorice strips into 10mm lengths and stick 1 behind each Jelly Tot, for the feelers.

MAKES 10

ANIMALS

Mini insects

You can make an assortment of mini insects and other creatures using a variety of sweets and some melted chocolate. These are quick to prepare and can be incorporated into many party themes, or even made as a special treat or a lunch box surprise. Use these ideas as guidelines and inspiration to get you going. (All the recipes use melted milk chocolate to stick the parts together.)

Spiders

chocolate balls
mini liquorice sweets
short liquorice strips

Stick the mini liquorice sweet to the front of the chocolate ball. Stick 8 liquorice 'legs', in different lengths, to the body.
Allow the chocolate to set before handling.

Ants

short liquorice strips
Jelly Babies

Cut the liquorice strips into small pieces. Stick 4 pieces on either side of the Jelly Baby, for the legs.
Allow the chocolate to set before handling.

Worms

flat, round sweets (7 or 8 per worm)
heart-shaped sweets or Smarties
Jelly Tots (halved)
oblong liquorice sweets (halved)
vermicelli

Stick the round sweets together, and place a heart-shaped sweet or Smartie at the front, for the face. Place half a Jelly Tot at the back and top it with a half liquorice sweet, for the tail. Draw a face using a non-toxic pen and add two vermicelli, for the feelers.

Snails

round marbled jelly sweets
Jelly Tots
vermicelli

Cut a thin piece off one side of the jelly sweet to create a flat edge. Stand the sweet on the cut edge, to form the body.
Stick a Jelly Tot to the front of the jelly sweet, for the head.
Stick 2 pieces of vermicelli on top of the Jelly Tot, for the feelers.
Allow the chocolate to set before handling.

58 ANIMALS

Hairy caterpillars

sour worms
vermicelli
icing tube

Spread melted chocolate over the sour worm (leaving one end clear for the head) and press the worm into the vermicelli. Use the icing tube to draw a face.
Allow the chocolate and icing to set before handling.

Ladybirds

Jelly Tots
round sugared jelly sweets
icing tube

Cut a piece off a Jelly Tot and stick the flat end to the round sugared jelly sweet, to form the head and body. Using the icing tube, draw eyes and wings on the body. Allow the chocolate and icing to set before handling.

Moths

round flat sweets (3 per moth)
Jelly Tots
jelly beans (halved)
heart-shaped sugared jelly sweets
sugar drops in various colours
vermicelli
icing in tubes

Stick 3 round flat sweets together. Place a Jelly Tot at the front, for the face, and half a jelly bean at the back, for the tail.
Cut the points off 2 heart-shaped sweets and stick these to the sides of the body, for the wings. Decorate with sugar drops. Place 2 pieces of vermicelli on top of the head, for the feelers, and draw a face using the icing tube. Allow the chocolate to set before handling.

Baby bugs

Jelly Tots
mini Astros or small chocolate buttons

Cut off a little bit of Jelly Tot and stick the mini Astro to the cut part, for the head. Allow the chocolate to set, then use a non-toxic pen to draw a face on the Astro.

ANIMALS

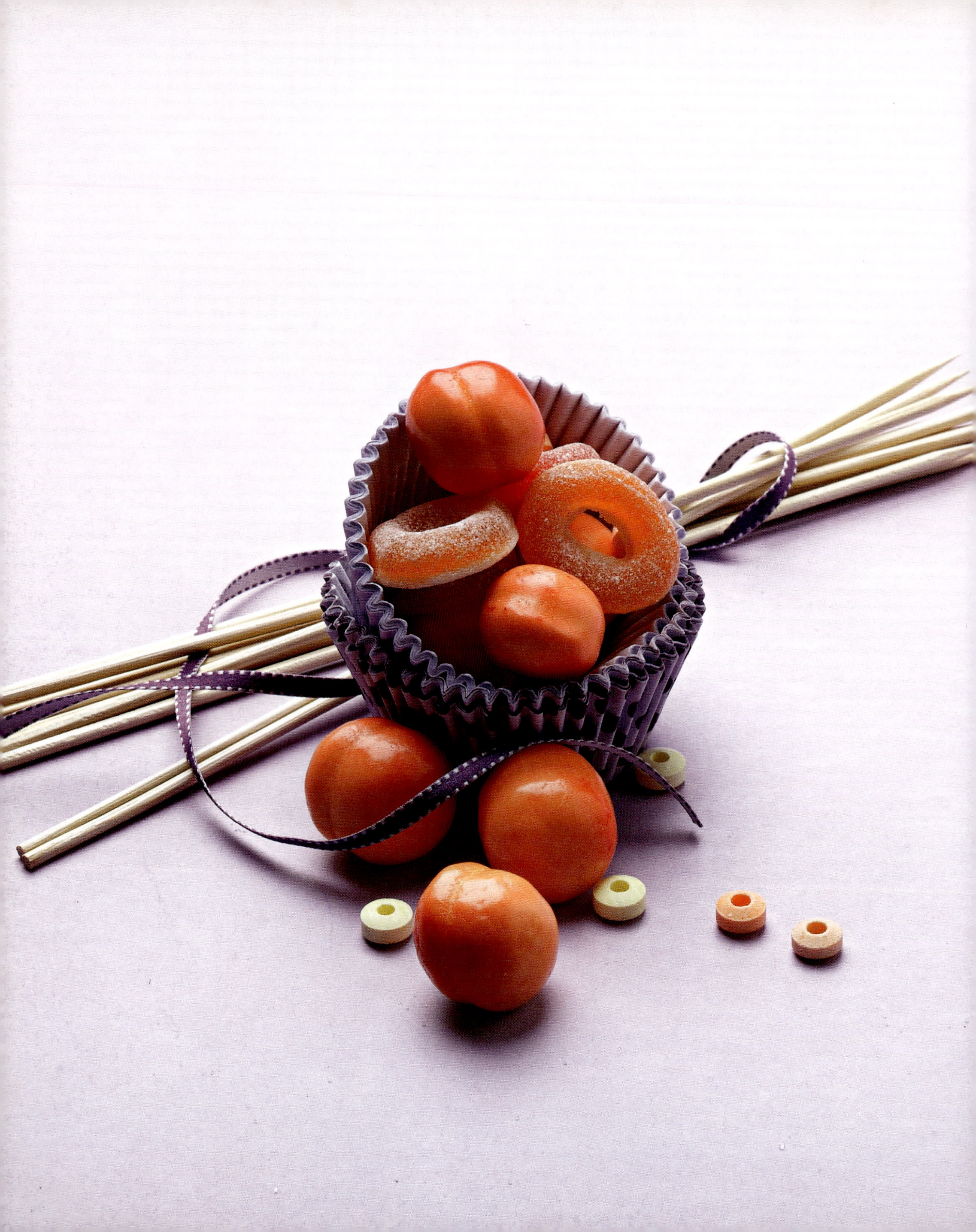

Little figures

Little figures

These little figures are quick to prepare and can be made with leftover sweets. Use these guidelines to make 16 different figures, or let your imagination run wild and see how many you can create. Exchange legs, feet, arms or heads, use other colour combinations, and substitute sweets if they not available or if your children don't like them. Use glacé icing to stick the separate parts together.

The first sweets listed form the legs or base of the figure, and the last sweets form the head. Unless otherwise stated, each set of instructions makes one figure, so multiply the sweets by the number of figures you require. Use an icing tube or a non-toxic (edible) pen to draw in the faces.

Soak wooden skewers or cocktail sticks beforehand, to make it easier and less sticky to thread the sweets onto them.

Twista man

Push a wooden skewer through the following:
square coconut marshmallow
jelly orange slice
round jelly sweet
marshmallow (threaded upright)
round jelly sweet
long marshmallow twist
2 small jelly rings
marshmallow (threaded sideways, for the face)
dome-shaped sweet (for the hat)

Marshmallow Maggie

Push a wooden skewer through the following, for the body:
3 marshmallows (2 pink and 1 white)
flat apricot sweet

4 yoghurt pretzel sticks
3 silver balls, for decoration

To finish off:
Press yoghurt pretzel sticks into the body for legs and arms. Stick 3 silver sugar balls onto the top marshmallow, for buttons. Draw a face using an icing tube or pen with edible ink.

62   LITTLE FIGURES

Little drummer boy

Push a wooden skewer through the following, for the body:
marshmallow
4 round, flat jelly rings
long sour worm
smaller marshmallow
Jelly Tot

For the legs, push a cocktail stick through the following (make 2):
long marshmallow

To finish off:
Press the cocktail sticks into the bottom marshmallow.
Draw a face using an icing tube or pen with edible ink.

Crazy clown

Push a wooden skewer through the following, for the body:
3 marshmallows
marshmallow face
flat sweet and a Jelly Tot (for the hat)

Push a cocktail stick through the following, for the legs (make 2):
jelly orange slice
long marshmallow

Push a cocktail stick through the top marshmallow and attach the following on either side, for the arms:
2 car-shaped marshmallows

silver balls, for decoration

To finish off:
Press the cocktail sticks into the bottom marshmallow, for the legs and feet. Stick 6 silver sugar balls to the top and middle marshmallows, for buttons. (If you don't have a marshmallow face, use a white marshmallow, on its side, and draw a face with an icing tube or non-toxic pen.)

LITTLE FIGURES   63

Mr Allsorts

Push a wooden skewer through the following, for the body:
2 square Allsorts
long liquorice sweet (threaded sideways)
3 jelly rings or ring-shaped sweets
round apricot sweet

Push a cocktail stick through the following, for the legs (make 2):
long liquorice sweet (threaded lengthwise)
small piece of liquorice sweet, for the feet

To finish off:
Press the cocktail sticks into the bottom liquorice square, to make the legs and feet. Press the top of the apricot sweet into glacé icing and then into sprinkles (100's & 1000's), to form the hair. Leave to set, then draw a face using a non-toxic pen.

Blue boy

Push a wooden skewer through the following, for the body:
white marshmallow
smaller, coloured marshmallow
2 round jelly sweets (blue or green)
small blue or green Fizzer (wrapped, threaded sideways)
round apricot sweet
round blue or green liquorice sweet, for the hat

Push a cocktail stick through the following, for the legs (make 2):
large Jelly Tot
5 jelly rings or ring-shaped sweets

To finish off:
Press the cocktail sticks into the bottom marshmallow, for the legs and feet. Use an icing tube or non-toxic pen to draw the face.

64   LITTLE FIGURES

Flipper foot

Push a wooden skewer through the following:
square coconut marshmallow
2 jelly feet
white marshmallow
circular (tyre-shaped) jelly sweet
white marshmallow
long liquorice sweet, threaded sideways
round jelly sweet
animal face-shaped sweet

Note: Skewer the jelly feet so that both feet rest on top of the coconut marshmallow.

Miss Fizzer

Push a wooden skewer through the following, for the body:
pink marshmallow (threaded sideways)
2 heart-shaped, pink marshmallows
small jelly ring
small pink Fizzer (wrapped, threaded sideways)
white marshmallow (threaded upright)
round Allsorts, for the hat

Push a cocktail stick through the following, for the legs (make 2):
shoe-shaped sweet
5 jelly rings or ring-shaped sweets

To finish off:
Press the cocktail sticks into the bottom marshmallow, for the legs and feet. Use an icing tube or non-toxic pen to draw the face.

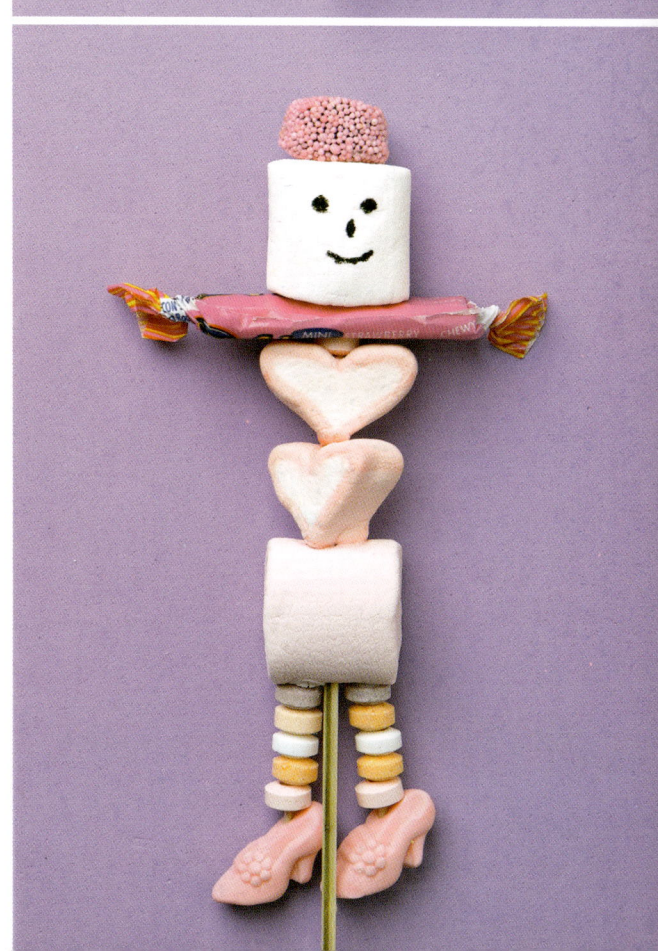

LITTLE FIGURES   65

Snow ghost

Push a wooden skewer through the following:
square coconut marshmallow
large jelly ring
white marshmallow
smaller jelly ring
white marshmallow
2 long liquorice sweets, threaded horizontally
white marshmallow
spinning top jelly sweet, for the hat

To finish off:
Stick a vampire teeth jelly sweet onto the body for the mouth. Draw a face and other details using an edible ink pen.

Uptown girl

Push a wooden skewer through the following, for the body:
coloured marshmallow
sugared jelly ring
coloured marshmallow
2 sugared jelly rings
long marshmallow, threaded sideways
sugared jelly ring
green-coloured apricot sweet, for the face

yellow butter icing (page 8), for the hair
mini marshmallow cone, for the hat

To finish off:
Fit an icing bag with a star-shaped nozzle, fill with butter icing and pipe some hair onto the apricot sweet. Place a mini marshmallow ice-cream cone upside down on top of the head, pressing down into the icing. Leave to set, then draw a face using a non-toxic pen.

66 LITTLE FIGURES

Water bug

Push a wooden skewer through the following, for the body:
white marshmallow (threaded sideways)
2 green jelly feet (threaded to overlap the marshmallow)
smaller blue marshmallow (threaded vertically)
red jelly snake with the head cut off (threaded sideways)
2 round green jelly sweets
flat apricot sweet

Push a cocktail stick through the following, for the feelers (make 2):
2 blue jelly rings or ring-shaped sweets
2 blue Jelly Tots

3 jelly rings or ring-shaped sweets (2 blue, 1 pink), to decorate

To finish off:
Press the cocktail sticks into the apricot sweet, for the feelers. Stick 3 small jelly rings to the front of the apricot sweet, for the mouth and eyes.

Cone-arm man

Push a wooden skewer through the following, for the body:
3 coloured marshmallows (thread the bottom and top marshmallows sideways and the centre one upright)
round apricot sweet

For the legs, push a cocktail stick through the following (make 2):
long marshmallow

2 mini marshmallow ice-cream cones
glacé icing (page 8)
rainbow vermicelli, to decorate

To finish off:
Press the cocktail sticks into the bottom marshmallow, for the legs. Using glacé icing, stick 2 mini marshmallow ice-cream cones to the top marshmallow, for the arms. Press the apricot sweet into the glacé icing and then into the rainbow vermicelli, for the hair. Draw a face onto the apricot sweet using an icing tube or a non-toxic pen.

LITTLE FIGURES

Jolly dolly

Push a wooden skewer through the following:
pink marshmallow
3 sugared jelly rings
pink marshmallow
small pink Fizzer (wrapped, threaded lengthwise)
2 small jelly rings or round sweets
1 Jolly Jammer biscuit

yellow butter icing (page 8), to decorate

To finish off:
Place yellow butter icing in an icing bag fitted with a star-shaped nozzle and pipe the hair onto the biscuit.

Tip: If you can't get Jolly Jammer biscuits, use a round filled biscuit and draw a face using an icing tube or a non-toxic pen.

Rocket man

Push a wooden skewer through the following, for the body:
2 marshmallows
mini Chomp (unwrapped, threaded lengthwise)
marshmallow
spinning top jelly sweet

Push a cocktail stick through the following, for the legs (make 2):
Jelly Tot
6 small jelly rings or ring-shaped sweets

pink mini marshmallow
blue mini marshmallow

To finish off:
Press the cocktail sticks into the bottom marshmallow, for the legs and feet. To make the face, use glacé icing to stick a pink mini marshmallow in place for the mouth, and cut a blue mini marshmallow in half for the eyes.

68   LITTLE FIGURES

Disco dancer

Push a wooden skewer through the following, for the body:
2 cerise-coloured apricot sweets
1 Jolly Jammer biscuit

Push cocktail sticks through the following, for the arms and legs (make 4):
sour worms (use matching worms for the arms and legs)

mini marshmallows
glacé icing (page 8)

To finish off:
Press 2 sour worms into the bottom apricot sweet, for the legs, and 2 into the top apricot sweet, for the arms. Using glacé icing, stick mini marshmallows to the top edge of the Jolly Jammer face, for the hair.

Tip: If you can't get Jolly Jammer biscuits, use a round filled biscuit and draw a face using an icing tube or a non-toxic pen.

Skeleton Sam

Push a wooden skewer through the following:
large sugared jelly ring (threaded sideways)
3 small white jelly rings or ring-shaped sweets
large sugared jelly ring (threaded sideways)
1 small white jelly ring or ring-shaped sweet
jelly skull

nylon fishing line or thread
28 small white jelly rings or ring-shaped sweets

To finish off:
Tie a small jelly ring or ring-shaped sweet to one end of a piece of nylon thread. String 9 small ring shaped sweets onto the nylon, then wind the thread twice around the skewer where it goes through the ring-shaped sweet. String another 9 small ring-shaped sweets to the other side and end off by tying a ring-shaped sweet to the end. Repeat this for the arms, but use 5 sweets and wind the nylon around the skewer where it was pushed through the top ring-shaped sweet.

Tip: To make the arms and legs sturdier, thread strips of liquorice through the ring-shaped sweets together with the nylon.

LITTLE FIGURES

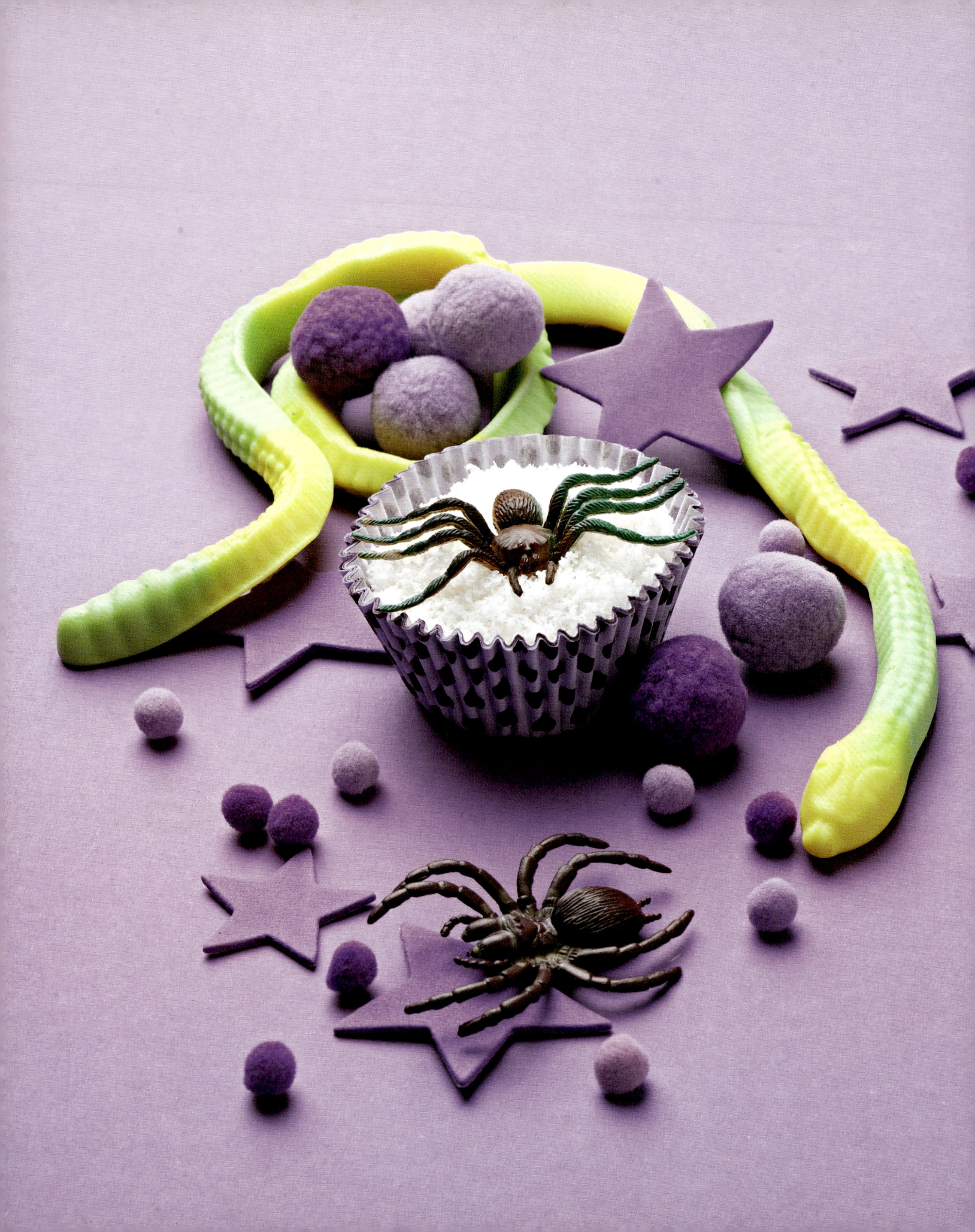

Aliens and creepy crawlies

Robots

40 cocktail sticks
50 Jelly Tots
120 ring-shaped sweets
10 white marshmallows
glacé icing (page 8)
non-toxic pen or icing tube
10 Marie biscuits
5 marshmallows, cut in half

To make the legs and feet, push a cocktail stick into a Jelly Tot, then thread on 4 ring-shaped sweets. Make 2 legs per robot. Push the legs into the long side of the marshmallow.

Place a Jelly Tot at one end of a cocktail stick, for a hand, and add 2 ring-shaped sweets, for an arm. Push the cocktail stick through the marshmallow and add 2 ring-shaped sweets and a Jelly Tot to the other end of the stick, for the other arm and hand.

Cut a Jelly Tot in half. Use glacé icing to stick the halves on top of the marshmallow, for antennae. Draw a face using a non-toxic pen.

Spread some glacé icing over a Marie biscuit. Cut a marshmallow in half, and place it on one side of the biscuit, to support the robot and prevent it from falling over. Stick the robot to the biscuit, resting it against the marshmallow. Leave to stand for the icing to set completely.

MAKES 10

Ghosts

white fondant
10 white marshmallows
non-toxic pen

Roll out the fondant and cut out circles. Drape each circle over a marshmallow, pressing down lightly. Allow to stand for a while and then draw faces using a non-toxic pen.

MAKES 10

Tip: Wet the marshmallows slightly to help the fondant stick.

Creepy brownies

fridge brownie recipe (page 12)
milk chocolate, for melting
various creepy jelly sweets

Prepare the brownie mixture and bake as normal. While the brownies are still warm, cut into squares, or use cookie cutters to cut shapes. Melt the chocolate and use dabs to stick the jelly sweets on top of the brownies.

Burrowing earthworms
Make these with leftover brownie bits. Place a layer of crumbled brownies at the bottom of a transparent plastic cup. Insert a jelly worm so that it is visible, then almost fill the cup with more crumbs (add chopped marshmallows or other crumbled biscuits to fill the cups, if necessary). Push one or two creepy sweets and another worm into the top of the crumbs.

ALIENS AND CREEPY CRAWLIES

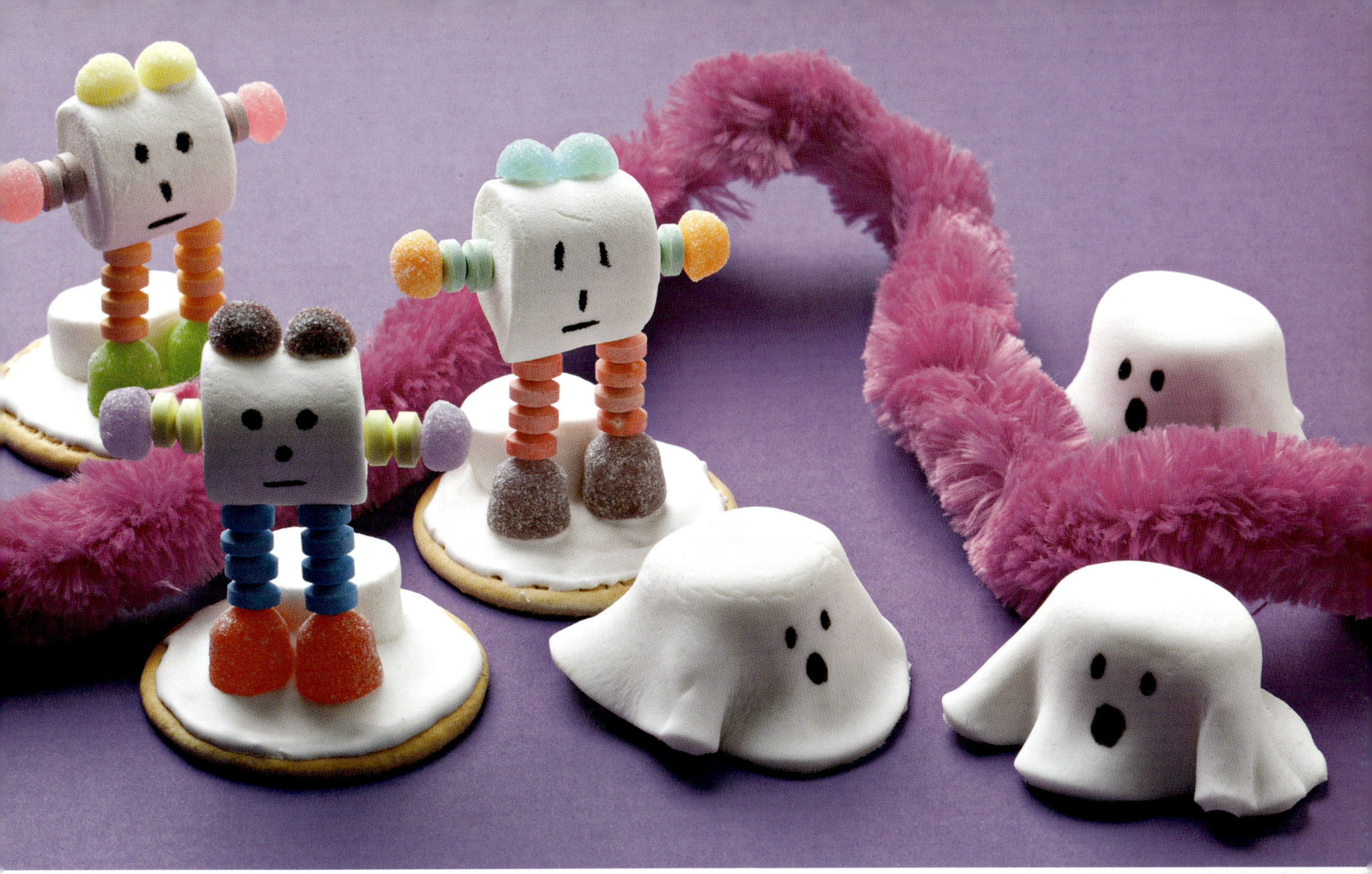

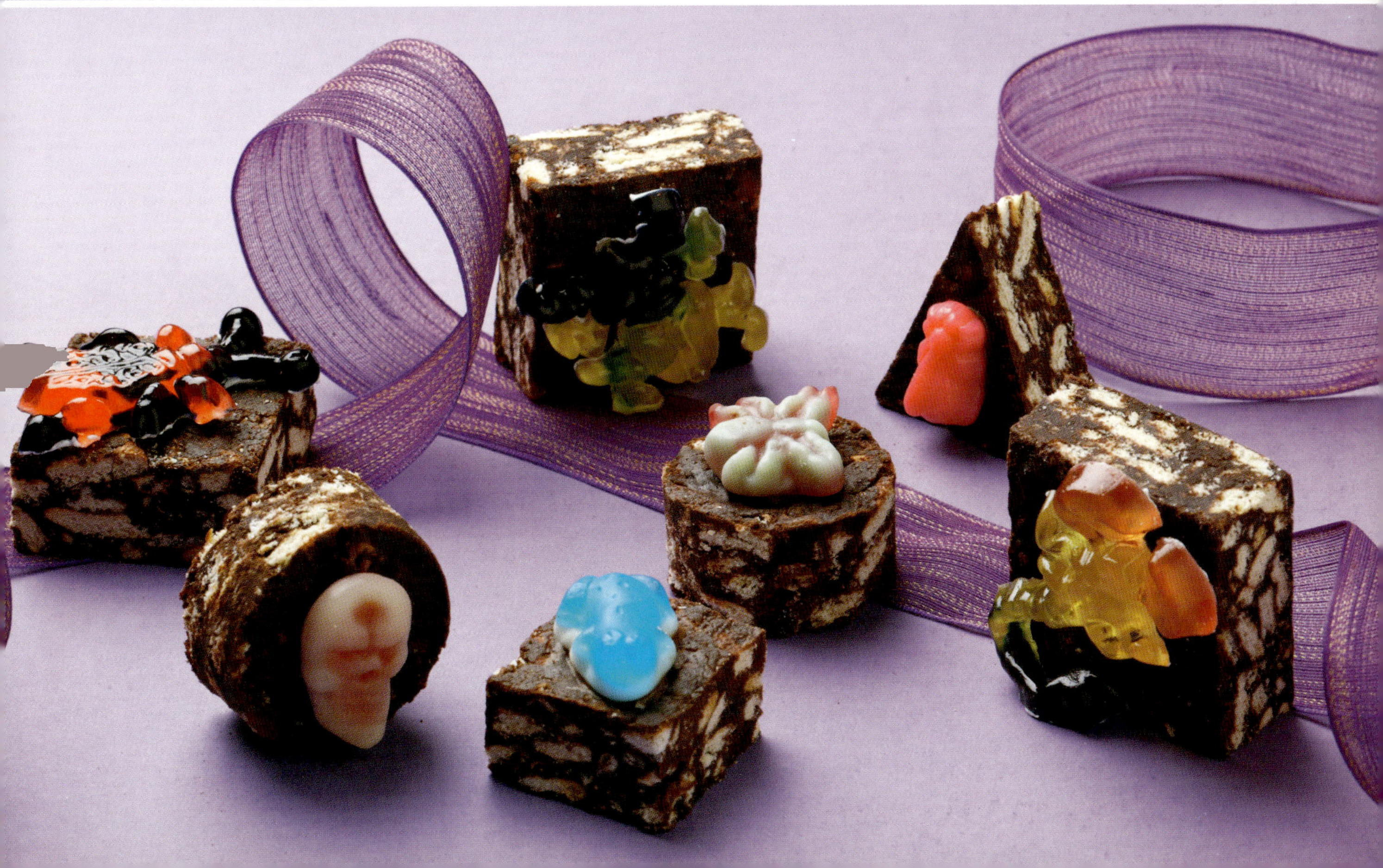

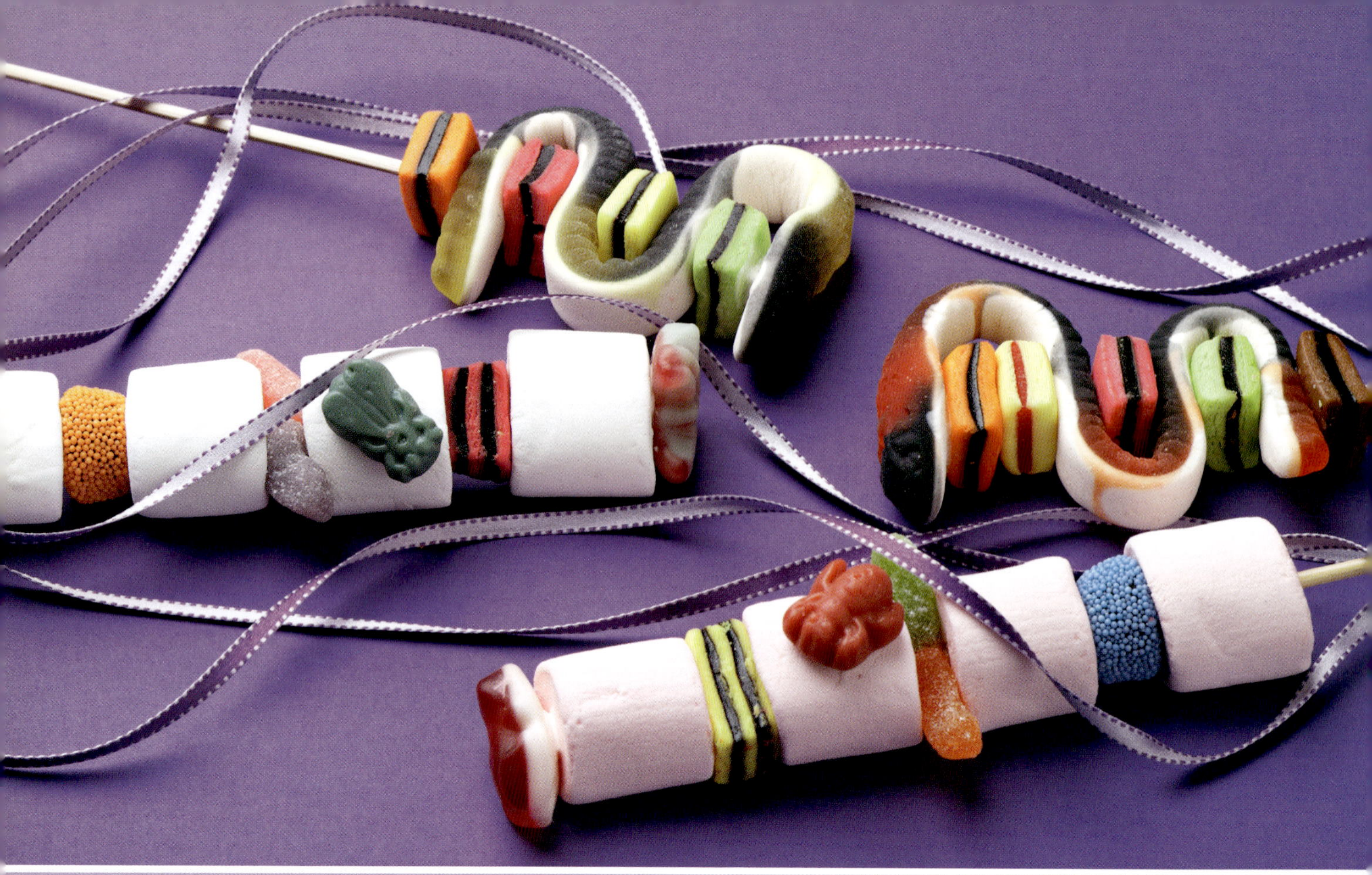

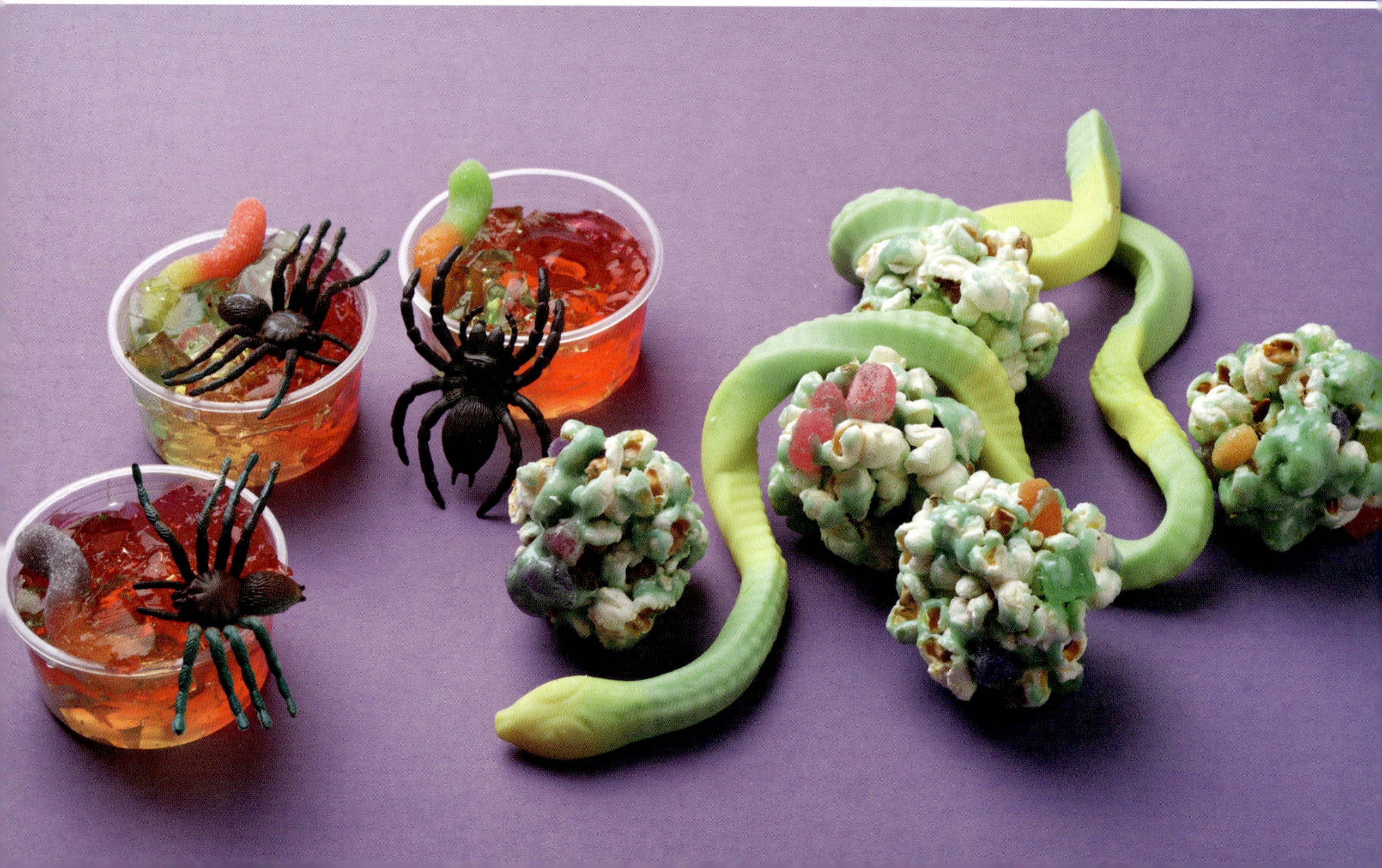

Kreepy kebabs

marshmallows (4 per kebab)
liquorice sweets
wooden skewers
various creepy jelly sweets
glacé icing (page 8)

Push wooden skewers through alternating marshmallows and other sweets. Using glacé icing, stick creepy jelly sweets to the sides of the marshmallows, and one on top. Leave to set.

Tip: Dipping the point of wooden skewers in lukewarm water makes it easier to push them through marshmallows and sticky sweets.

Ssssnake skewers

large jelly snakes
liquorice sweets
wooden skewers

Starting at the tail of the jelly snake, thread a wooden skewer through the snake, making an 'S' shape and alternating with liquorice sweets, as in the picture.

Slime cups

3 packets of jelly powder (green, yellow and orange)
10 plastic cups
10 sour worms
10 plastic spiders

Prepare each colour jelly according to the packet instructions and allow to set. Cut or stir up the jelly so it isn't solid and smooth anymore.

Spoon some of each colour jelly into a cup, mixing gently to combine the colours. Insert a sour worm so it is half in and half out of the jelly, and position a plastic spider on top of the slime.

MAKES 10

Slime balls

62.5ml (¼ cup) popcorn
sunflower oil (to pop corn)
Jelly Tots (± 4–5 per ball)
16 marshmallows
20g (1T) butter
30ml (1T) green jelly powder

Pop the popcorn (in oil or in the microwave, as preferred). Allow to cool. Place the cooled popcorn in a large bowl and add the Jelly Tots.

Melt the marshmallows and butter together in the microwave. Add the jelly powder and stir the colour through. Pour the melted marshmallow mixture over the popcorn and stir well. Quickly roll into small balls, and leave to set.

MAKES 12

ALIENS AND CREEPY CRAWLIES

Friendly aliens

10 Marie biscuits
glacé icing (page 8)
20 feet-shaped jelly sweets
10 marshmallows
20 Jelly Tots
70 small ring-shaped sweets
10 large ring-shaped sweets
10 apricot sweets
10 mini liquorice sweets
non-toxic pen

Spread glacé icing over the Marie biscuit and stick 2 feet on top. With another dab of icing, stick a marshmallow upright on top of the feet. Leave to stand until set.

For the arms, thread a Jelly Tot and 2 small ring-shaped sweets onto one end of a cocktail stick. Push the cocktail stick through the marshmallow and add another 2 small ring-shaped sweets and a Jelly Tot.

For the head, thread a mini liquorice sweet onto one end of a cocktail stick, followed by a small ring-shaped sweet, apricot sweet and a large ring-shaped sweet. Push the other end of the cocktail stick into the marshmallow.

Stick 2 small ring-shaped sweets to the front of the apricot sweet, for the eyes. Draw a mouth and nose using a non-toxic pen.

MAKES 10

Angry aliens

green butter icing (page 8)
silver and blue sugar crystals
10 Marie biscuits
15 marshmallows
glacé icing (page 8)
20 Astros or chocolate buttons
10 silver sugar balls
liquorice strips

Spread green butter icing over the Marie biscuit. Press a marshmallow into the centre and decorate the edges with coloured sugar crystals. (Make some aliens bigger by using 2 marshmallows, stuck together with a little glacé icing.)

Use a wet sosatie skewer to make 3 holes in the marshmallow. Using a little glacé icing, insert 2 Astros for the eyes and a sugar ball for the nose.

Make 2 holes on top of the marshmallow. Cut the liquorice strips into small pieces, dip one end into some glacé icing and insert them into the holes to resemble antennae.

MAKES 10

Space dwarves

Jelly Babies
glacé icing (page 8)
silver sugar balls
liquorice strips

Using a sharp knife, cut the heads off the Jelly Babies. 'Mix and match' by placing a head of one colour onto a body of another colour. (The sweets should be sticky enough for the heads to stay in place, but if not, use a little glacé icing and allow to set.)

Using glacé icing, stick 2 silver sugar balls to the face, for the eyes. Cut the liquorice strips into small pieces and stick two to the top of the head, for the antennae.

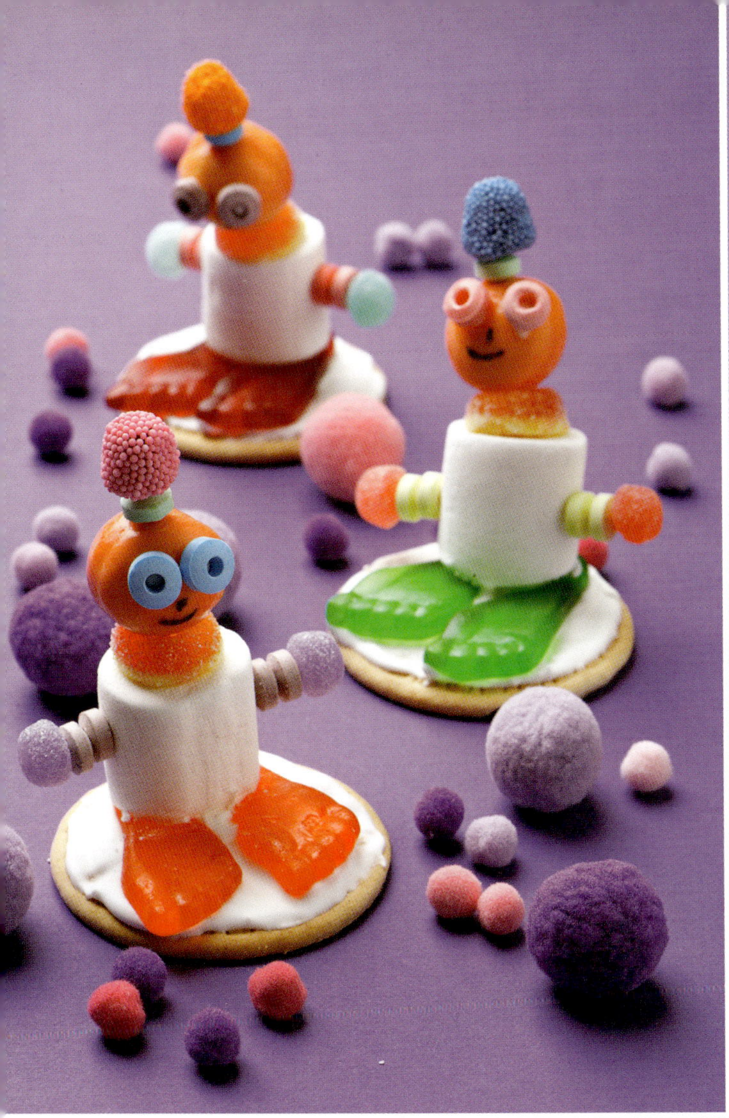
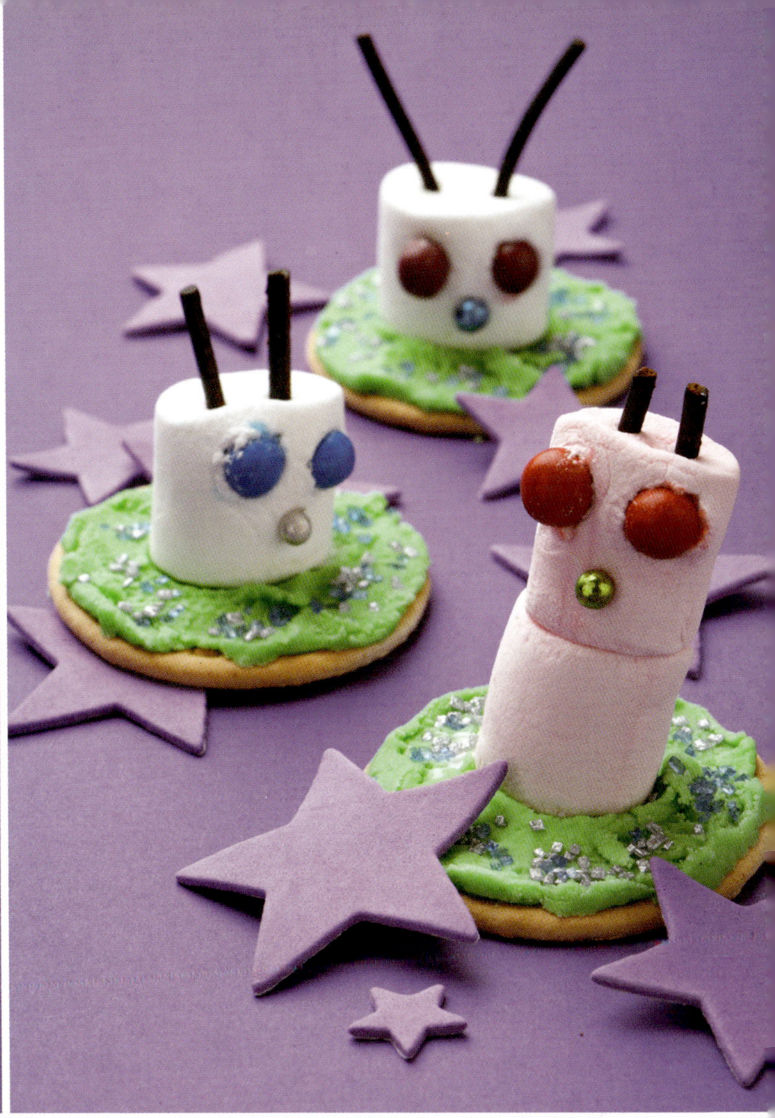
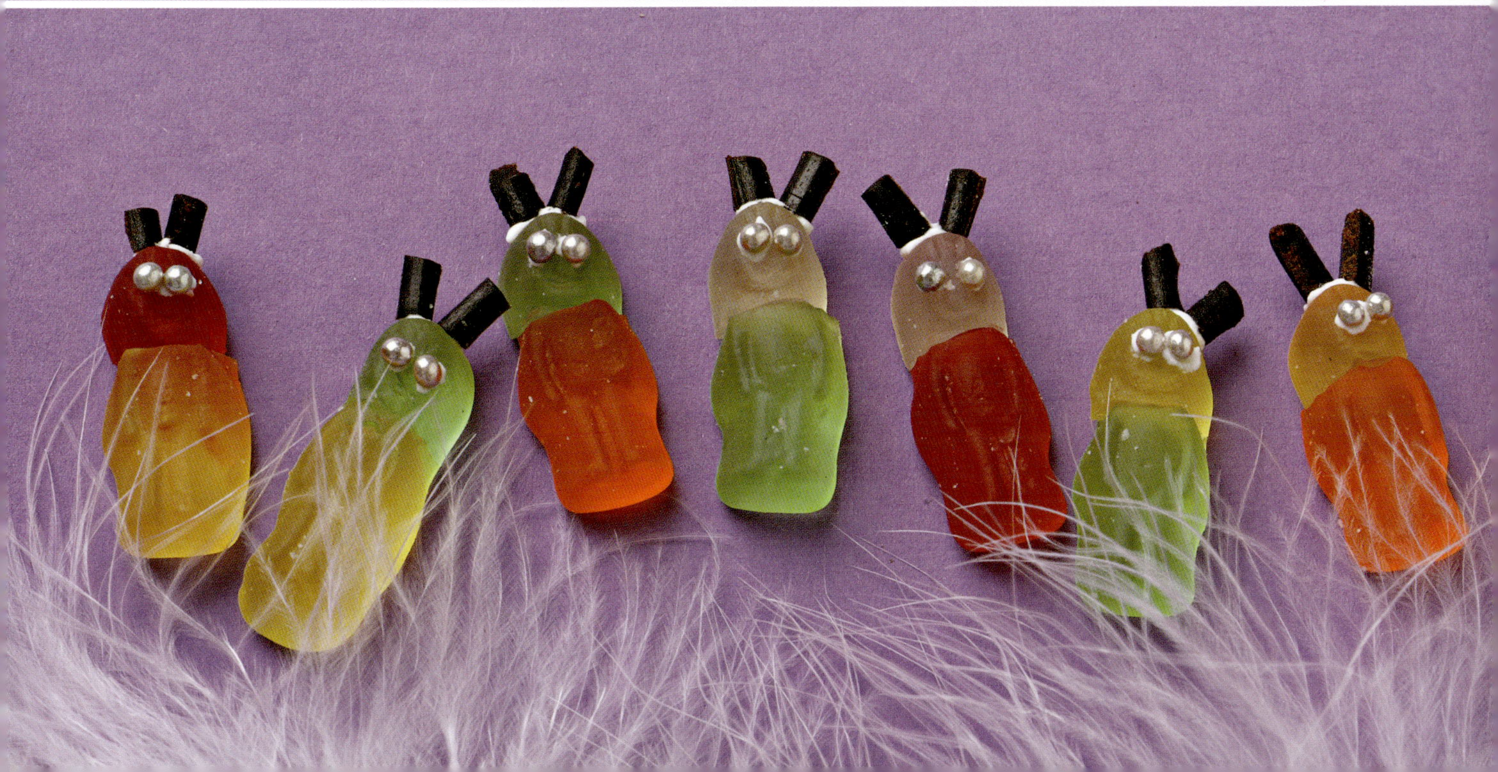

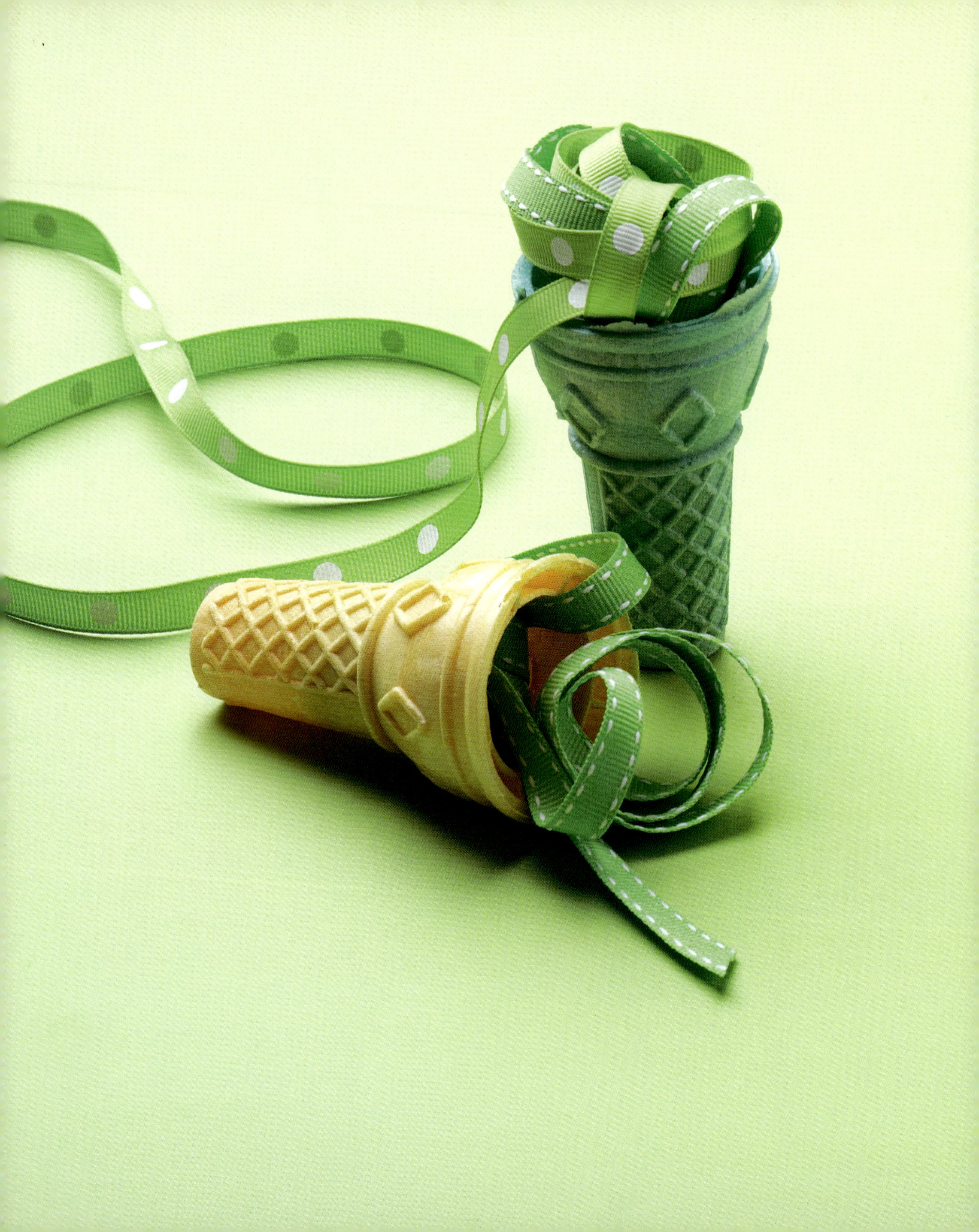

Cone figures

Flower girl

10 ice-cream cones
variety of small sweets
butter icing (page 8)
10 Marie biscuits
5 marshmallows or 5 apricot sweets
dome-shaped sugared jelly sweets
long marshmallows or sour worms
sugar flowers, cake beads, Smarties or
    other sweets for decorating
non-toxic pen

Fill the ice-cream cones with a variety of small sweets.
Fit an icing bag with a star-shaped nozzle, fill with butter icing and pipe a border around the edge of a Marie biscuit. Press the biscuit onto the cone. Place in a standing position and leave to set.

Use a non-toxic pen to draw faces on the marshmallows or apricot sweets. Cut off the tip of the cone. Use butter icing to stick a marshmallow or apricot sweet onto the cone, for the head. Stick a dome-shaped jelly sweet on top, for a hat.

Using butter icing, stick two long marshmallows or sour worms to the sides of the cone, for the arms. Pipe 2 butter icing stars on the front of each cone and stick sugar flowers or other sweets on top, for decoration.

Leave to stand for the icing to set completely.

MAKES 10

Lady with a handbag

10 apricot sweets
glacé icing (page 8)
chocolate vermicelli
10 ice-cream cones
butter icing (page 8)
10 Marie biscuits
variety of small sweets
pearl cake beads
10 handbag-shaped sweets
white and pink pearl sprinkles
non-toxic pen

Dip half the apricot sweet into the glacé icing and then into the chocolate vermicelli, for the hair. Leave to stand for the icing to set, then draw a face using a non-toxic pen. Cut the tip off the ice-cream cone.

Fit an icing bag with a star-shaped nozzle, fill with butter icing and pipe a border around the edge of a Marie biscuit. Press the biscuit onto the cone and leave until the icing sets. Pour small sweets into the open end of the cone.

Pipe a circle of butter icing around the open end of the cone and set the head on top. Press pearl cake beads into the icing, to make a necklace. Pipe butter icing around the base of the cone. Stick the handbag-shaped sweet to the front and cover the rest of the icing with sprinkles. Leave to stand for the icing to set completely.

MAKES 10

Lady with a hat

10 ice-cream cones
variety of small sweets
butter icing (page 8) in yellow and other colours
10 Marie biscuits
cake beads
10 marshmallows
10 edible cupcake cases
butterfly sprinkles
20 long marshmallows
Smarties
non-toxic pen

Fill the ice-cream cone with a variety of small sweets.

Fit an icing bag with a star-shaped nozzle, fill with yellow butter icing and pipe a border around the edge of a Marie biscuit. Press the biscuit onto the cone. Place in a standing position, press cake beads into the icing and leave to set.

Use a wet sosatie skewer to make a hole in one side of a marshmallow and push the tip of the cone into the marshmallow, for the head.

Fit a piping bag with a thin star-shaped nozzle and fill with yellow butter icing. Pipe icing around the top and sides of the marshmallow, for the hair.

Place an edible cupcake case on top of the hair, for a hat. Using a different coloured butter icing, pipe stars along the edge of the cupcake case and decorate with cake beads and butterfly sprinkles.

Use a dab of icing to stick a long marshmallow onto either side of the ice-cream cone, for the arms. Pipe 2 or 3 icing stars on the front of the cone and stick Smarties to the stars. Use a non-toxic pen to draw a face on the marshmallow.

Leave to stand for the icing to set completely.

MAKES 10

Beach babes

10 ice-cream cones
variety of small sweets
yellow and green butter icing (page 8)
10 Marie biscuits
10 marshmallows
sugar flowers
10 paper umbrellas
20 thin long marshmallows
20 Smarties
cake beads
non-toxic pen

Fill the ice-cream cone with a variety of small sweets. Fit an icing bag with a round nozzle, fill with green butter icing and pipe a border around the edge of a Marie biscuit. Press the biscuit onto the cone, place in a standing position, and leave to set.

Cut the tip off the ice-cream cone and stick a marshmallow on top, for the head. Fit an icing bag with a thin, star-shaped nozzle and fill with yellow butter icing. Pipe long lines of icing over the top and sides of the marshmallow, for the lady's hair, and shorter bristles for the man's hair. Place a sugar flower in the lady's hair. Using a non-toxic pen, draw the faces, then push an open paper umbrella into the back of the marshmallow, so it stands away from the head.

Stick a long marshmallow to either side of the ice-cream cone, for the arms. Using a star-shaped nozzle and green butter icing, pipe a pair of trousers for the man and a bikini top and skirt for the lady. Decorate the lady's top with 2 Smarties and her skirt with cake beads. Leave to stand for the icing to set completely.

MAKES 10

Pearly princess

10 ice-cream cones
variety of small sweets
yellow and white butter icing (page 8)
10 Marie biscuits
10 marshmallows
star-shaped sweets or sugar flowers
pearl cake beads
non-toxic pen

Fill the ice-cream cone with a variety of small sweets. Fit an icing bag with a round nozzle, fill with butter icing and pipe a border around the edge of a Marie biscuit. Press the biscuit onto the cone, place in a standing position and leave to set.

Cut the tip off the ice-cream cone, but don't throw it away. Using a dab of icing, stick the marshmallow onto the cut end of the cone, for the head. Fit an icing bag with a thin, star-shaped nozzle and fill with yellow butter icing. Pipe icing onto the top and sides of the marshmallow, for the hair. Before the icing sets, press the tip of the cone into the hair, for a hat. Use dabs of icing to stick star-shaped sweets or sugar flowers to the hat and in the hair.

Using a round nozzle, pipe white butter icing in swirls around the base of the cone. Decorate with pearl cake beads in various colours. Pipe 3 blobs of icing on the front of the cone and press a cake bead onto each blob, for buttons.
Leave to stand for the icing to set. Draw a face using a non-toxic pen.

MAKES 10

Rock stars

10 ice-cream cones
variety of small sweets
yellow butter icing (page 8)
10 Marie biscuits
glacé icing (page 8)
10 round lollipops
liquorice logs
20 cocktail sticks
small star-shaped sweets
small chocolate buttons or Smarties
cake beads or silver balls
blue and orange round sugar sprinkles
non-toxic pen

Fill the ice-cream cone with a variety of small sweets.

Fit an icing bag with a star-shaped nozzle, fill with butter icing and pipe a border around the edge of a Marie biscuit. Press the biscuit onto the cone, place in a standing position and leave to set.

Cut the tip off the ice-cream cone (or make a small hole in the tip). Unwrap a lollipop and push the stick into the hole (use a little glacé icing to hold the lollipop in place). Leave to set.

For the arms, cut the liquorice logs into short lengths. Push a cocktail stick through the cone and place a liquorice strip on each end. Pipe icing stars on top of the liquorice strips and place a cake bead on top of each star.

Using butter icing, pipe a pair of trousers on the front of the cone, and decorate with star-shaped sweets or cake beads. Pipe 3 or 4 butter icing stars on the front of each cone and stick chocolate buttons or Smarties on top.

Pipe upright lines on top of the lollipop, for 'punk' hair.

Position sugar sprinkles for the eyes and nose. The lollipop should be sticky enough but if not, stick down using a little glacé icing. Draw a mouth using a non-toxic pen.

Leave to stand for the icing to set completely.

MAKES 10

One-eyed aliens

10 ice-cream cones
variety of small sweets
yellow and white butter icing (page 8)
10 Marie biscuits
silver cake beads
10 twisted marshmallows
short liquorice strips
mini Allsorts, halved
cocktail sticks
20 sugared jelly rings
20 dome-shaped sugared jelly sweets
30 ring-shaped sweets

Fill the ice-cream cone with a variety of small sweets. Fit an icing bag with a star-shaped nozzle, fill with butter icing and pipe a border around the edge of a Marie biscuit. Press the biscuit onto the cone and place in a standing position. Press silver cake beads into the butter icing and leave to set.

Cut the tip off the ice-cream cone. Use a dab of white butter icing to stick the twisted marshmallow to the top of the cone. Using glacé icing, stick a piece of liquorice strip onto the marshmallow, for a mouth, and half a mini Allsorts, for an eye. Push 2 liquorice strips into the top of the marshmallow, for antennae.

Push a cocktail stick through the cone and place a sugared jelly ring and a dome-shaped sugared jelly sweet on either end, for the arms. Pipe 3 blobs of butter icing on the front of the cone and top with ring-shaped sweets and a cake bead. Leave to stand for the icing to set completely.

MAKES 10

Spaceships

10 ice-cream cones
variety of small sweets
butter icing (page 8)
10 Marie biscuits
20 wafer biscuits
cake beads
dome-shaped sugared jelly sweets
Smarties
sugar stars

Fill the ice-cream cone with a variety of small sweets. Fit an icing bag with a star-shaped nozzle, fill with butter icing and pipe a border around the edge of a Marie biscuit. Press the biscuit onto the cone, place in a standing position and leave to set.

Cut the wafer biscuits in half diagonally. Use some butter icing to stick 4 wafer halves to each cone, for the fins. Cut the tip off the ice-cream cone. Use a dab of butter icing to stick a dome-shaped sugared jelly sweet to the cone, and another small dab to position a silver cake bead on top of the jelly sweet.

Pipe blobs of butter icing between each wafer biscuit and top with Smarties. On the front of the spaceship, pipe a blob of butter icing just below the nose-cone and add a sugar star, for decoration.
Leave to stand for the icing to set completely.

MAKES 10

CONE FIGURES

Clowns

10 ice-cream cones
purple or red butter icing (page 8)
10 Marie biscuits
variety of small sweets
10 marshmallows
small chocolate buttons or Smarties
non-toxic pen

Cut the ice-cream cone in half (keeping both halves). Fit an icing bag with a star-shaped nozzle, fill with butter icing and pipe a border around the edge of a Marie biscuit. Press the top of the cone onto the biscuit and leave to set.

Pour small sweets into the cone. Pipe butter icing around the edge of the cone and place the marshmallow on top, for the face. Leave to set.

Pipe butter icing around the open edge of the lower part of the ice-cream cone and press it onto the marshmallow, for a hat. Using butter icing, pipe stars around the joins, and a star on the tip of the hat. Leave to set.

Using a non-toxic pen, draw a face. Add a red butter icing star for the nose. Pipe 2 butter icing stars below the marshmallow and 3 stars on the hat and decorate with small chocolate buttons or Smarties.

Leave to stand for the icing to set completely.

MAKES 10

F1 racing cones

10 ice-cream cones
variety of small sweets
red butter icing (page 8)
10 Marie biscuits
silver cake beads
racing car-shaped jelly sweets
tyre-shaped jelly sweets

Fill the ice-cream cone with a variety of small sweets.

Fit an icing bag with a star-shaped nozzle, fill with red butter icing and pipe a border around the edge of a Marie biscuit. Press the biscuit onto the cone and place in a standing position. Press cake beads onto the butter icing border and leave to set.

Use a dab of icing to stick the racing car sweet to the front of the cone. Hang the tyre-shaped sweet over the tip of the cone.

Pipe red butter icing stars over the cones, to decorate.
Leave to stand for the icing to set completely.

MAKES 10

CONE FIGURES

Bears

10 ice-cream cones
variety of small sweets
green butter icing (page 8)
10 Marie biscuits
cake beads
sugar flowers
yellow and black fondant icing

Fill the ice-cream cone with a variety of small sweets.

Fit an icing bag with a star-shaped nozzle, fill with butter icing and pipe a border around the edge of a Marie biscuit. Press the biscuit onto the cone and place in a standing position. Press cake beads and sugar flowers onto the border. Leave to set.

Use the fondant icing to make the head, eyes, ears, nose and mouth.

To assemble, place the head onto the tip of the cone, then attach the eyes, ears and nose (use a little water if the parts won't stick). Use a cocktail stick to make indentations for the ears and nose. For the mouth, use a paperclip that has been bent into a curve.

Leave to stand for the icing to set completely.

MAKES 10

Dalmatians (Spotty dogs)

10 ice-cream cones
variety of small sweets
butter icing (page 8)
10 Marie biscuits
black and white fondant icing
bone-shaped sweets
non-toxic pen

Fill the ice-cream cone with a variety of small sweets.

Fit an icing bag with a star-shaped nozzle, fill with butter icing and pipe a border around the edge of a Marie biscuit. Press the biscuit onto the cone, place in a standing position and leave to set.

Use the fondant icing to make the head and ears and nose.

To assemble, place the head onto the tip of the cone, then attach the ears and nose. Use a non-toxic pen to draw the eyes, mouth and 'spots'.

Pipe blobs of butter icing over the cone and stick bone-shaped sweets on top. Leave to stand for the icing to set completely.

MAKES 10

Cats

10 ice-cream cones
variety of small sweets
butter icing (page 8)
10 Marie biscuits
grey, black, white, red and pink fondant
fish-shaped sweets

Fill the ice-cream cone with a variety of sweets.

Fit an icing bag with a star-shaped nozzle, fill with butter icing and pipe a border around the edge of a Marie biscuit. Press the biscuit onto the cone, place in a standing position and leave to set.

Use the fondant icing to make the head, eyes, ears, nose and mouth.

To assemble, place the head onto the tip of the cone, then attach the eyes, ears, nose and mouth (use a little water if the parts won't stick). Use a cocktail stick to make 2 holes in the nose and draw in the whiskers, as shown, using a non-toxic pen.

Pipe blobs of butter icing over the cone and stick fish-shaped sweets on top.

Leave to stand for the icing to set completely.

MAKES 10

Monkeys

10 ice-cream cones
variety of small sweets
butter icing (page 8)
10 Marie biscuits
brown, cream and white fondant
non-toxic pen
banana-shaped sweets

Fill the ice-cream cone with a variety of small sweets.

Fit an icing bag with a star-shaped nozzle, fill with butter icing and pipe a border around the edge of a Marie biscuit. Press the biscuit onto the cone, place in a standing position and leave to set.

Use the fondant icing to make the head, eyes, ears, nose and mouth.
To assemble, place the head on the tip of the cone, then attach the eyes, ears, nose and mouth (use a little water if the parts won't stick). Use a non-toxic pen to draw a small black dot on the eyes, and a cocktail stick to make indentations on the ears, and holes for the nose. For the mouth, use a paperclip that has been bent open to make a nice 'smile'.

Pipe blobs of butter icing onto the front of the cone and stick 1 or 2 banana-shaped sweets on top. Leave to stand for the icing to set completely.

MAKES 10

CONE FIGURES

Cows

10 ice-cream cones
variety of small sweets
green and white butter icing (page 8)

10 Marie biscuits
grey, black, white, red and pink fondant
sugar flowers

Fill the ice-cream cone with a variety of small sweets.

Fit an icing bag with a star-shaped nozzle, fill with butter icing and pipe a border around the edge of a Marie biscuit. Press the biscuit onto the cone, place in a standing position and leave to set.

Use the fondant icing to make the head, eyes, ears, nose, spots and hair. To assemble, place the head onto the tip of the cone, then attach the eyes, ears, nose, hair and spots (use a little water if the parts don't stick). Place a sugar flower next to one ear. Use a cocktail stick to make 2 holes for the nose and bent-open paperclip to make a curve for the mouth.

Pipe green butter icing leaves over the cone and add sugar flowers.

Leave to stand for the icing to set completely.

MAKES 10

Pigs

10 ice-cream cones
green and white butter icing (page 8)
10 Marie biscuits

variety of small sweets
black and pink fondant
sugar flowers

Fill the ice-cream cone with a variety of small sweets.

Fit an icing bag with a star-shaped nozzle, fill with white butter icing and pipe a border around the edge of a Marie biscuit. Press the biscuit onto the cone, place in a standing position and leave to set.

Use the fondant icing to make the head, eyes, ears and nose.

To assemble, place the head on the tip of the cone, then attach the eyes, ears and nose (use a little water if the parts won't stick). Make 2 holes for the nose using a cocktail stick.

Pipe blobs of green butter icing over the cone and stick sugar flowers on top.

Leave to stand for the icing to set completely.

MAKES 10

88   CONE FIGURES

Fly-catcher cones

black and red coloured chocolate, melted (page 8)
insect-shaped chocolate moulds
10 ice-cream cones
red butter icing (page 8)
10 Marie biscuits
variety of small sweets
black sugar sprinkles

Pour melted black chocolate into insect-shaped moulds and place in the fridge until set. Remove from the moulds and place on wax paper.

Fill the ice-cream cone with a variety of small sweets. Fit an icing bag with a star-shaped nozzle, fill with red butter icing and pipe a border around the edge of a Marie biscuit. Press the biscuit onto the cone, place in a standing position and leave to set.

Drizzle the melted red chocolate down the sides of the cone and scatter with black sugar sprinkles while the chocolate is still soft. Leave to stand for the chocolate to set. Use dabs of melted chocolate to stick the insects to the cone.
Leave to stand for the icing to set completely.

MAKES 10

Tip: If you can't get insect-shaped chocolate moulds, buy sugar insects from a specialist baking store. Another option is to buy plastic insects from a toy shop, but remember to warn the children not to eat them!

Volcanoes

10 ice-cream cones
variety of small sweets
butter icing (page 8)
10 Marie biscuits
milk chocolate, for melting
orange coloured chocolate (page 8)
black sugar sprinkles
red sugar sprinkles
dinosaur jelly sweets

Fill the ice-cream cone with a variety of small sweets.

Fit an icing bag with a star-shaped nozzle, fill with butter icing and pipe a border around the edge of a Marie biscuit. Press the biscuit onto the cone, place in a standing position and leave to set.

Place the cones on a wire rack set over a bowl or tray to catch the excess chocolate. Melt the milk chocolate in the microwave, stirring often. Pour the melted chocolate over the cones until they are completely covered. Leave to set. Melt the orange chocolate, and let it drip down from the tip of the cone. Sprinkle red sugar sprinkles on the tip of the cone while the chocolate is still soft.

Use a little melted chocolate to stick down the dinosaur jelly sweets.
Leave to stand for the icing to set completely.

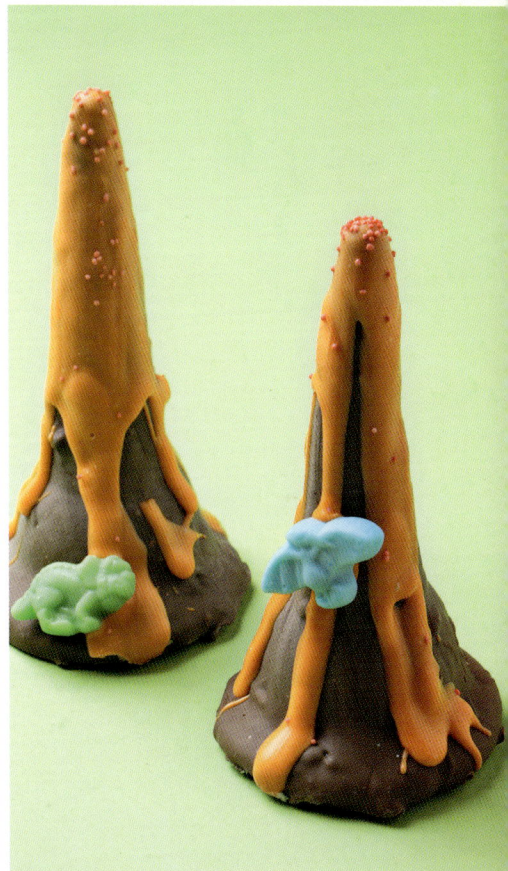

MAKES 10

CONE FIGURES

Vases

10 Marie biscuits
white and pink butter icing (page 8)
10 flat-bottomed ice-cream cones
10 sugar butterflies
pearl cake beads
30 flat green lollipops
30 large sugar flowers
small ring-shaped sweets
small sugar flowers (optional)

Spread pink butter icing over the Marie biscuit and place the ice-cream cone upright in the centre of the biscuit. Place a sugar butterfly in the icing and sprinkle cake beads around the edge. Leave to stand for the icing to set completely.

Use a dab of white butter icing to stick a large sugar flower onto each lollipop. Leave to stand for the icing to set.

Place a layer of ring-shaped sweets at the bottom of the cone, add three lollipops, then fill the cone with more ring-shaped sweets.

MAKES 10

Optional: Pipe blobs of white butter icing over the cone and stick small sugar flowers on top.

Trees

10 ice-cream cones
variety of small sweets
green butter icing (page 8)
10 Marie biscuits
brown fondant
red or orange cake beads

Fill the ice-cream cone with a variety of small sweets.

Fit an icing bag with a star-shaped nozzle, fill with green butter icing and pipe a border around the edge of a Marie biscuit. Press the biscuit onto the cone, place in a standing position and leave to set.

Cover the bottom half of the cone with brown fondant. Using a cocktail stick, draw lines in the fondant to resemble bark. Using the green butter icing and a star-shaped nozzle, pipe stars close together all around the cone (piping each star outwards) to form the leaves. Place red or orange cake beads between the leaves.

Leave to stand for the icing to set completely.

MAKES 10

Windmills

10 ice-cream cones
variety of small sweets
green and white butter icing (page 8)
10 Marie biscuits
flower sprinkles
10 wafer biscuits
10 Smarties

Fill the ice-cream cone with a variety of small sweets.

Fit an icing bag with a star-shaped nozzle, fill with green butter icing and pipe a border around the edge of a Marie biscuit. Press the biscuit onto the cone. Stand the cone upright, and place flower sprinkles around the edge of the butter icing. Leave to set.

Cut each wafer biscuit lengthwise in two. Using a small blob of white butter icing, stick 2 wafer halves in an 'X' shape, to form the sails of the windmill. Use another blob of icing to stick a Smartie to the middle of each sail. Leave to set.

Use white butter icing to stick the sails to the front of the cone.

Leave to stand for the icing to set completely.

MAKES 10

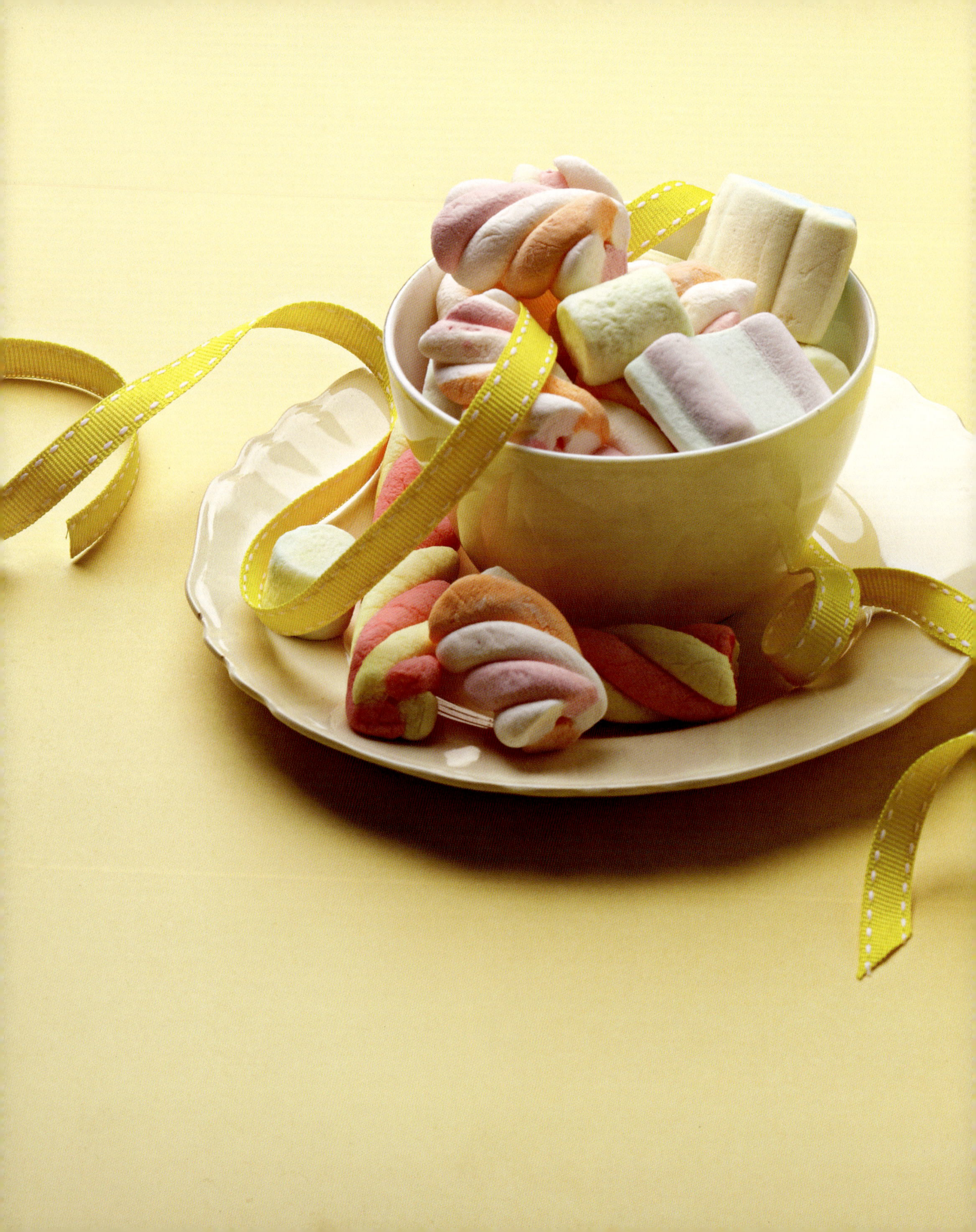

Marshmallows

Marshmallow love bears

**10 wooden skewers
20 large white marshmallows
glacé icing (page 8)
40 pink mini marshmallows
30 yellow mini marshmallows
10 large sugar hearts
30 small sugar hearts
non-toxic pen**

Push a wooden skewer lengthwise through a large white marshmallow for the body and add a second marshmallow on its side, on the tip of the skewer, for the bear's face. For the legs and arms, use glacé icing to stick 4 pink mini marshmallows to the body.

Using glacé icing, stick 2 yellow mini marshmallows on top of the head, for the ears. Cut one yellow mini marshmallow in two and stick one half to the face, for the nose. Leave to stand until the glacé icing sets and the marshmallows stick firmly to each other.

Using glacé icing, stick a large sugar heart to the body and a small sugar heart to each ear and the nose. Use a non-toxic pen to draw the eyes and mouth.

MAKES 10

Marshmallow bunnies

**wooden skewers
40 large white marshmallows
glacé icing (page 8)
30 white mini marshmallows
5 pink mini marshmallows
pink sprinkles
10 red heart-shaped sprinkles
20 blue dot sprinkles
non-toxic pen**

Push a wooden skewer lengthwise through a large white marshmallow, for the body, and place a second marshmallow on its side, on the tip of the skewer, for the face. Cut a white mini marshmallow in half and use glacé icing to stick the two halves to the face, for the cheeks.

Use glacé icing to stick 2 white mini marshmallows to the body, for the front legs. For the feet, cut a large marshmallow in half and half again to form 4 semi-circles. Make two light cuts in the curves of each semi-circle, for the toes. Cut the pink mini marshmallows in half and stick one half to each foot.

For the ears, cut a large white marshmallow lengthwise in two and press the sticky side into the pink sprinkles (if the sprinkles won't stick, coat the marshmallow with a thin layer of glacé icing).

Use glacé icing to stick 2 feet and 2 ears to the body.
Leave to stand until the icing sets and the marshmallows stick firmly to one another.

Use the heart-shaped and blue dot sprinkles to create the face. Draw whiskers onto the cheeks using a non-toxic pen.

MAKES 10

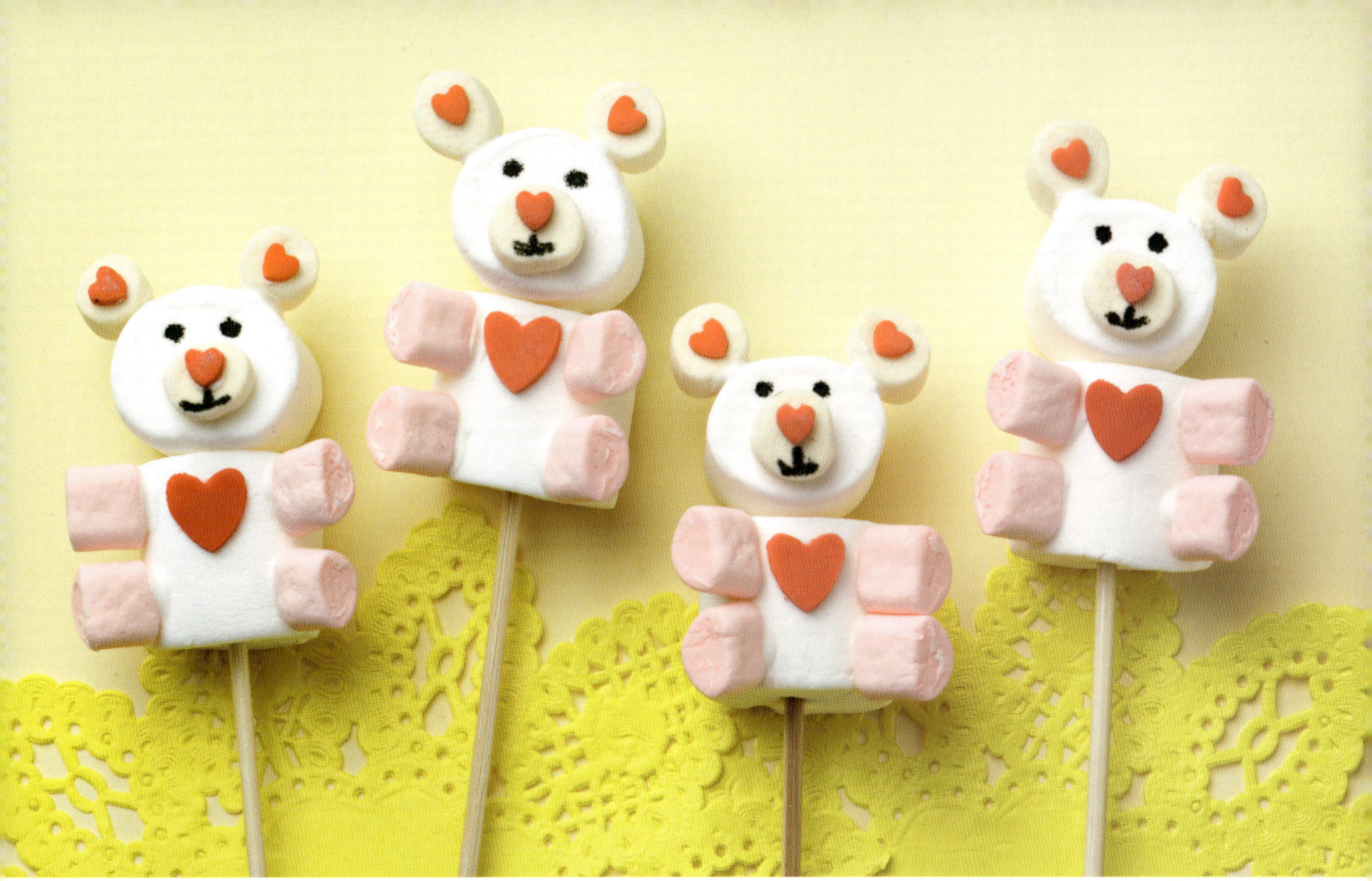
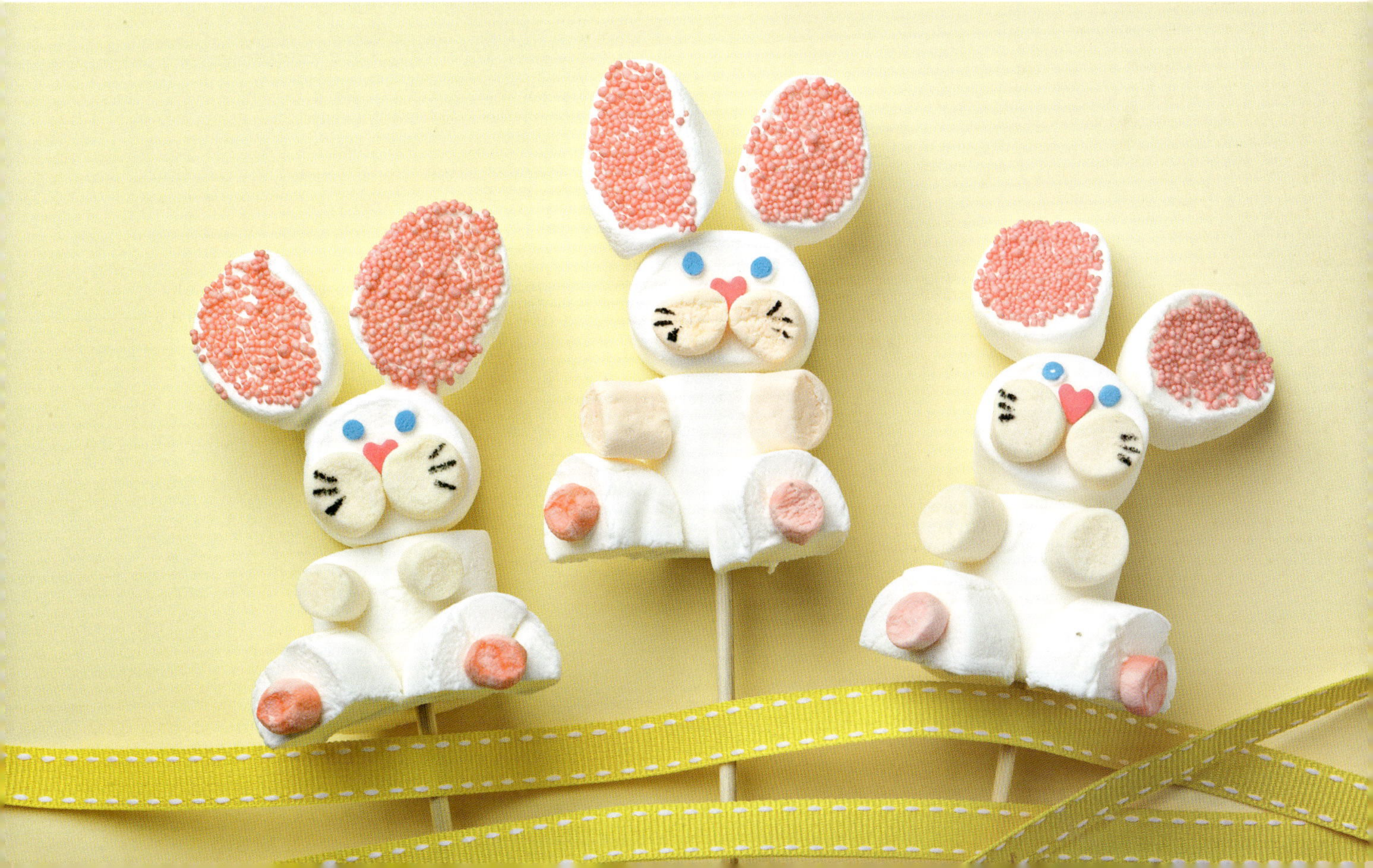

Quick marshmallow animals

Use marshmallows, jelly beans, glacé icing and a non-toxic pen to make these characters. Each set of instructions makes one animal.

Hoppity bunnies

Use a large white marshmallow for the body. For the feet, cut 2 mini marshmallows in half and use glacé icing to stick them to the body. For the ears, cut 2 slices at an angle from the sides of a large marshmallow and use glacé icing to stick them down, with the sticky sides towards the back. For the tail, use part of a marshmallow and stick it to the back of the body with glacé icing. Leave until the icing sets and all the marshmallows stick firmly to one another. Use a non-toxic pen to draw the eyes, nose and whiskers.

Pink piglets

Use a large pink marshmallow for the body. For the legs, cut 2 pink jelly beans in half and use glacé icing to stick them to the body. For the snout, cut a pink mini marshmallow in half and stick one half to the front of the body. For the ears, cut another pink mini marshmallow in two lengthways and stick the pieces down, using glacé icing. Leave until the icing sets and all the marshmallows stick firmly to one another. Use a non-toxic pen to draw the eyes and nose.

Little lambs

Use a large white marshmallow for the body. For the legs, cut 2 black jelly beans in half and use glacé icing to stick them to the body. Cut a slice of marshmallow for the head. Cut another slice into four and use 2 pieces for the ears (*see* picture), sticking them to the head with glacé icing. Stick the head to the body with glacé icing and leave until the icing sets and all the marshmallows stick firmly to one another. Use glacé icing to stick a small heart-shaped sweet to the centre of the face, for the nose, and draw the eyes and mouth with a non-toxic pen.

Chirpy chicks

Use a large yellow marshmallow for the body. For the head, cut a large yellow marshmallow in half, then cut out a curve so the head fits onto the body. Use glacé icing to stick the head to the body. Cut 2 orange jelly beans in two and use glacé icing to stick them in place for the wings and beak. Draw the eyes using a non-toxic pen.

MARSHMALLOWS

Marshmallow lollipops

10 marshmallows
10 lollipop sticks
100g coloured chocolate (page 8)
variety of sugar decorations (sprinkles, Smarties and other small sweets)

Press the lollipop sticks into the marshmallows.

Melt the chocolate in a small bowl in the microwave. Dip the top of each marshmallow into the melted chocolate. Holding it upside down, allow any excess chocolate to drip back into the bowl.

While the chocolate is still wet, dip the marshmallow into the sprinkles or place a Smartie or a sugar decoration of your choice on top. See picture for ideas.

Leave to set.

MAKES 10

Rainbow mini marshmallows

white chocolate
coloured mini marshmallows
sprinkles (100's & 1000's)

Melt the chocolate in the microwave, stirring often. Dip one end of each mini marshmallow into the melted chocolate, allowing most of the chocolate to drip away, then press it into the sprinkles.

Stand the marshmallows on the undipped end until the chocolate sets.

Marshmallow name lollies

marshmallows
wooden skewers
non-toxic pens

Using 1 marshmallow per letter, push a wooden skewer through enough marshmallows for each guest's name. (If the name is too long for one skewer, use two, and push the tip of the second skewer through the last marshmallow of the first skewer.)
Write the name on the marshmallows, using a non-toxic pen.

Tip: Dipping the tip of a skewer in warm water makes it easier to push through the marshmallows.

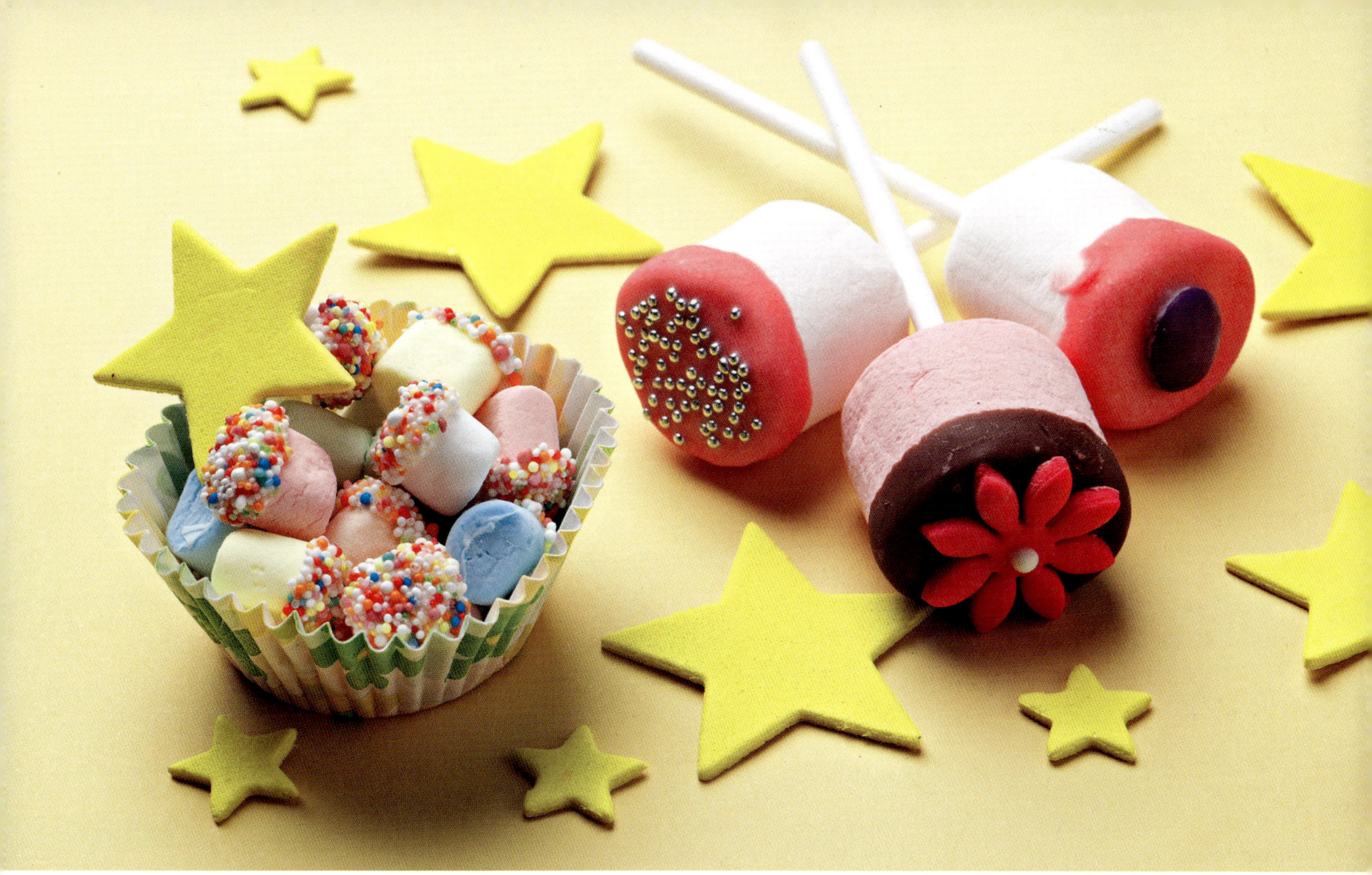

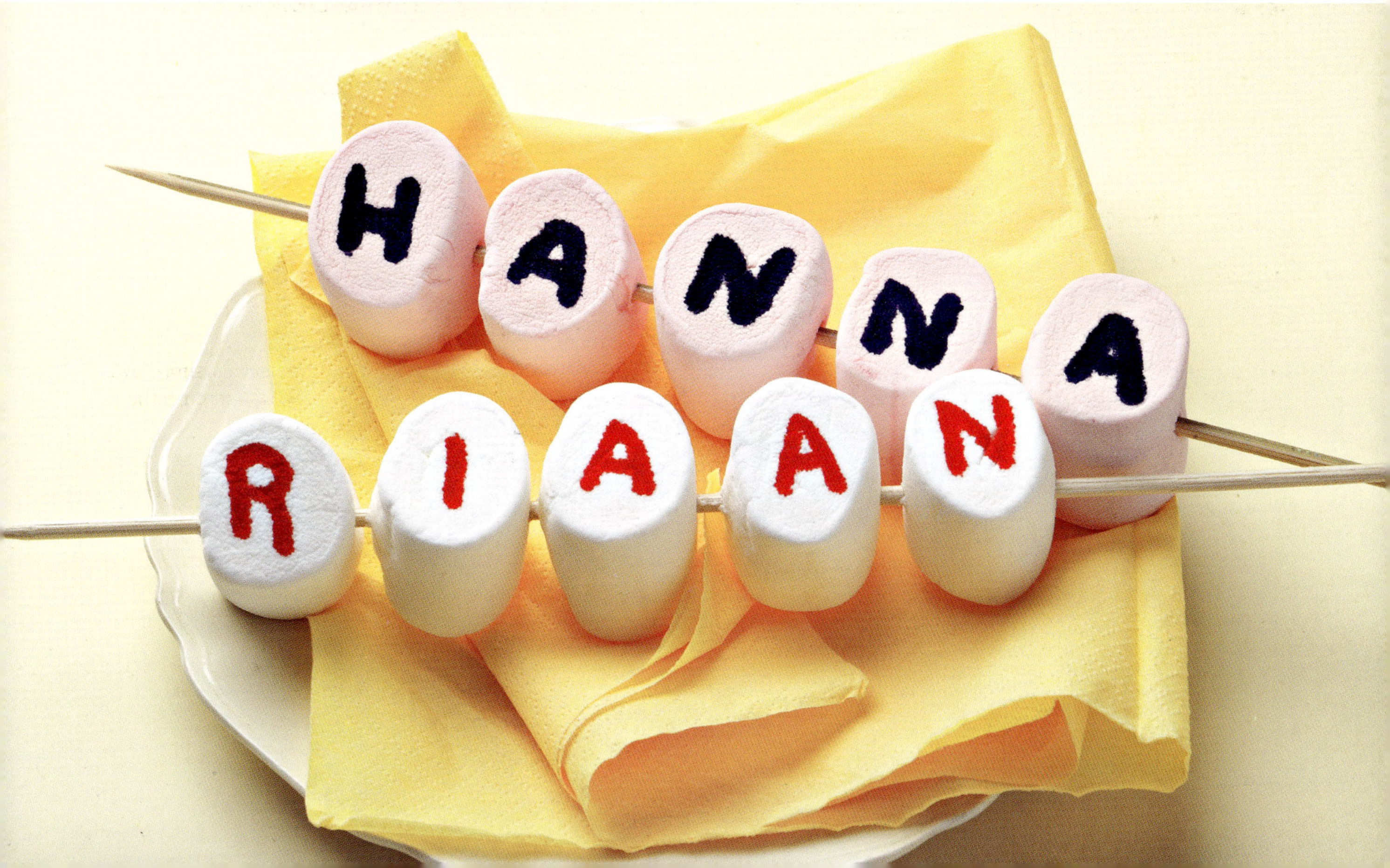
HANNA
RIAANA

Marshmallow kebabs

Marshmallow kebabs are easy to prepare. All you need is wooden skewers, different coloured marshmallows, chocolate for melting, sweets, sugar decorations and sprinkles. Use these ideas as an inspiration; you'll find you can make kebabs to suit any theme.

Tip: Dipping the tip of a skewer in warm water makes it easier to push through the marshmallows.

Twirly kebabs

marshmallows
wooden skewers
milk chocolate
sprinkles or 100's & 1000's

Push a wooden skewer through 3 marshmallows, keeping them close together. Melt the chocolate in the microwave, stirring often. Pour the sprinkles onto a flat plate. Use a fork to drip chocolate onto the marshmallows while turning the skewer. Wait a few seconds, then roll the kebab in the sprinkles. Leave to set.

Jelly kebabs

marshmallows
wooden skewers
variety of sugared jelly sweets

Thread alternate marshmallows and jelly sweets onto the wooden skewer, ending with a jelly 'hat'. Allow 3 marshmallows per skewer.

Sherbet kebabs

marshmallows
sherbet-filled straws
variety of sugared jelly rings

Use a wet skewer to make a hole through a marshmallow and then push a sherbet-filled straw through the marshmallow. Add a sugared jelly ring and another marshmallow.

With this kebab you can enjoy both the sweets and the skewer!

Chocolate kebabs

marshmallows
wooden skewers
milk chocolate
Smarties or Astros (candy-coated biscuit bites)

Push a wooden skewer through 3 or 4 marshmallows. Melt the chocolate in a bowl in the microwave, stirring often. Dip the marshmallows into the melted chocolate, holding the kebab upside down over the bowl of to allow most of the chocolate to drip down. Before the chocolate sets completely, decorate with Smarties or Astros.

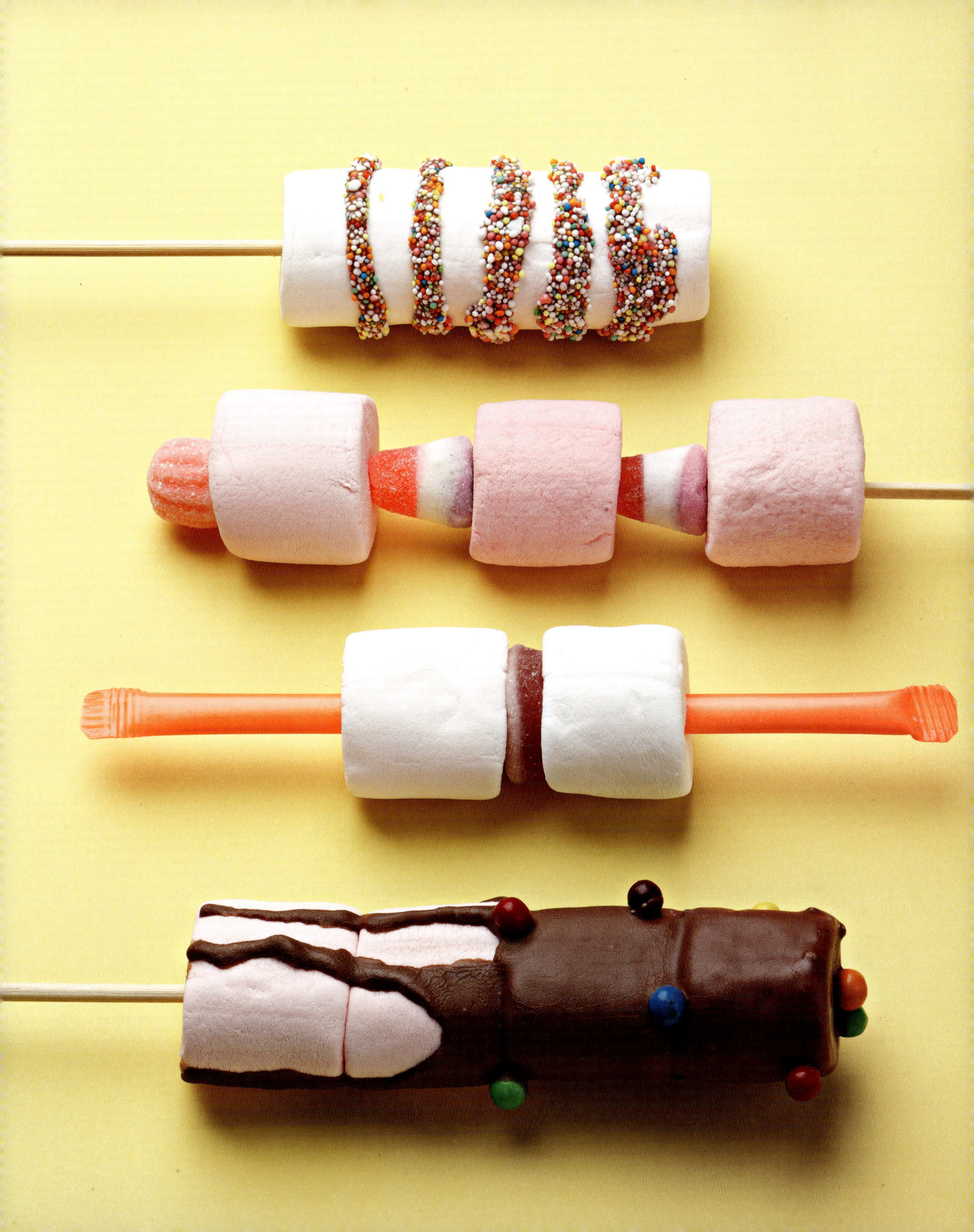

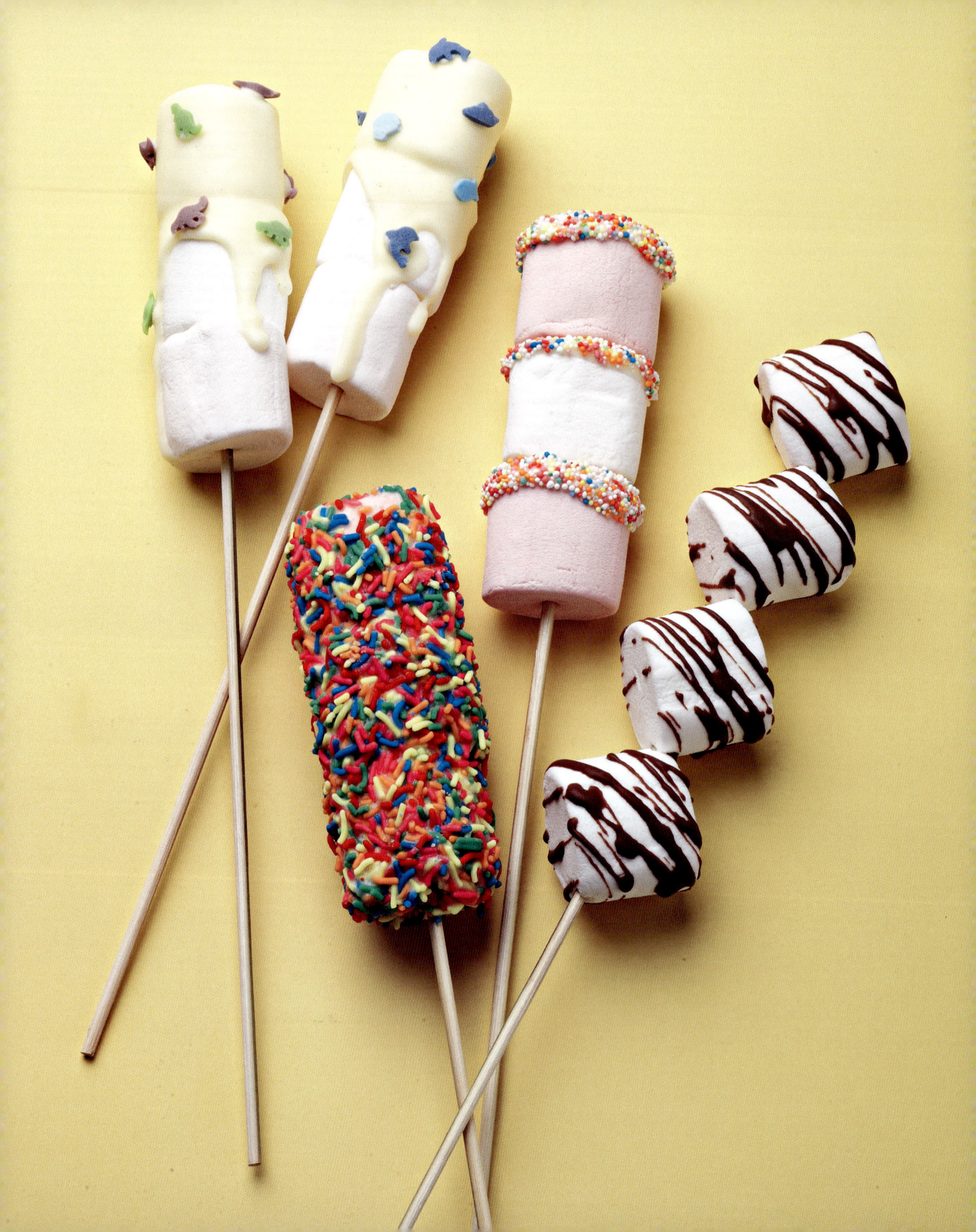

Dino kebabs

marshmallows
wooden skewers
white chocolate
dinosaur sprinkles

Push a skewer through 3 marshmallows, keeping them close together. Melt the chocolate in a bowl in the microwave, stirring often. Dip the marshmallows into the melted chocolate, holding the kebab upside down over the bowl to allow most of the chocolate to drip down.

Before the chocolate sets completely, sprinkle over the dinosaurs.

Tip: Instead of dinosaurs, use any other shape to match your party theme.

Rainbow kebabs

marshmallows
wooden skewers
white chocolate
rainbow vermicelli

Push a skewer through 3 marshmallows, keeping them close together. Melt the chocolate in a bowl in the microwave, stirring often. Pour the rainbow vermicelli onto a flat plate. Dip the marshmallows completely in the melted chocolate, holding the kebab upside down over the bowl to allow most of the chocolate to drip down.

Before the chocolate sets, roll the kebab in the vermicelli until it is well coated. Leave to set.

Sprinkle kebabs

white chocolate
marshmallows
wooden skewers
sprinkles or 100's & 1000's

Melt the chocolate in the microwave, stirring often. Pour the sprinkles onto a flat plate. Dip one end of each marshmallow into the melted chocolate and then into the sprinkles or 100's & 1000's. Stand the marshmallows on their undipped sides until set. Push a skewer through 3 dipped marshmallows.

Marbled kebabs

marshmallows
wooden skewers
milk chocolate

Push a skewer diagonally through 3 or 4 marshmallows. Melt the chocolate in the microwave, stirring often. Using a fork, drip melted chocolate over the marshmallows to make marble-like streaks. Leave to set.

Tip: Use both milk and white chocolate for a rainbow effect.

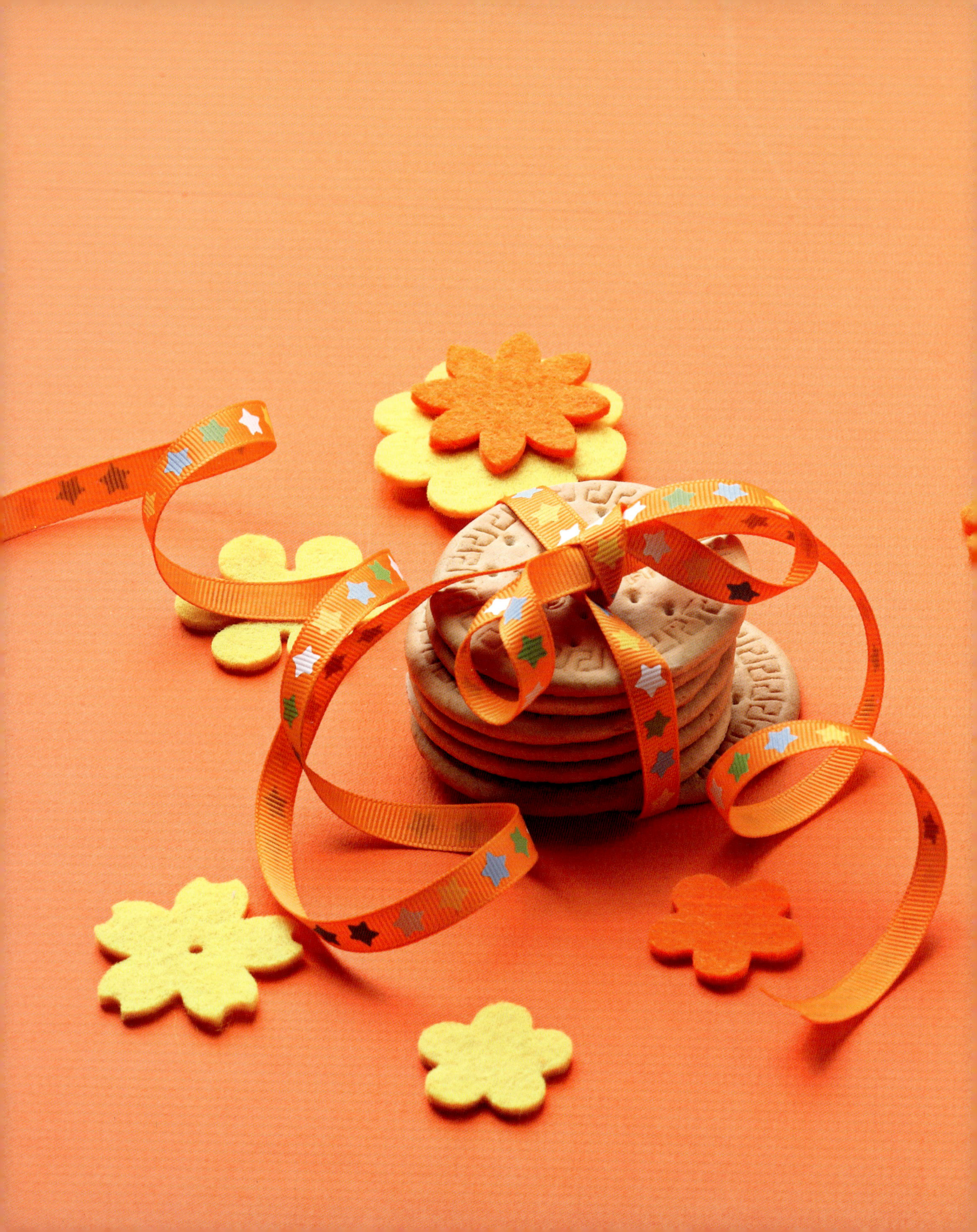

Marie biscuits

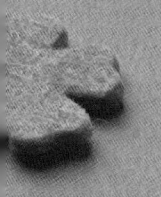

Clown faces

royal icing (page 8)
20 Marie biscuits
variety of small sweets (Smarties, jelly beans, Jelly Tots, mini allsorts, sour worms, etc.)
variety of cake beads, sprinkles and vermicelli

Spread royal icing over the Marie biscuits.

Use a variety of sweets and cake beads to make eyes, noses and mouths.
Add sprinkles, vermicelli or other cake decorations to put hair on some of the faces.

Leave to stand until the icing sets.

MAKES 20

Curious clams

pink royal icing (page 8)
20 Marie biscuits
20 chewy white peppermints
pearl cake beads

Spread royal icing over 10 of the Marie biscuits and allow to set slightly.

Spread royal icing over the other 10 biscuits, one at a time. Immediately place a chewy peppermint flat, towards the back of the just-iced biscuit, and another peppermint upright in front of it.

Place one of the previously iced biscuits on top, to form a 'hinged shell'.
Leave to stand until the icing sets.

Use a dab of icing to stick 2 pearl cake beads to the edge of the top biscuit, for the eyes.

MAKES 10

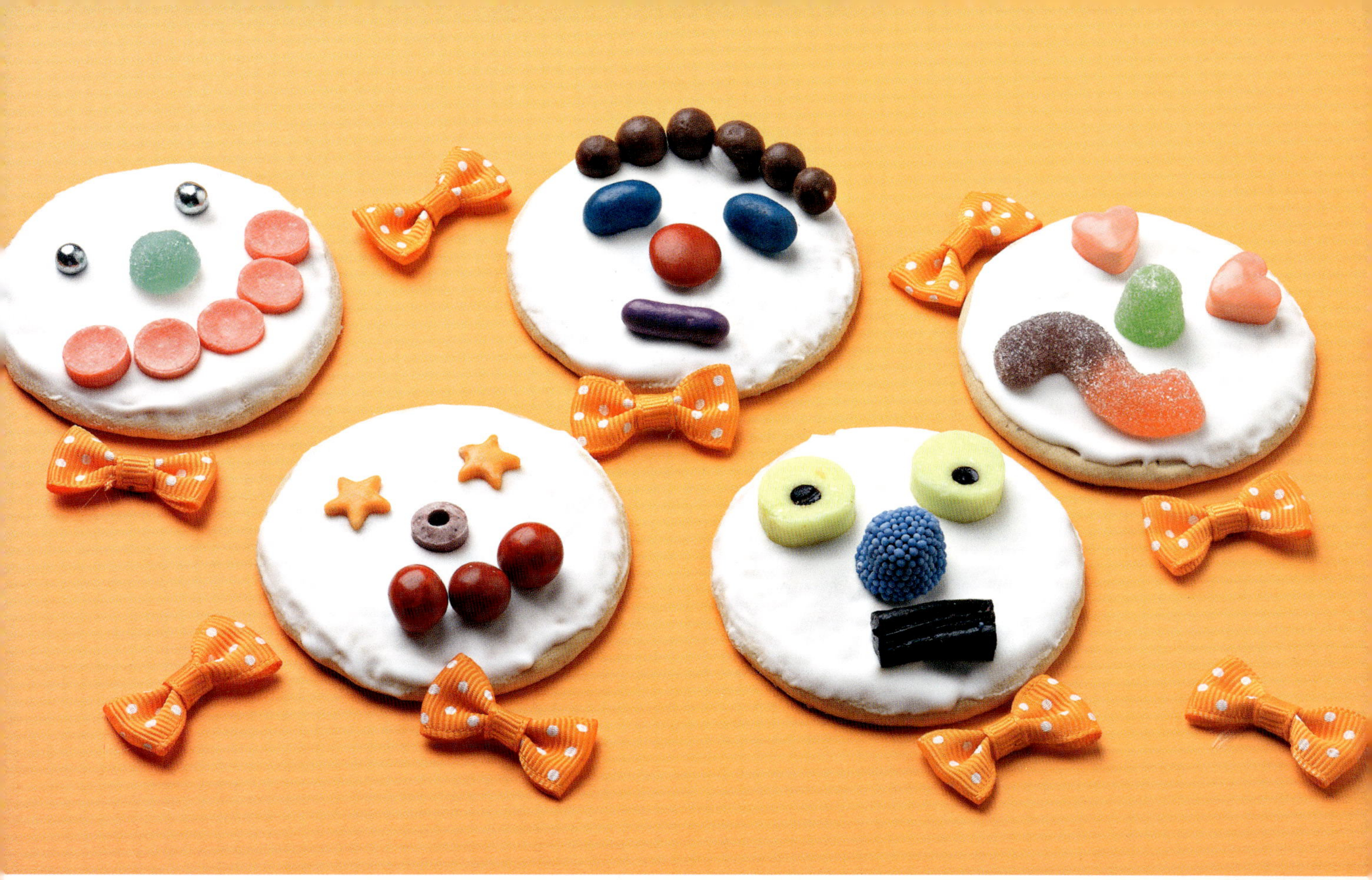

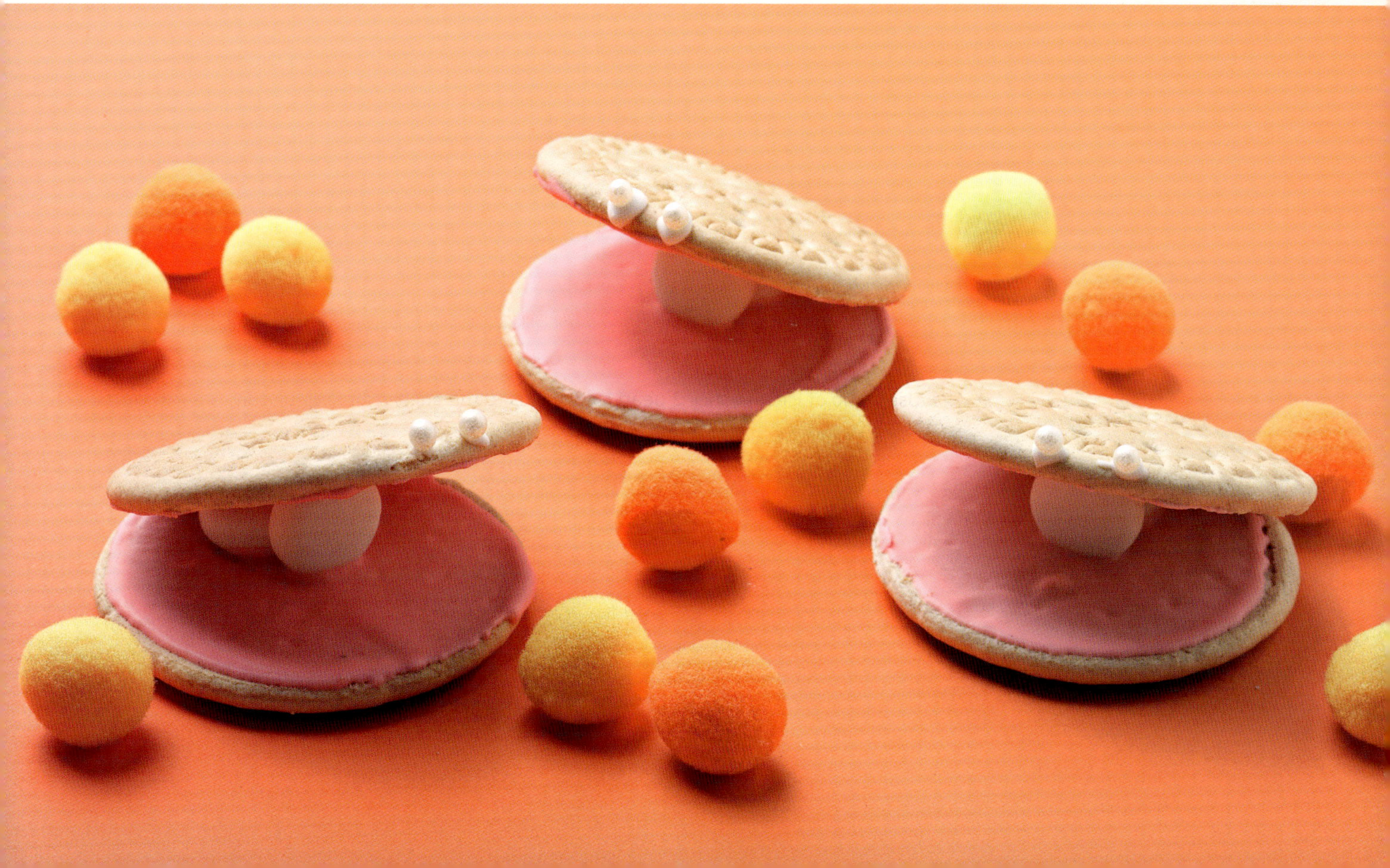

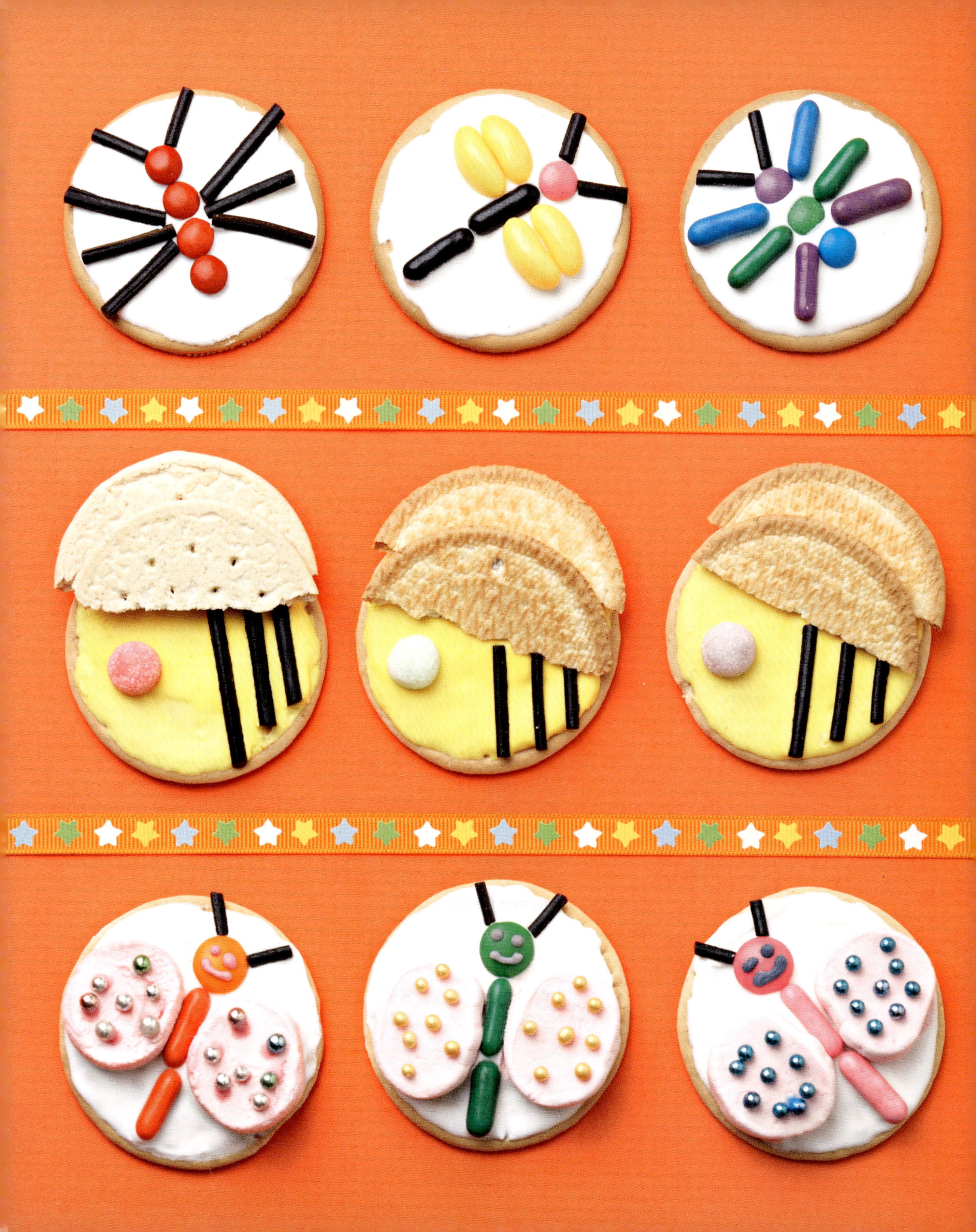

Crunchy bugs

royal icing (page 8)
20 Marie biscuits
variety of sweets (Smarties, Astros, jelly beans, allsorts, etc.)
liquorice strips

Spread royal icing over the Marie biscuits.

While the icing is still soft, use liquorice strips and a variety of different sweets to make the bugs' heads, bodies, legs and wings (see picture for guidelines).

Leave to stand until the icing sets.

MAKES 10

Bee biscuits

yellow royal icing (page 8)
20 Marie biscuits
10 Jelly Tots
liquorice strips

Spread royal icing over half the Marie biscuits.

Cut 10 un-iced biscuits in half (for the wings) and use extra dabs of icing to stick them in place, as shown in the picture.

Stick down a Jelly Tot for the eye. Cut the liquorice strips into three different lengths and stick them below the wings, for the bee's stripes.

Leave to stand until the icing sets.

MAKES 10

Butterfly biscuits

10 Marie biscuits
royal icing (page 8)
10 marshmallows
10 Smarties
20 oblong liquorice sweets
liquorice strips
cake beads
icing tube

Spread royal icing over the Marie biscuits.
Cut the marshmallow in half and place the pieces on the biscuit for the wings.
Place 2 oblong sweets and a Smartie between the marshmallows, for the body and head. Cut 2 short pieces of liquorice strip and place them above the Smartie, for the feelers.

Decorate the wings with cake beads (use small dabs of icing to stick them down).
Draw a face on the Smartie using the icing tube.

Leave to stand until the icing sets.

Tip: Dip the scissors into warm water before cutting the marshmallows.

MAKES 10

Ladybirds

royal icing (page 8)
20 Marie biscuits
liquorice strips
30 red or brown Smarties
silver cake beads

Spread royal icing over the Marie biscuits.

Cut liquorice strips to the desired lengths. Place 1 strip across at the top of the biscuit and another down the centre (in a 'T' shape).

Place 3 or 4 Smarties on either side of the liquorice strip, for the wings. Place 2 silver cake beads at the top, for the eyes.

Leave to stand until the icing sets.

MAKES 10

Katie the cat

royal icing (page 8)
10 Marie biscuits
5 marshmallows
10 Smarties
round liquorice sweets
liquorice strips
red jelly sweets

Spread royal icing over the Marie biscuits.

Cut each marshmallow into 3 slices and then cut each slice in half, and half again, for the ears (use scissors dipped in warm water to cut the marshmallows).

Stick 2 ears to the top of the biscuit, and a Smartie in the centre, for the nose. Cut a round liquorice sweet into small pieces and position 2 pieces for the eyes. Place 3 pieces of liquorice strip on either side of the Smartie, for the whiskers, and 2 small pieces below the Smartie. Cut a slice of red jelly sweet for the mouth and stick this below the Smartie.

Leave to stand until the icing sets.

MAKES 10

Percy piglet

10 pink marshmallows
royal icing (page 8)
10 Marie biscuits
liquorice strips
20 Smarties
20 Jelly Tots

Cut 5 marshmallows in half, for the noses (use scissors dipped in warm water). Cut the other 5 marshmallows into 3 slices, then cut each slice in half, for the ears.

Spread royal icing over the Marie biscuits.

Place the nose and ears on the biscuit. Cut the liquorice strips into pieces. Place 1 piece below the nose, for the mouth.
Use 2 Smarties for the eyes, and stick 2 Jelly Tots on top of the nose.

Leave to stand until the icing sets.

MAKES 10

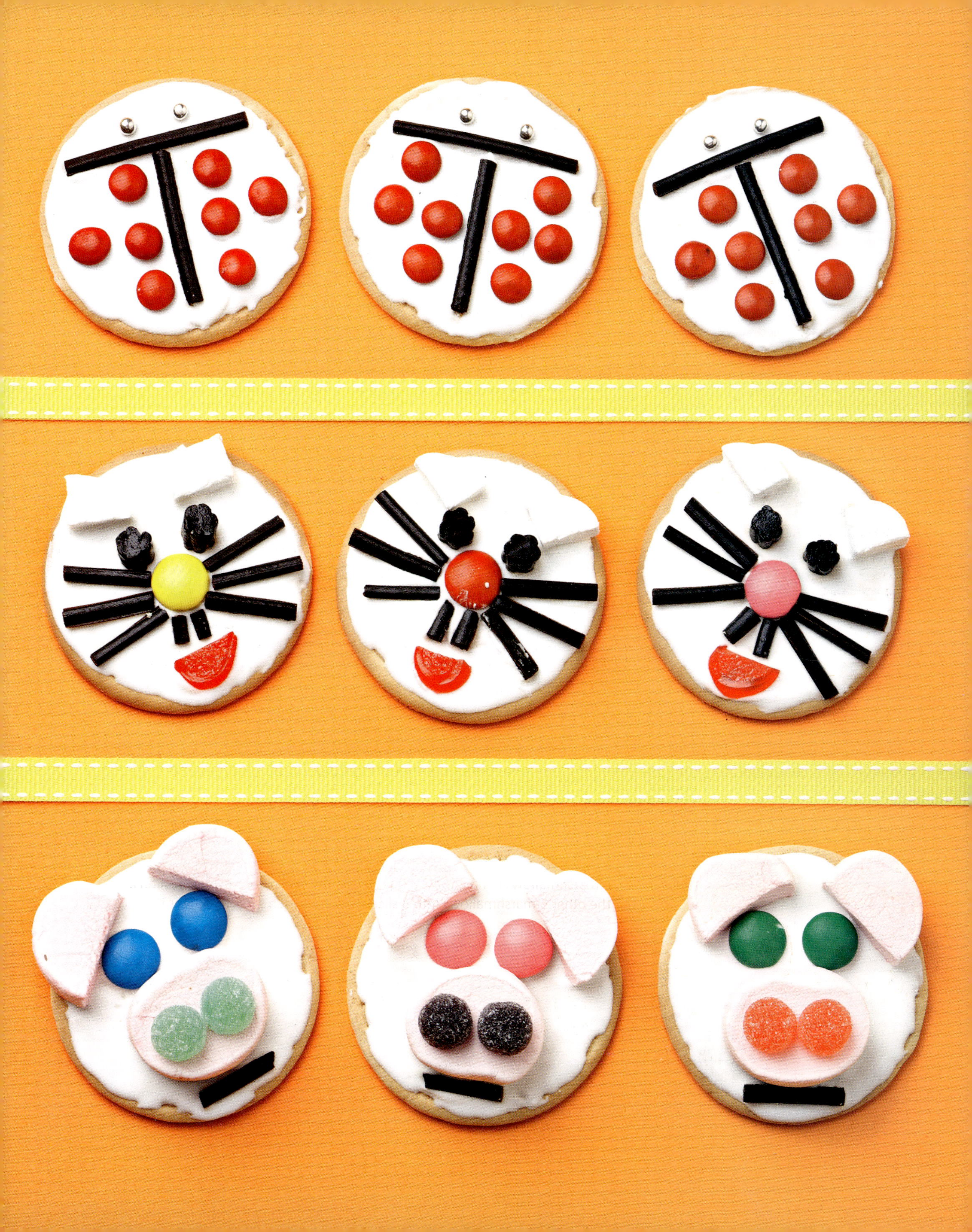

Cowabunga

royal icing (page 8)
10 Marie biscuits
sprinkles or 100's & 1000's
5 white marshmallows
10 pink marshmallows
20 Smarties
10 Jelly Tots
non-toxic pen

Spread royal icing over the Marie biscuit and add a layer of sprinkles or 100's & 1000's.

Cut a white marshmallow in half, for the nose.
Place a pink marshmallow upright on the biscuit, for the head. Using royal icing, stick half a white marshmallow in front of the pink marshmallow. Cut slits in the edge of the pink marshmallow and place a Smartie in each slit, for the ears. Use a dab of royal icing to stick a Jelly Tot between the ears.

Draw the face, using a non-toxic pen. Leave to stand until the icing sets.

MAKES 10

Feeesh

10–20 wafer biscuits
yellow royal icing (page 8)
10 Marie biscuits
small ring-shaped sweets
10 Jelly Tots
liquorice strips

Cut the wafer biscuits into triangles. (Take care when cutting, as wafer biscuits break easily; allow for extra wafers in case some of them break. You need 30 triangles.)

Spread royal icing over the Marie biscuits. Place 2 triangles (flat edges inwards) on the top and bottom of the Marie biscuit, for the fins, and 1 triangle at the back, with the tip pointing forwards, for the tail.

Place a ring-shaped sweet at the front, for the eye. Cut the Jelly Tot in half and cut out a small piece, then place the Jelly Tot at the front, for the mouth. Cut the liquorice strips into short pieces and place 3 pieces in the centre of the biscuit, for the gills.

Leave to stand until the icing sets.

MAKES 10

Crawly crabs

10 Marie biscuits
blue royal icing (page 8)
sprinkles (optional)
5 apricot sweets, halved
100 small banana-shaped sweets
blue or silver cake beads

Spread royal icing over the Marie biscuit. Scatter with sprinkles if desired.

Place half an apricot sweet in the centre of the biscuit, for the body. Place 4 banana-shaped sweets on either side of the body, for the legs, and 2 at the front, for the claws. Place 2 cake beads between the claws, for the eyes.

Leave to stand until the icing sets.

MAKES 10

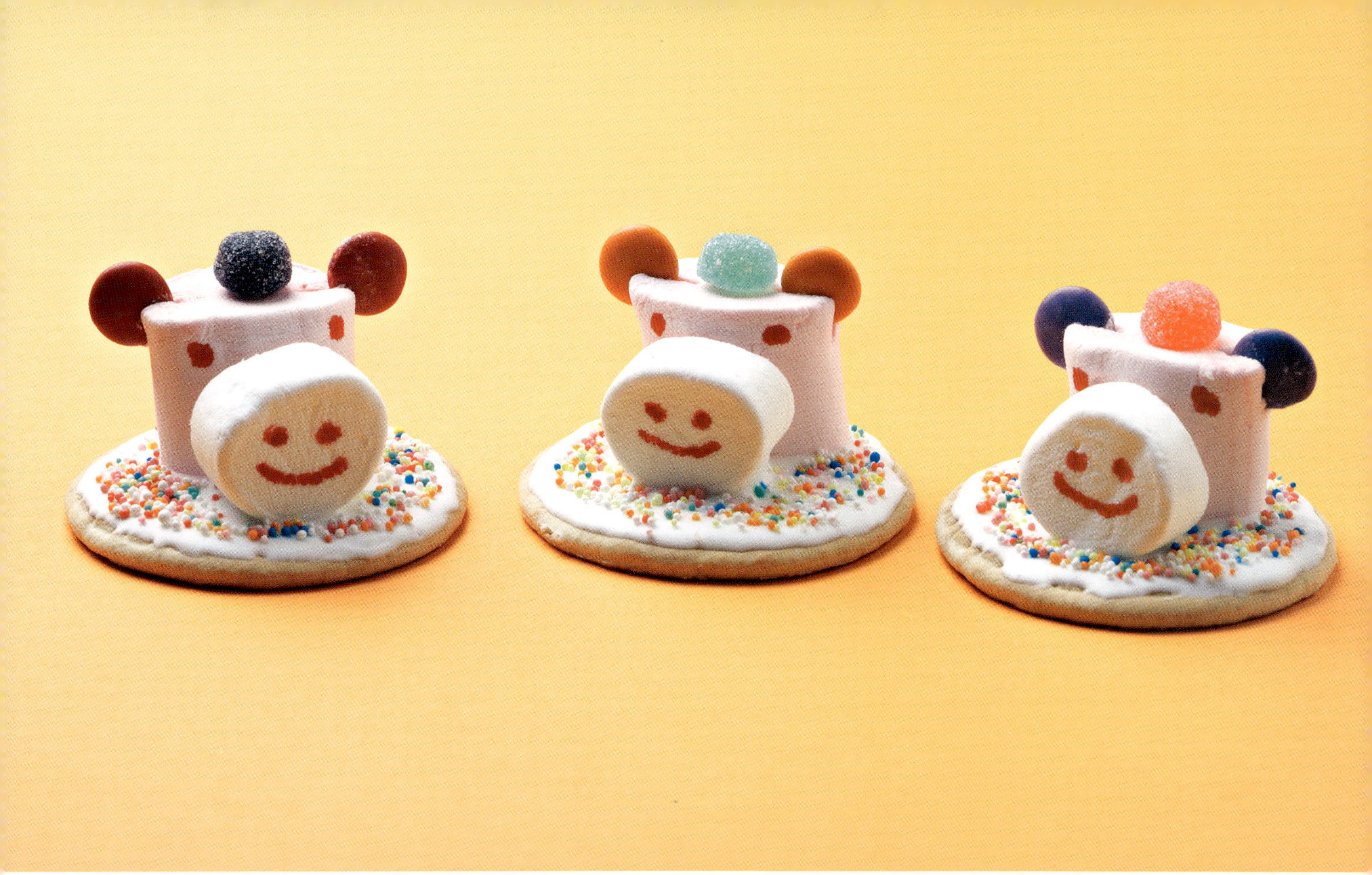

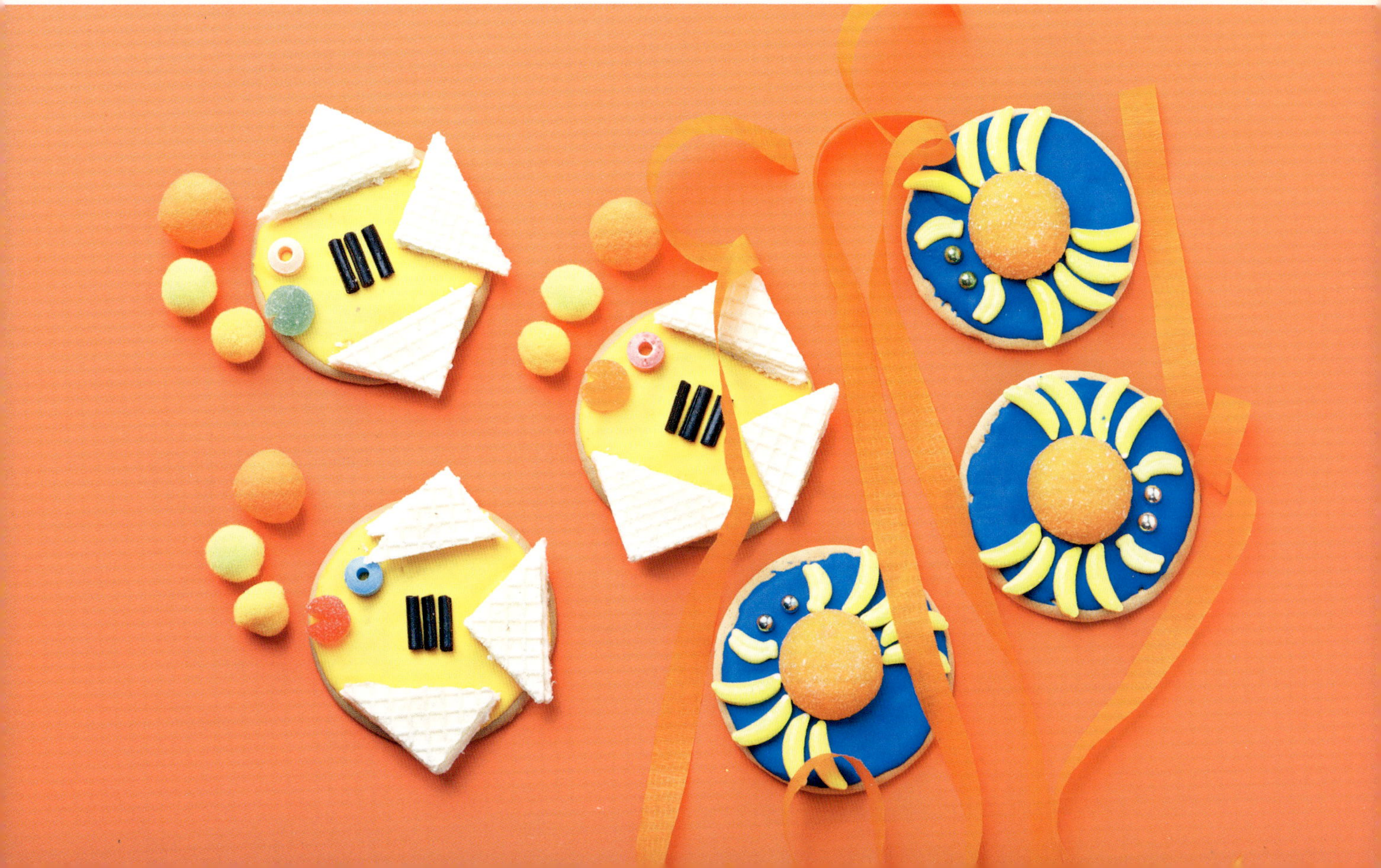

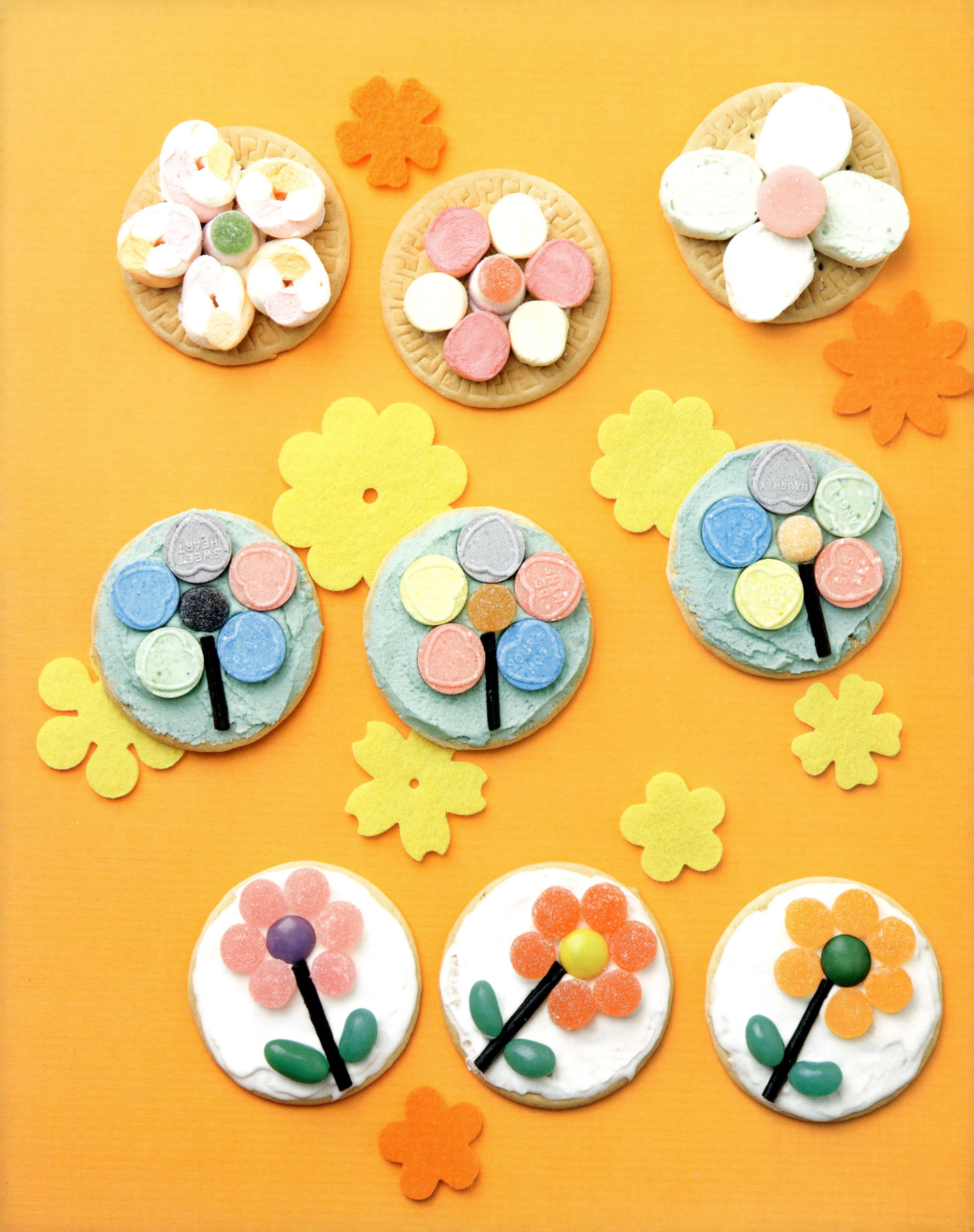

Mallow flowers

variety of marshmallows
glacé icing (page 8)
10 Marie biscuits
dome-shaped sugared jelly sweets
butterfly-shaped sweets

Spread glacé icing over the Marie biscuits.

Cut large marshmallows into slices, for flower petals. Place 4 petals onto a biscuit and stick a jelly sweet to the centre of the petals, using a dab of icing.

For the smaller marshmallows, place a jelly sweet in the centre of the biscuit and place 5 or 6 mini marshmallows in a circle around it.

Leave to stand until the icing sets.

MAKES 10

Tip: Use a dab of icing to stick a butterfly sweet on top of a petal.

Daisy delights

green butter icing (page 8)
10 Marie biscuits
10 Jelly Tots
50 round flat sweets
liquorice strips

Spread green butter icing over a Marie biscuit.

Place a Jelly Tot in the centre of the Marie biscuit, surrounded by 5 round flat sweets. Position a piece of liquorice strip for the stem.

Leave to stand until the icing sets.

MAKES 10

Jelly Tot flowers

royal icing (page 8)
10 Marie biscuits
10 Smarties
60 Jelly Tots
liquorice strips
20 green jelly beans

Spread royal icing over the Marie biscuit. Place the Smartie towards the top of the biscuit, surrounded by 6 Jelly Tots.

Position a piece of liquorice strip for the stem, and 2 green jelly beans on either side of the stem, for the leaves.

Leave to stand until the icing sets.

MAKES 10

Springtime

10 Marie biscuits
royal icing (page 8)
green vermicelli
30 small flower-shaped sweets
30 small flat round green sweets
icing tube (light grey)

Spread royal icing over the Marie biscuit.
Sprinkle vermicelli at the bottom of the biscuit, for the grass. Place 3 flower-shaped sweets towards the top of the biscuit and 3 round sweets in the centre, for the leaves.

Leave until the icing has set, then use the icing tube to draw the stems (see picture).

MAKES 10

Fireworks

10 Marie biscuits
royal icing (page 8)
variety of sweets (Smarties, Jelly Tots, oblong liquorice sweets, mini Astros, etc.)
cake beads

Spread royal icing over the Marie biscuits.

Use a variety of different sweets and coloured cake beads to decorate each biscuit (see picture for ideas).

Leave to stand until the icing sets.

MAKES 10

Marshmallow sandwich

20 Marie biscuits
10 marshmallows
sprinkles or 100's & 100's

Place a marshmallow in the centre of a Marie biscuit. Place on a microwaveable plate and microwave on full power for a few seconds, keeping an eye on it constantly.

As soon as the marshmallow puffs up, remove the biscuit and flatten the marshmallow by pressing down gently with a second Marie biscuit, to make a 'sandwich' (the marshmallow should ooze around the edges of the biscuit).

Pour the sprinkles or 100's & 100's onto a plate. While the marshmallow is still hot, roll the edges of the sandwich in the sprinkles.

Leave to stand until the marshmallow is cool.

MAKES 10

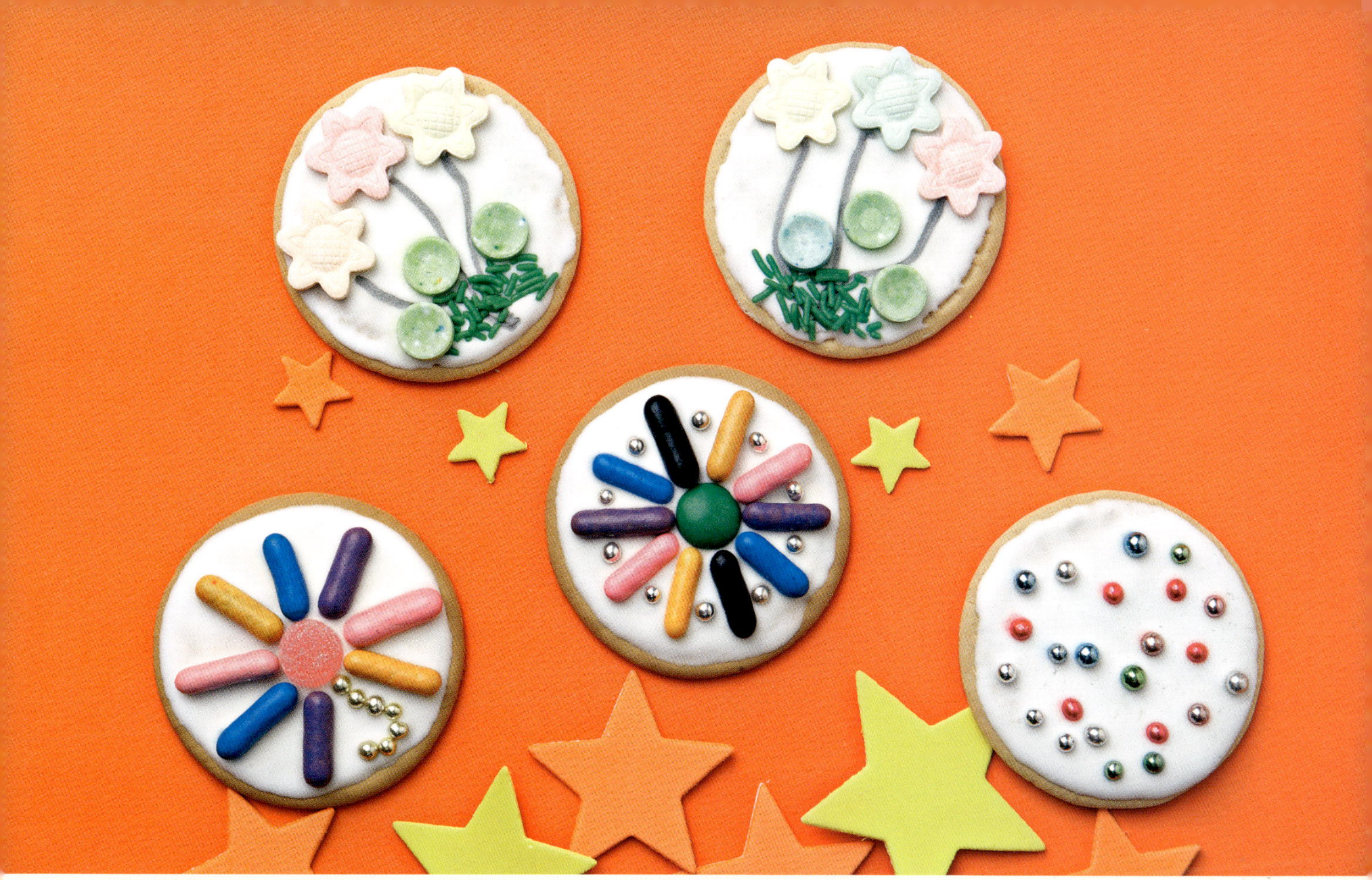

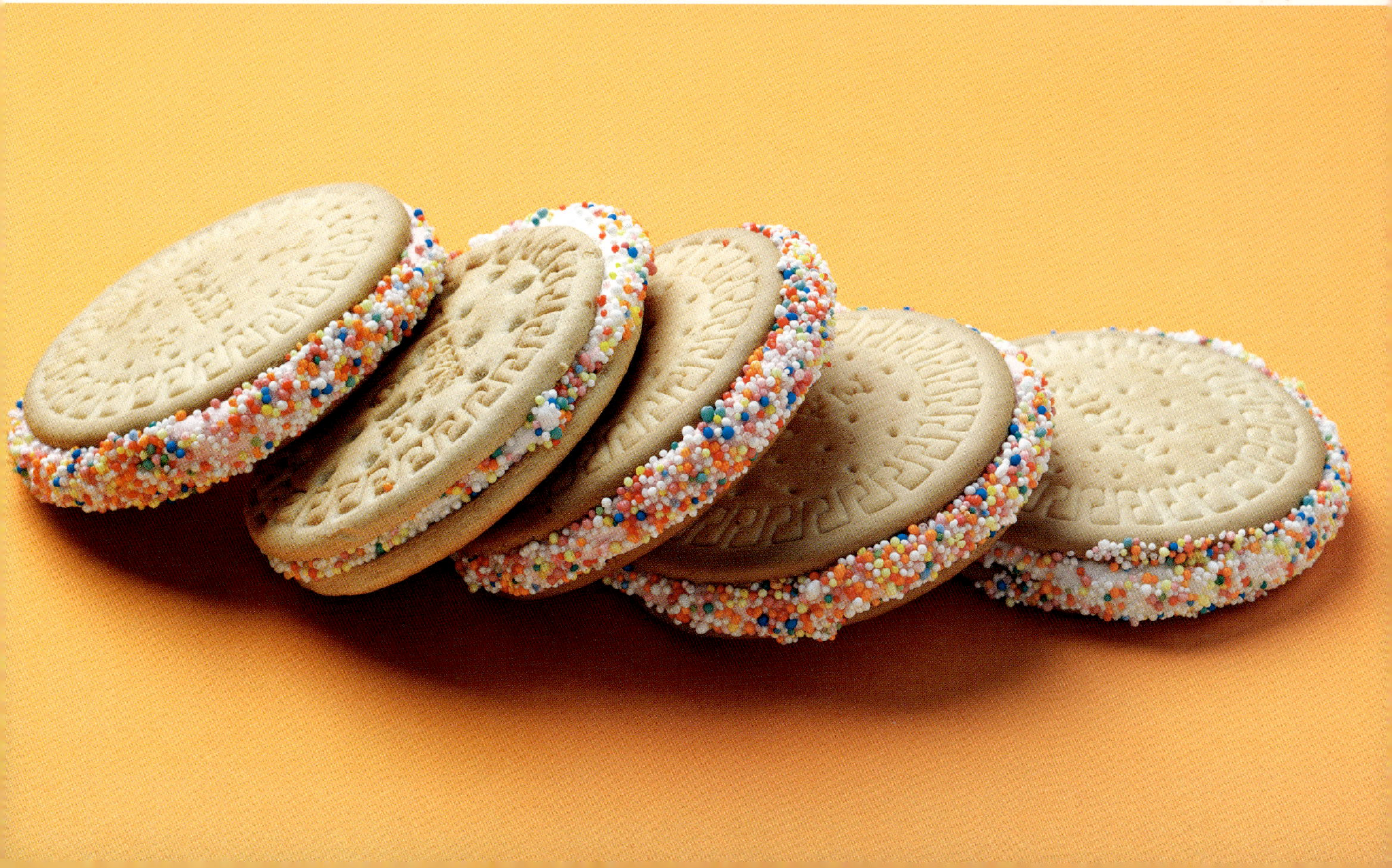

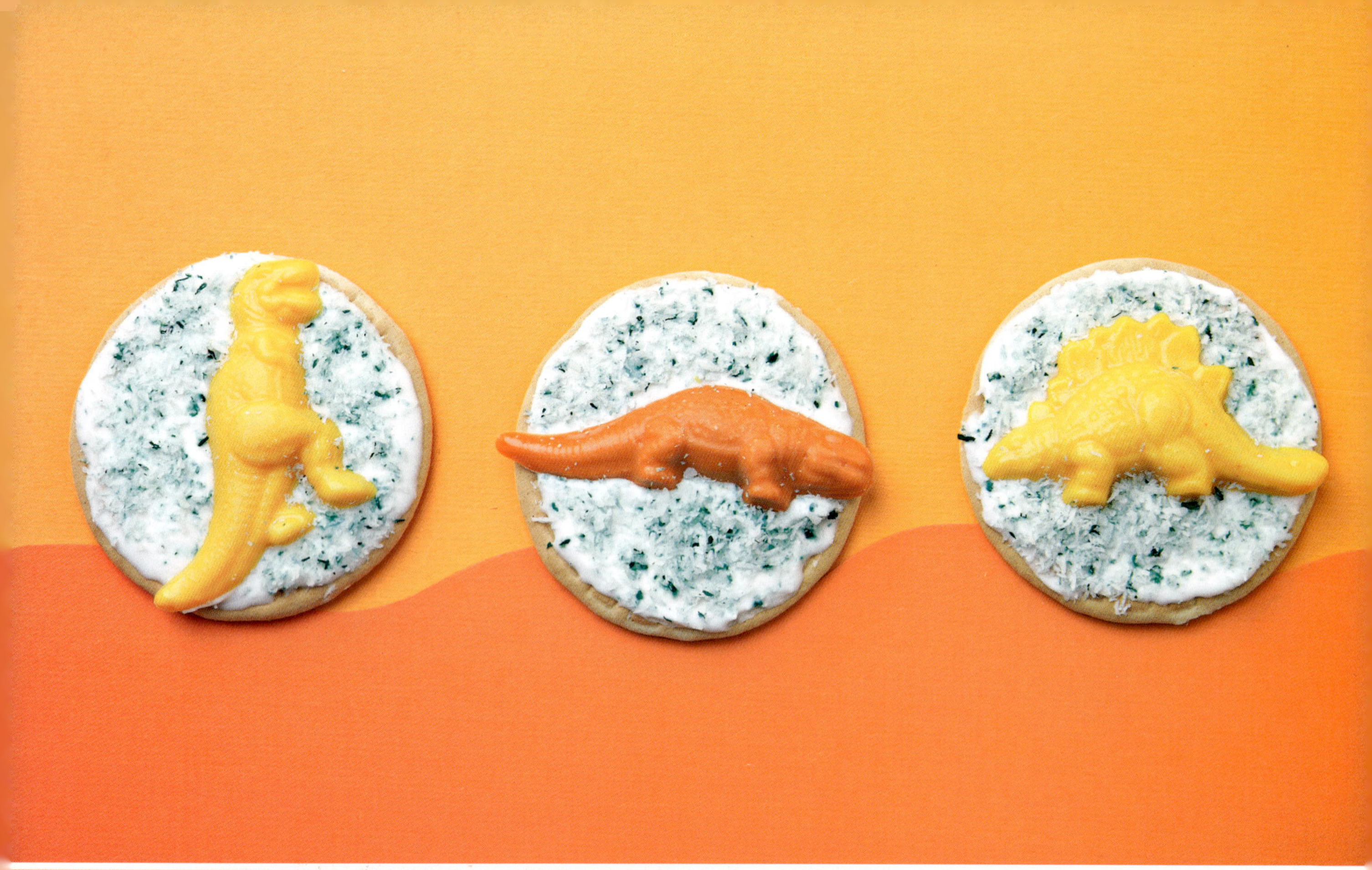
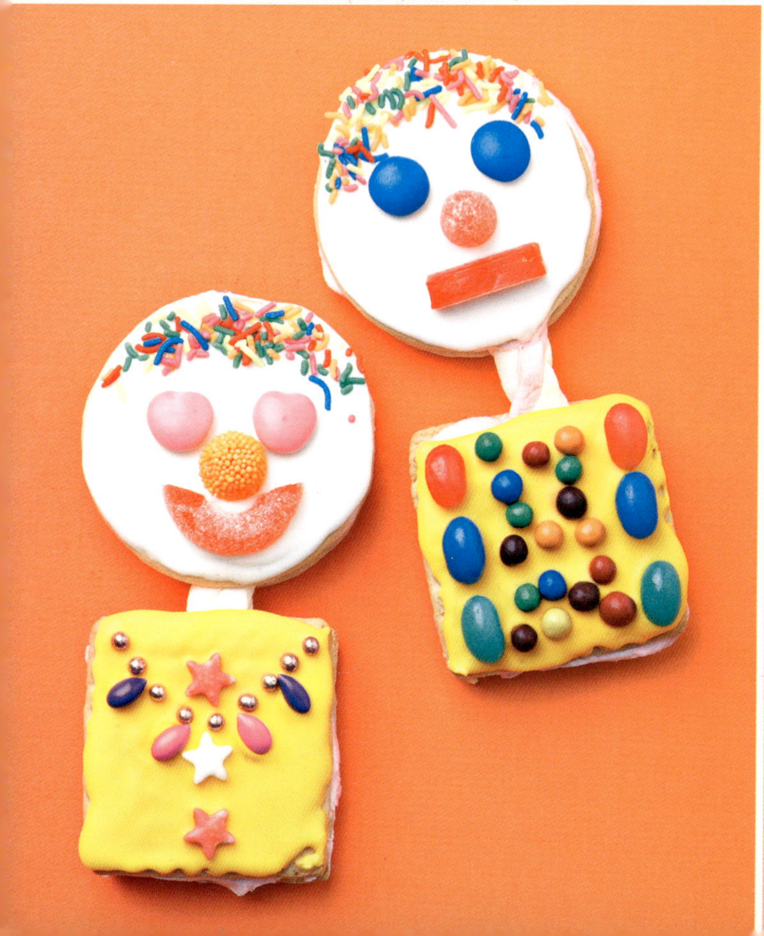
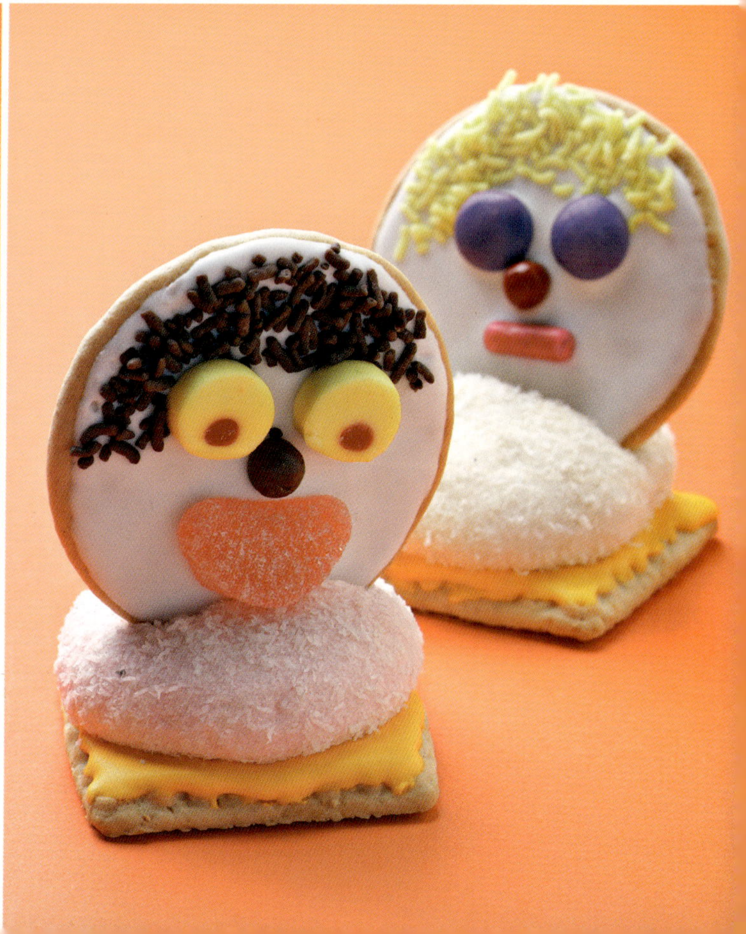

Dinosaur days

yellow and orange coloured
    chocolate (page 8)
dinosaur-shaped chocolate moulds
desiccated coconut
green food colouring
glacé icing (page 8)
10 Marie biscuits

Melt the coloured chocolate in the microwave, stirring often. Pour the chocolate into the dinosaur-shaped moulds and place in the fridge to set. Remove from the moulds when set and set aside until needed.

Place the dessicated coconut in a small bowl. Mix in the green food colouring, one drop at a time, until the coconut is the desired shade of green.

Spread glacé icing over the Marie biscuits. While the icing is still wet, place a dinosaur chocolate in the centre of each biscuit and sprinkle over some coloured coconut.

Leave to stand until the icing sets.

MAKES 10

Girls 'n guys

20 marshmallows
20 Marie biscuits
10 long marshmallows
20 Tennis biscuits
white and coloured royal icing
    (page 8)
rainbow vermicelli
small sweets and cake beads

For the head, place 1 marshmallow on top of a Marie biscuit and microwave for a few seconds, keeping an eye on it. As soon as the marshmallow puffs up, remove the biscuit from the microwave. Place a long marshmallow on the edge of the Marie biscuit and flatten the puffed up marshmallow by pressing down with a second Marie biscuit.

For the body, repeat with 2 Tennis biscuits, placing the other end of the long marshmallow between the Tennis biscuits, to join both sets of biscuits (see picture).

Spread white royal icing over the front of the Marie biscuits, for the head. Create the face and hair with small sweets and vermicelli. For the body, spread coloured royal icing over the Tennis biscuits and decorate with a variety of sweets and cake beads.

Leave to stand until the icing sets.

MAKES 10

Funny faces

10 Tennis biscuits
royal icing in white and yellow
    (page 8)
10 large coconut marshmallows
10 Marie biscuits
vermicelli
variety of sweets for decorating

Spread yellow royal icing over a Tennis biscuit and place a coconut-covered marshmallow in the centre. Leave to stand until the icing sets..

Spread white royal icing over the Marie biscuit. Decorate with sweets and vermicelli for the face and hair. Leave to stand until the icing sets.

Cut a slit in the coconut marshmallow and push the Marie biscuit face into the slit, so that it stands upright.

MAKES 10

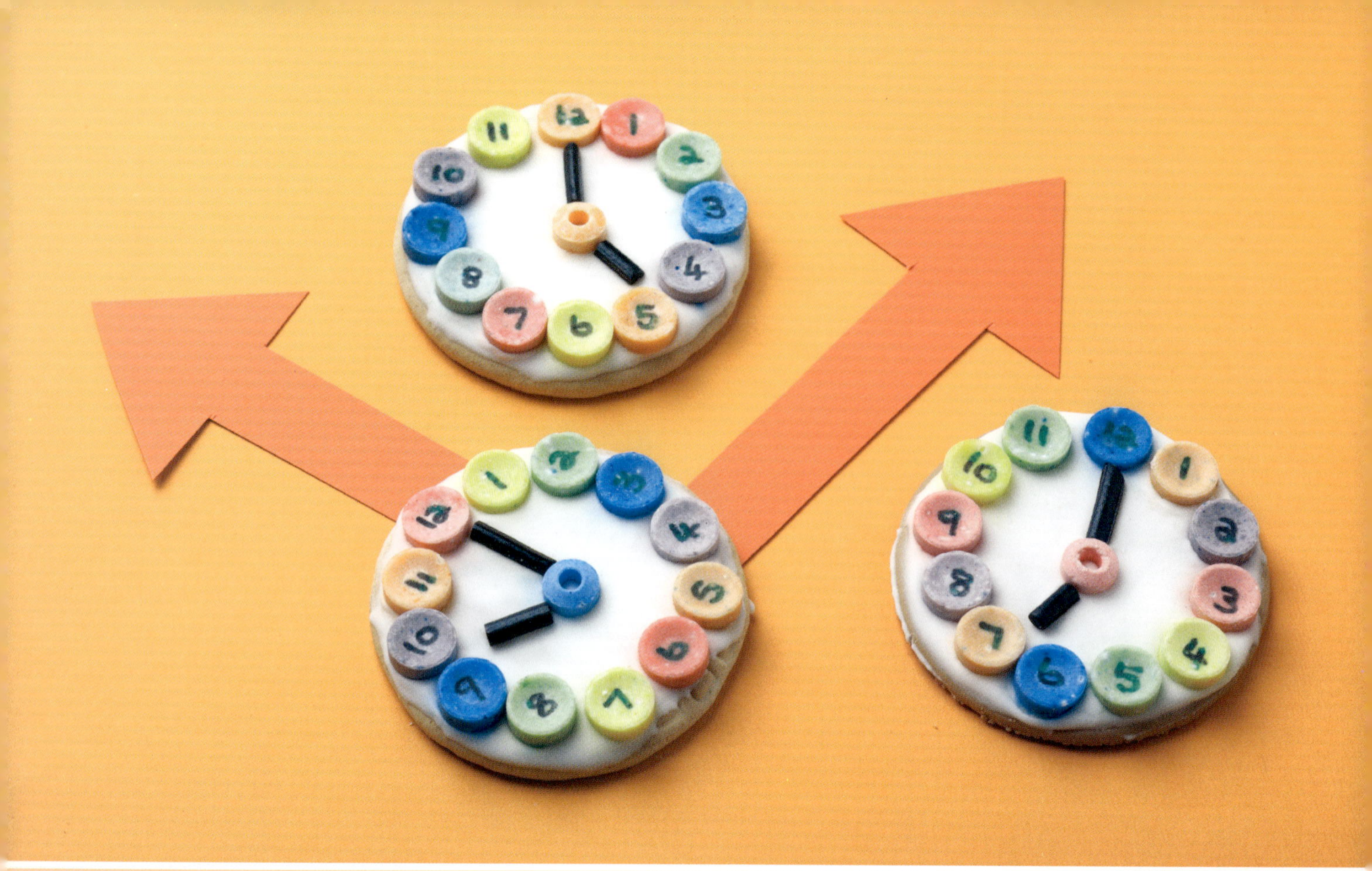

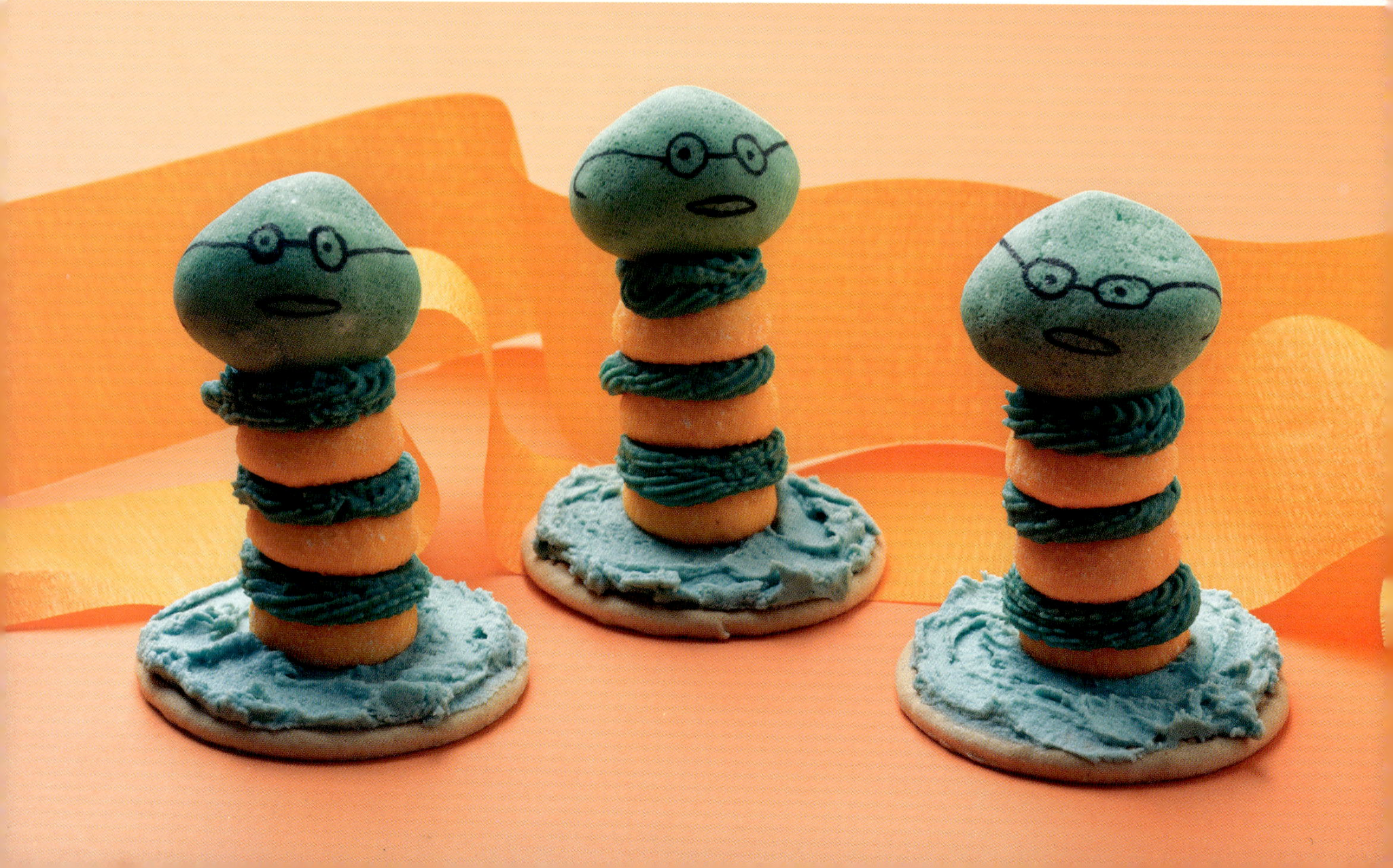

Tick tock clock

white glacé icing (page 8)
10 Marie biscuits
120 small flat round sweets
10 small ring-shaped sweets
20 liquorice strips
non-toxic pen

Spread glacé icing over a Marie biscuit.

Place 12 flat round sweets around the edge of the biscuit. Place 1 ring-shaped sweet in the centre and stick 2 liquorice strips to it, for the clock hands.

Leave to stand until the icing sets.

Use a non-toxic pen to write the numbers on the flat sweets.

MAKES 10

Bookworms

green butter icing (page 8)
10 Marie biscuits
15 apricot sweets, halved
10 green apricot sweets
non-toxic pen

Spread butter icing over the Marie biscuits and place half an apricot sweet in the centre of each biscuit.

Place the remaining butter icing into an icing bag fitted with a star-shaped nozzle. Pipe a blob of icing onto the halved apricot sweet and place another halved apricot sweet on top. Repeat, so you have 3 halved apricot sweets sandwiched with icing.

Pipe a blob of icing on the last apricot sweet and top with a green apricot sweet.

Leave to stand until the icing sets.

Use a non-toxic pen to draw a face on the green sweet.

MAKES 10

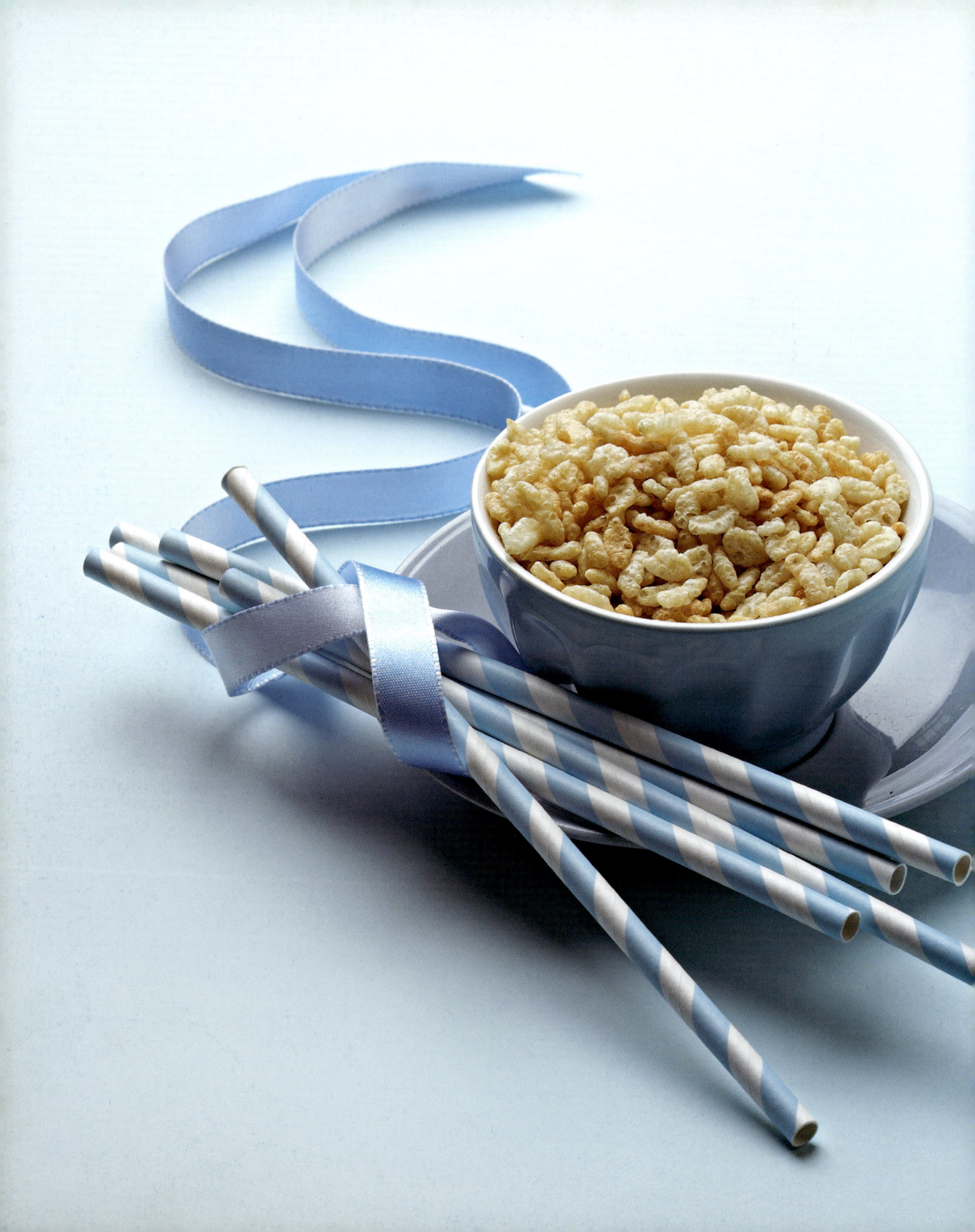

Rice Krispies

Freight train

1 Rice Krispies mix (page 11)
12 rectangular wafer biscuits
white chocolate
16 large flat round sweets
2 small flat round sweets
3 flat-bottomed ice-cream cones
variety of sweets for decorating

Prepare the Rice Krispies mix, pour onto baking paper and press down to flatten. Leave to set then, using a wafer biscuit as a template, cut 8 blocks.

Melt the chocolate in the microwave, stirring often. Coat 1 wafer biscuit with melted chocolate and place a Rice Krispies block on top. Coat another biscuit with melted chocolate and place it, chocolate side down, on the Rice Krispies block. Brush the top of the wafer with more chocolate and add a second Rice Krispies block. Coat the final wafer biscuit with chocolate and place it, chocolate side down, on the Rice Krispies block. Repeat, so you have one locomotive and three carriages.

Using melted chocolate, stick 2 large round sweets to each side of the locomotive and the carriages, for the wheels. Stick 2 small round sweets to the front of the locomotive, for the headlights.

Using melted chocolate, stick a flat-bottomed ice-cream cone to the top of the locomotive, for the funnel. Cut off the top of a second ice-cream cone and stick this to the third carriage. Cut the base off the cone and stick it behind the main funnel. Cut the base off the third ice-cream cone and stick it, upside down, to the back of the last carriage. Fill the open cones with sweets and decorate the carriages by sticking different sweets on top, using melted chocolate.

MAKES 1 TRAIN

Seashore scene

1 Rice Krispies mix (page 11)
blue coloured chocolate (page 8)
variety of sweets in the shape of
    fish and other marine creatures
white chocolate

Prepare the Rice Krispies mix using white marshmallows. Pour the mixture onto baking paper and press to flatten. Leave to set, then cut the sides neatly, to form a rectangle.

Melt the blue chocolate in the microwave, stirring often. Coat half the Rice Krispies block with the melted chocolate, for the sea, swirling it to create texture. Before the blue chocolate sets, position the fish and other creatures that belong in the sea.

Melt the white chocolate in the microwave, stirring often. Use dabs of white chocolate to stick marine creatures (like penguins and turtles) onto the beach.

MAKES 1 SCENE

Krispie cupcakes

1 Rice Krispies mix (page 11)
silicone cupcake cases
butter or margarine for greasing
100g white chocolate
rainbow vermicelli
10 birthday candles
10 paper cupcake cases

Prepare the Rice Krispies mix. Grease the silicone cupcake cases well with butter. Fill with the mixture and press down well. Leave until the mixture sets completely.

Melt the chocolate in the microwave, stirring often. Remove the 'cupcakes' from the silicone cases and spread the top with melted chocolate. Sprinkle over the vermicelli. Press a birthday candle into the cupcake and leave to stand until the chocolate sets completely. Serve in a paper cupcake case.

MAKES 10

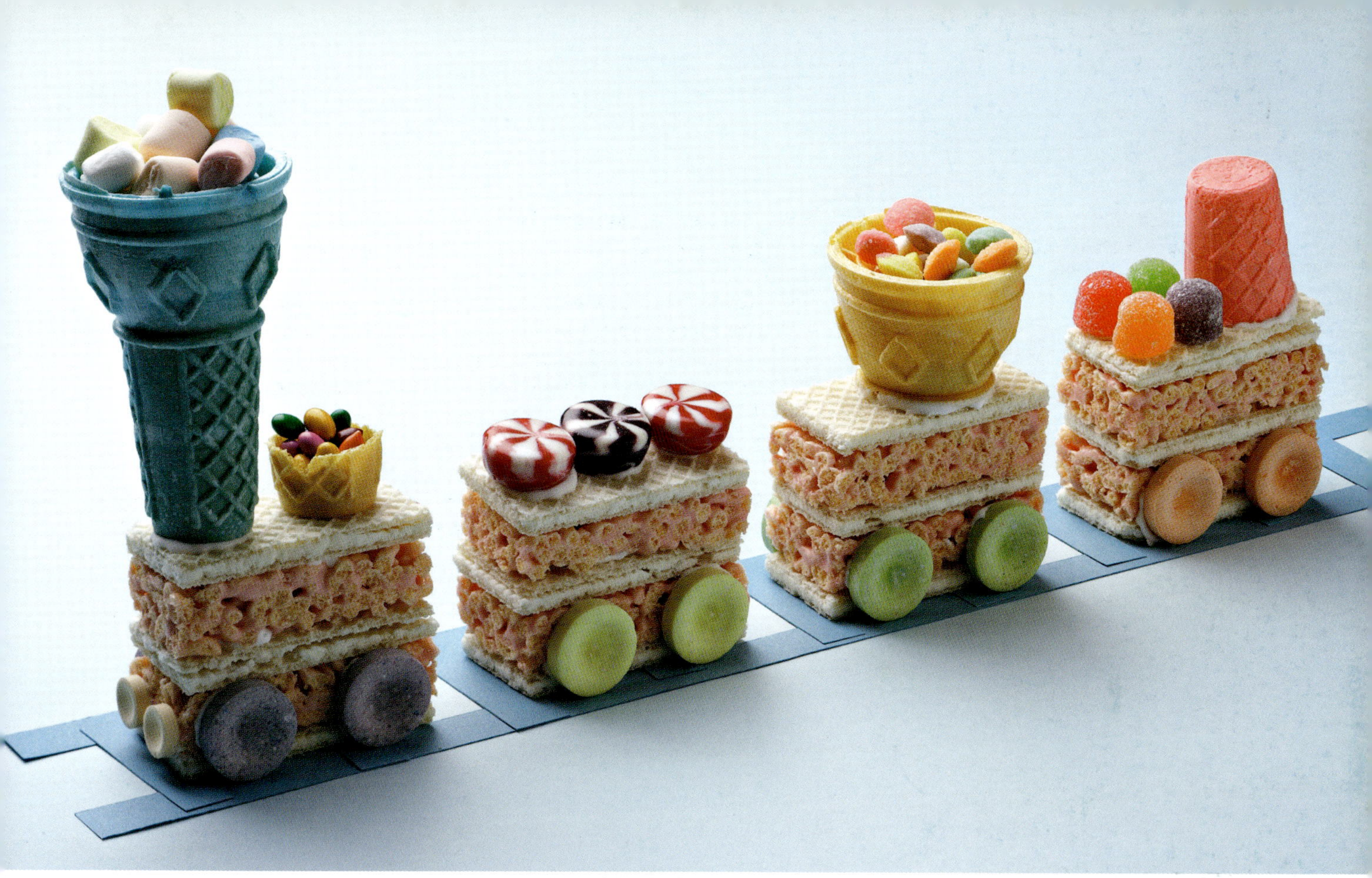

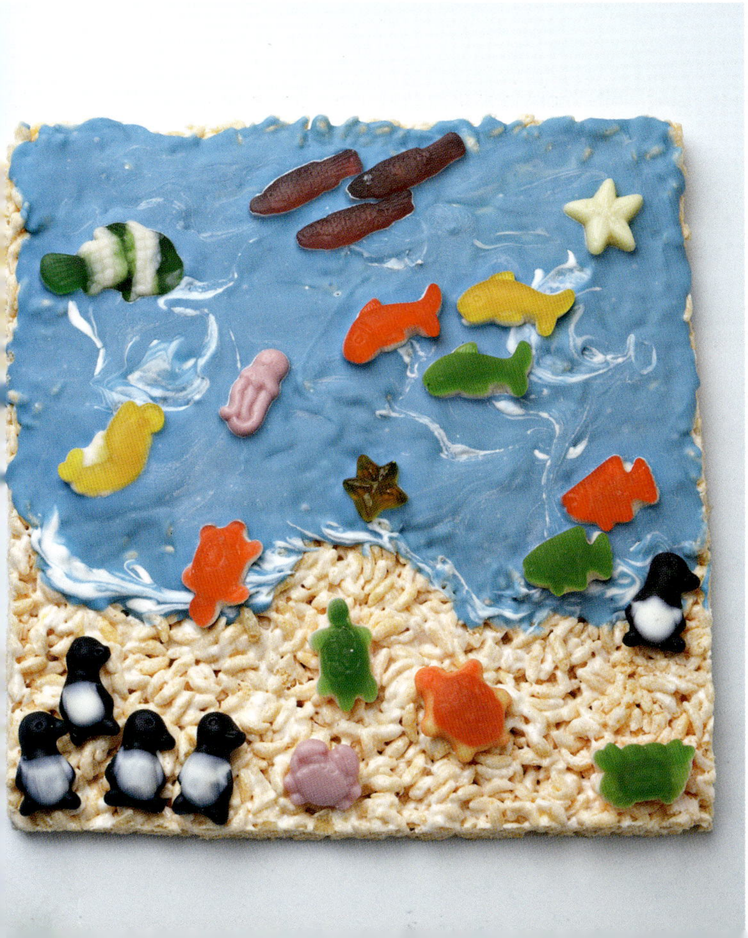

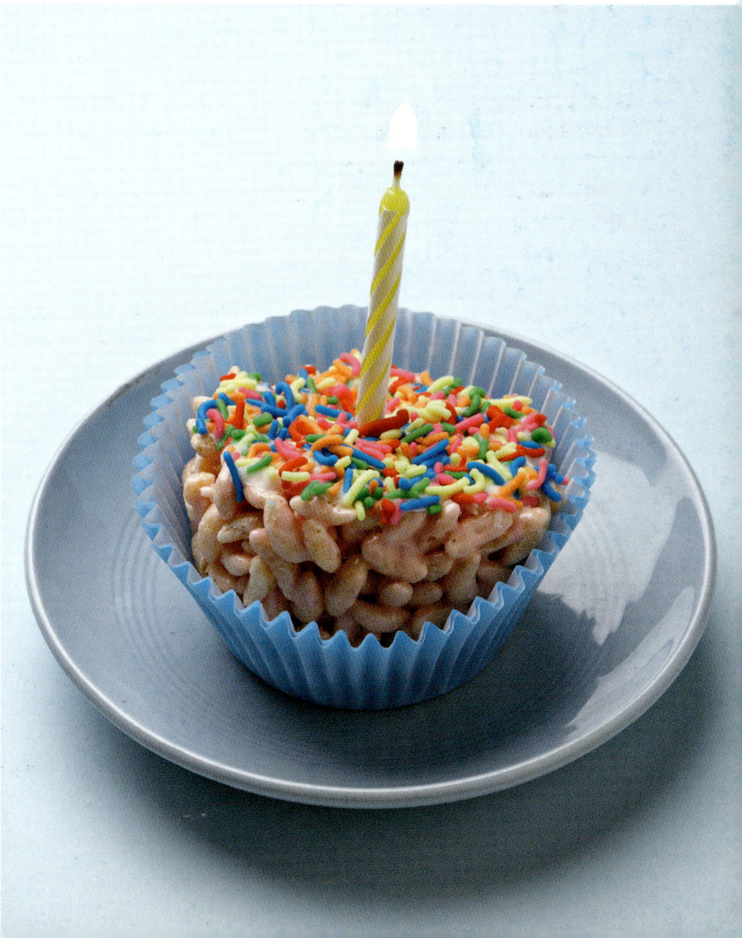

Mock rice cakes

1 Rice Krispies mix (page 11)
50g milk chocolate
50g white chocolate
green vermicelli

Pour the Rice Krispies mix onto baking paper and press to flatten. Leave to set, then cut out rounds.

Melt the chocolate separately in the microwave, stirring often. Spread milk chocolate over half the rounds (to look like Marmite). Spread white chocolate over the other half and sprinkle over green vermicelli (to resemble savoury cottage cheese).

Chocolate hearts

1 Rice Krispies mix (page 11)
100g milk chocolate

Pour the Rice Krispies mix onto baking paper and press to flatten. Leave to set, then cut out heart shapes.

Melt the chocolate in the microwave, stirring often.
Dip half of each heart into the melted chocolate. Place on a sheet of baking paper until completely set.

Flowers and butterflies

1 Rice Krispies mix (page 11)
white chocolate
variety of small sweets

Pour the Rice Krispies mix onto baking paper and press to flatten. Leave to set, then cut out flowers and butterflies.

Melt the chocolate in the microwave, stirring often.
Use dabs of melted chocolate to stick sweets onto the shapes, for decoration.

Krispie balls

1 Rice Krispies mix (page 11)
butter or margarine for greasing
100g white chocolate
lollipop sticks
rainbow vermicelli

Prepare the Rice Krispies mix. Grease your hands well to prevent the mixture from sticking, and form small balls. Leave to set.

Melt the chocolate in the microwave, stirring often. Dip the tip of a lollipop stick into the chocolate, push it into a Rice Krispie ball and leave upside down until the chocolate sets.

Melt the chocolate again. Dip the balls halfway into the chocolate and then into the rainbow vermicelli. Place the balls on a sheet of baking paper and leave until completely set.

MAKES 12

Colourful Krispie cups

½ Rice Krispies mix (page 11)
small chocolate-coated sweets
mini paper cupcake cases

Prepare the Rice Krispies mix using white marshmallows. While the mixture is still soft, mix in the chocolate-coated sweets. Spoon the mixture into the cupcake cases and leave until completely set.

MAKES 12

Krispie caramel cups

360g can ready-made caramel
1 box of Rice Krispies
24 edible cupcake cases

In a large mixing bowl, combine the caramel and Rice Krispies. Spoon the mixture into edible cupcake cases and decorate, if desired, to suit the party theme.

Tip: By adding more Rice Krispies the mixture won't be too sweet and you will be able to fill more cups.

Crunchy worms

½ Rice Krispies mix (page 11)
butter or margarine for greasing
white chocolate
liquorice strips

Prepare the Rice Krispies mix using white marshmallows. Grease your hands with butter and roll the mixture into small balls of equal size. Leave to set.

Melt the chocolate in the microwave, stirring often. Use dabs of melted chocolate to stick 4 balls together, for the body.
Cut the liquorice strips into different lengths. Use dabs of melted chocolate to place the liquorice on the front ball, for the eyes, nose and feelers.

Tree stumps

½ chocolate Rice Krispies mix
    (page 11)
butter or margarine for greasing
milk chocolate
red fondant
brown mini Astros or small
    chocolate-coated sweets
non-toxic pen
green butter icing (page 8)
sugar butterflies

Prepare the Rice Krispies mix. Grease your hands with butter and roll the mixture into small log shapes. Place on baking paper to set.
Melt the chocolate in the microwave, stirring often. Drizzle a spiral of chocolate on one end of the tree stump, for tree rings. Leave to set.

To make a ladybird, roll the red fondant into a ball and flatten slightly. Use a dab of chocolate to attach a brown mini Astro for the head. Draw wings using a non-toxic pen. Fill an icing bag with green butter icing and fit a small round nozzle. Pipe leaves and vines onto the tree stump. Place the ladybird and sugar butterfly while the icing is still wet. Allow to set very well before handling.

Bear faces

½ chocolate Rice Krispies mix
    (page 11)
butter or margarine for greasing
milk chocolate
brown Smarties
blue mini Astros
brown mini Astros
icing in a tube

Prepare the Rice Krispies mix. Grease your hands with butter and roll the mixture into balls, flattening them slightly. Place on baking paper to set.

Melt the chocolate in the microwave, stirring often. Cut off one edge of the brown Smarties and use melted chocolate to stick these to the ball, for the ears.

Use melted chocolate to stick 2 blue Astros to the ball, for the eyes, and 1 brown Astro, for the nose. Draw the mouth using an icing tube.

Smiley spiders

½ chocolate Rice Krispies mix
    (page 11)
butter or margarine for greasing
milk chocolate
liquorice strips
20 red Astros or small
    chocolate-coated sweets
red jelly strips

Prepare the Rice Krispies mix. Grease your hands with butter and roll the mixture into balls, flattening them slightly. Place on baking paper to set.

Melt the chocolate in the microwave, stirring often. Use dabs of chocolate to stick 8 liquorice strips to the bottom of each ball, for the legs. On top, stick 2 Astros for the eyes, and a red jelly strip for the mouth.

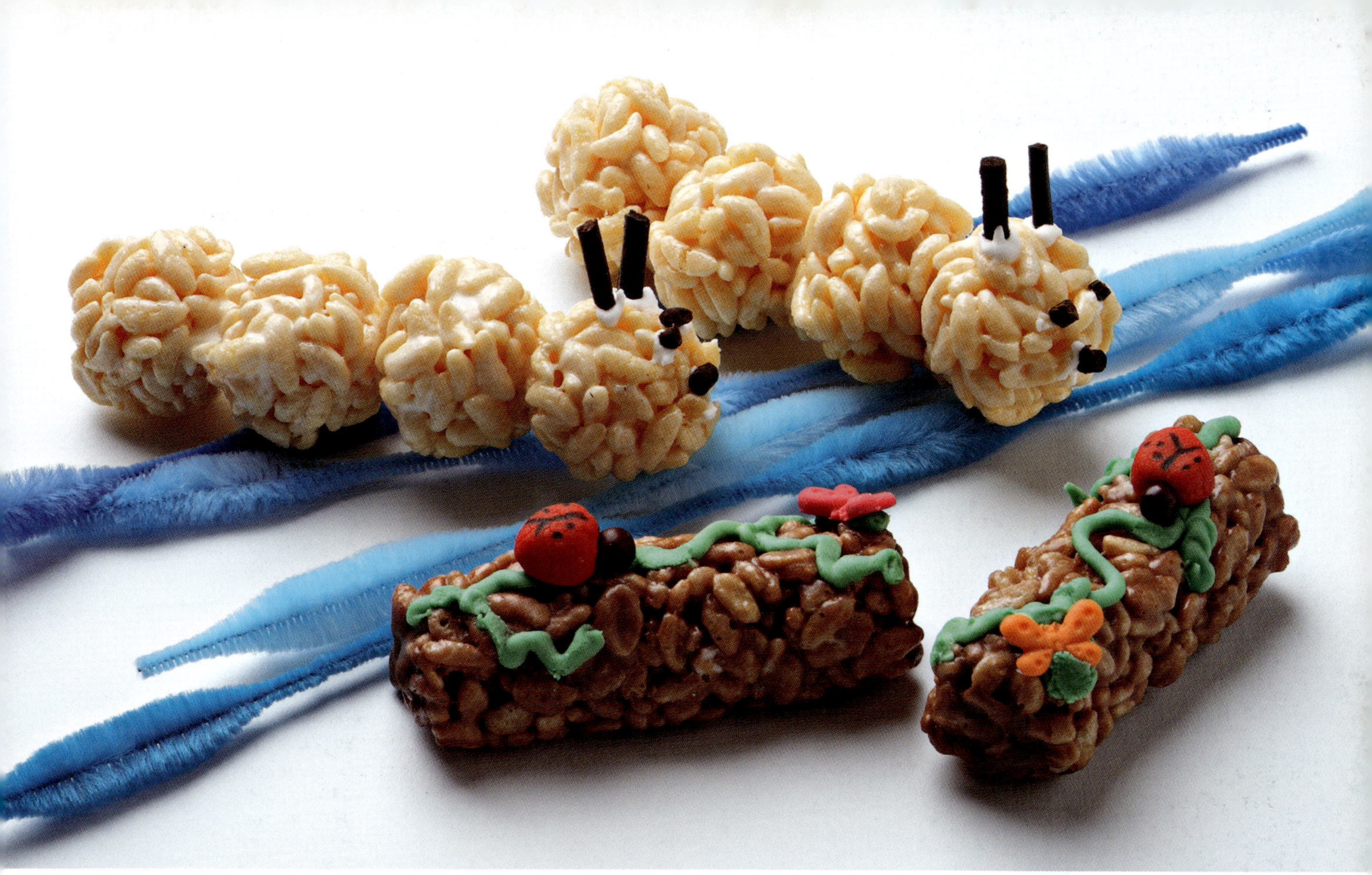

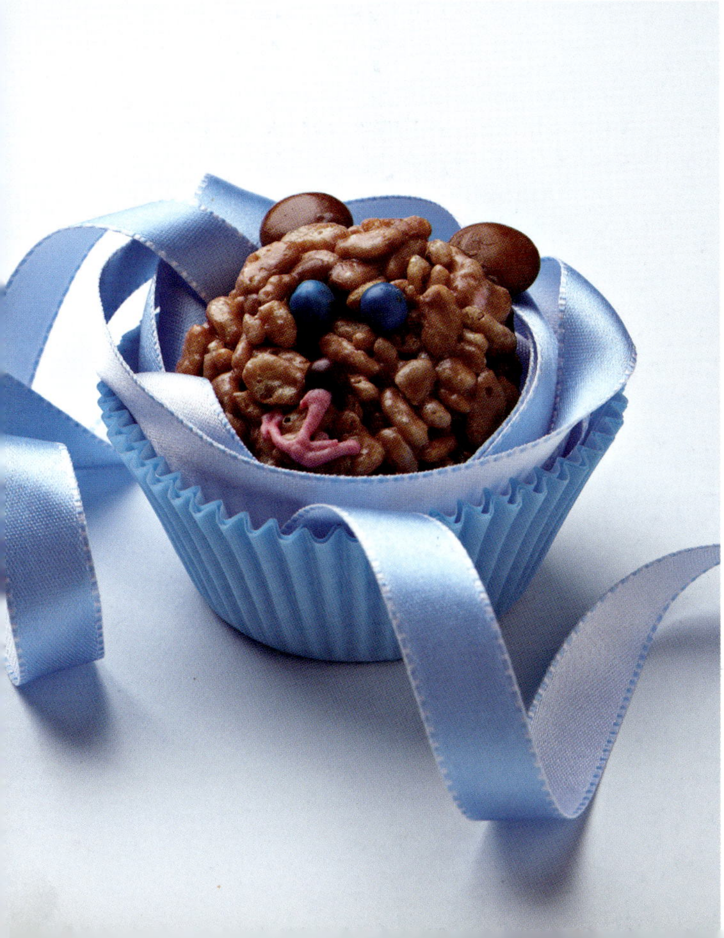

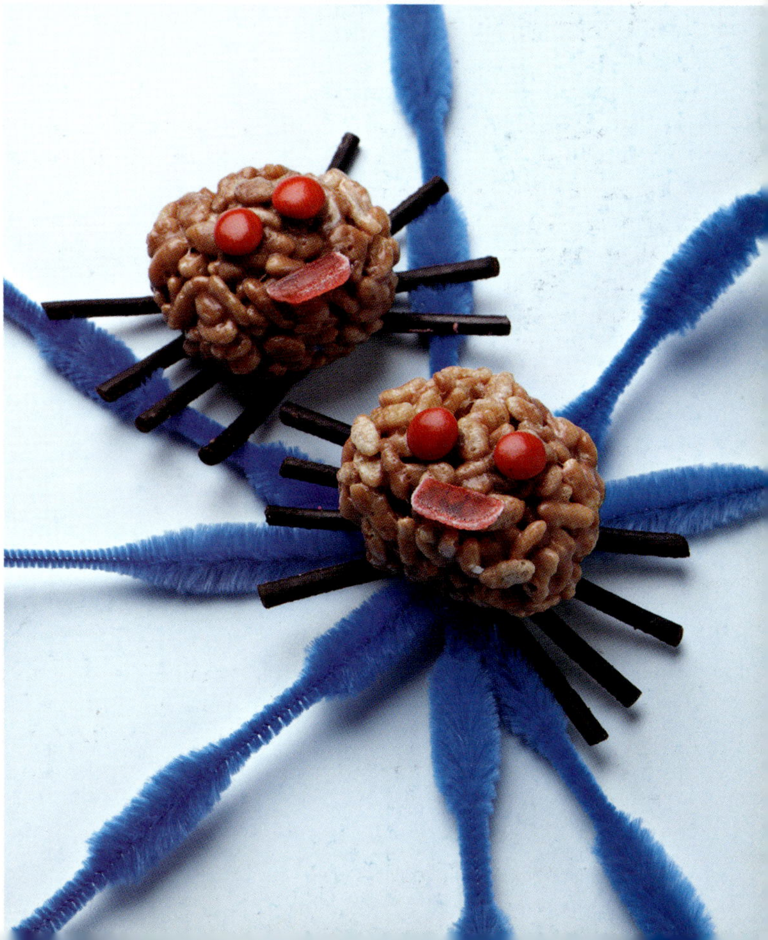

Hen and chicks

½ Rice Krispies mix (page 11)
¼ chocolate Rice Krispies mix (page 11)
butter or margarine for greasing
white chocolate
plain (unsalted) pretzels
sprinkles or 100's & 1000's
small blue chocolate sweets
orange Jelly Tots
yellow Smarties
red oblong liquorice sweets
blue mini Astros or small chocolate-coated sweets
extra milk chocolate
small banana-shaped sweets

Prepare the Rice Krispies mix using white marshmallows.
Grease your hands with butter to prevent the mixture from sticking and form a triangle shape for each hen and 2 balls for each chick, making one ball slightly smaller than the other. Melt the white chocolate in the microwave, stirring often. Drizzle some chocolate in a spiral on one end of the larger balls, to enable them to stand. Leave to set.

Follow the instructions below to finish off the hens and chicks.

Hen

Dip 2 pretzels into the melted white chocolate and scatter over the sprinkles. Place the pretzels on baking paper to set (or in the fridge to set quickly).

Use a dab of melted chocolate to stick down 2 small blue chocolate sweets for the eyes. Cut a wedge out of the orange Jelly Tot and stick it in place for the beak.

Use dabs of melted chocolate to position the dipped pretzels for the feet.

Chick

Use a dab of melted chocolate to stick the smaller Rice Krispie ball on top of the larger one and leave to set.

Cut an edge off 2 Smarties and use melted chocolate to stick them on either side of the bottom ball, for the wings. Cut the oblong liquorice sweet in two and stick one half down for the mouth. Stick down 2 mini Astros for the eyes.

Nest

Prepare the chocolate Rice Krispies mix. Grease the inside of a mould (a glass or plastic container works well) with butter or margarine. Spoon the mixture into the container and press down to cover the base and sides. Leave to set completely, then carefully remove the nest from the mould.

Melt the milk chocolate in the microwave, stirring often. Cover the outside of the nest with melted chocolate and leave until set.

Place banana-shaped sweets inside the nest and place a chick on top (use a dab of melted chocolate to hold it in place, if necessary).

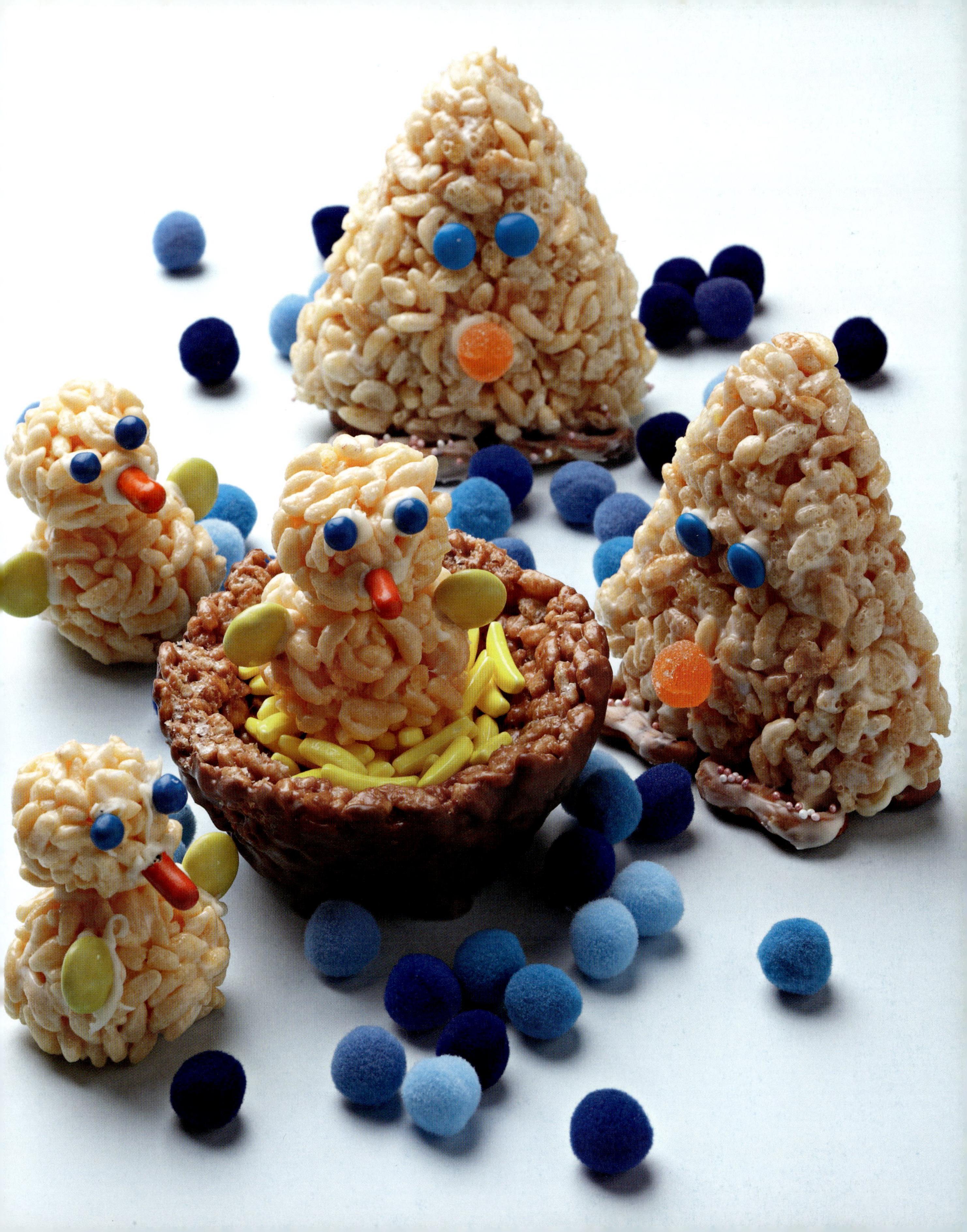

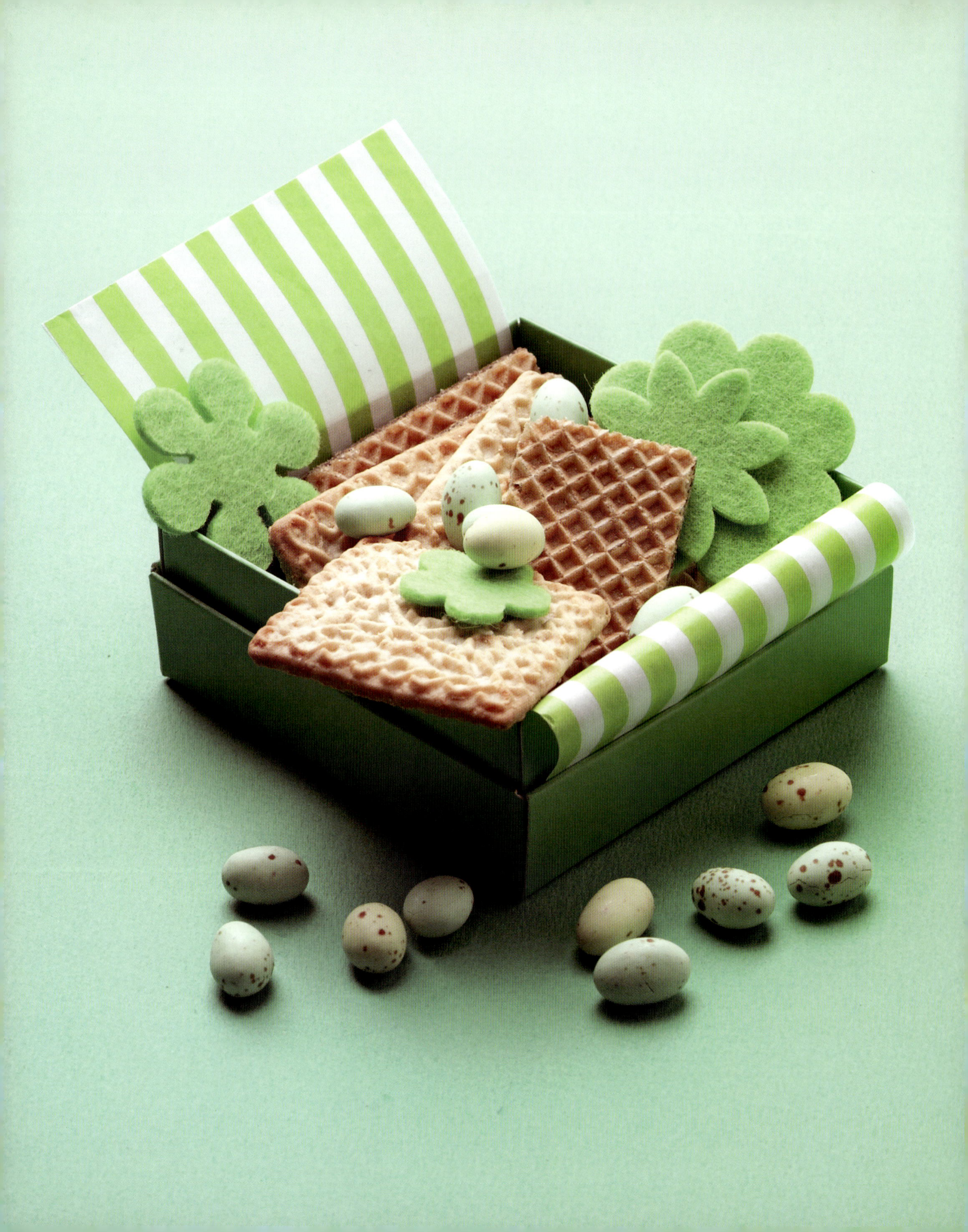

Miscellaneous

Chocolate paintboxes

fondant in various colours
10 x 100g white chocolate slabs
extra white chocolate, for melting

Roll out the different colours of fondant and cut out circles (about 8 per paintbox). Use grey and brown fondant to make 10 paintbrushes.

Remove the chocolate slabs from their packaging. Melt the extra chocolate and stick the fondant circles to the smooth side of the slabs, and the fondant brush in the centre. Leave until the chocolate sets.

Package in transparent plastic bags and tie with ribbon.

MAKES 10

Painted biscuits

basic butter biscuit mix (page 12)
liquid food colouring
glacé icing (page 8) in three or four colours

Preheat the oven to 180°C.
Roll out the biscuit dough to 5mm thick and cut into squares (±15 x 15cm).
Bake for 12–15 minutes or until golden brown. Leave until completely cooled.

Using food colouring and a thin brush, draw pictures on the cooled biscuits.

Prepare the glacé icing just before use. Place small amounts in saucers or individual containers, provide paintbrushes, and let each child colour in the picture on a biscuit. Leave to set.

These make a perfect 'take home' gift after the party.

Chocolatey bread

1 loaf of sliced white bread
1 tub chocolate spread
coloured vermicelli

Spread each slice of bread with chocolate spread. Use cookie cutters to cut out different shapes. Sprinkle over coloured vermicelli and serve.

Note: An average sliced loaf yields about 20 slices. With large cookie cutters, you'll probably only get one shape per slice; smaller cookie cutters will give more shapes.

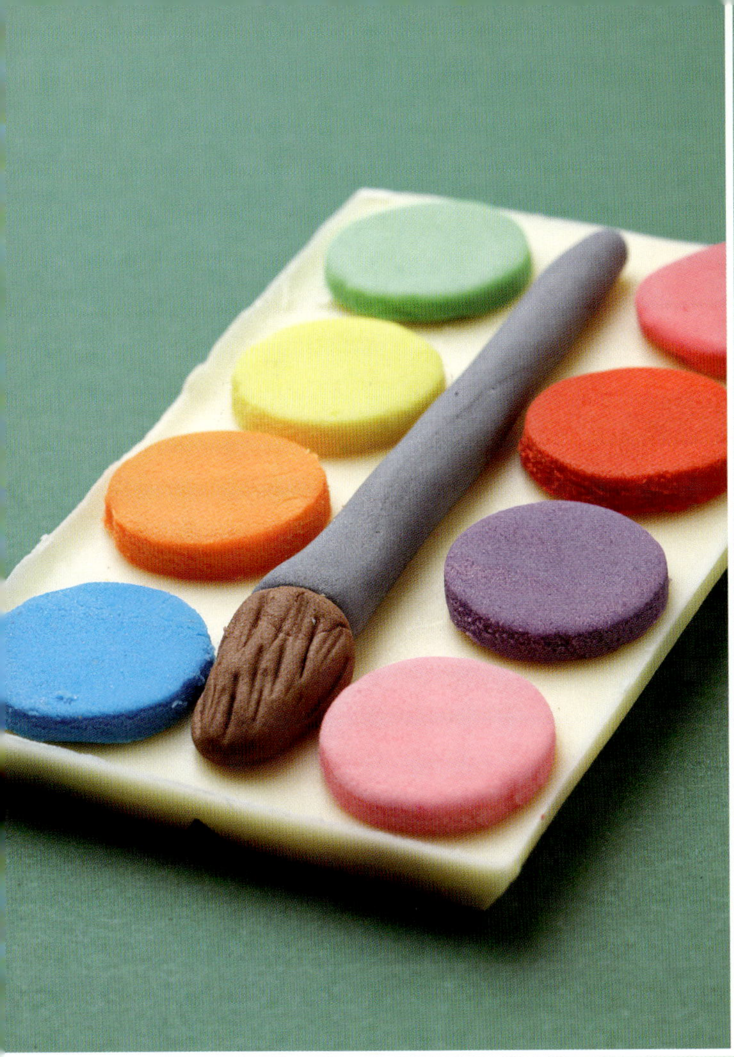
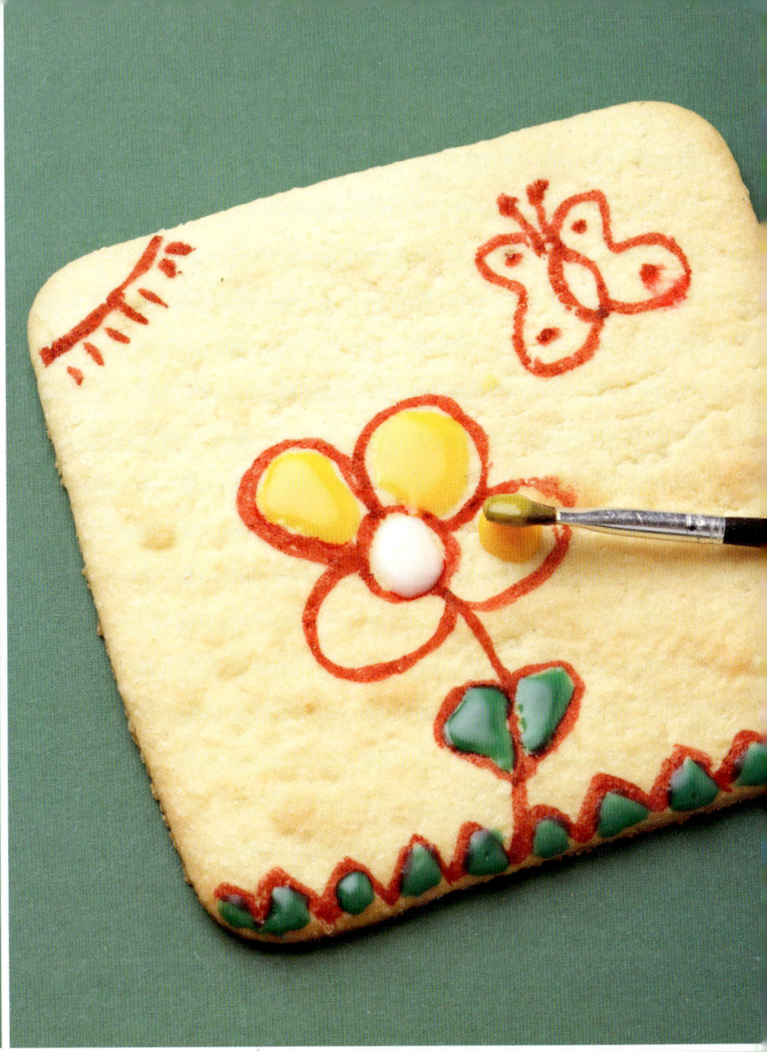
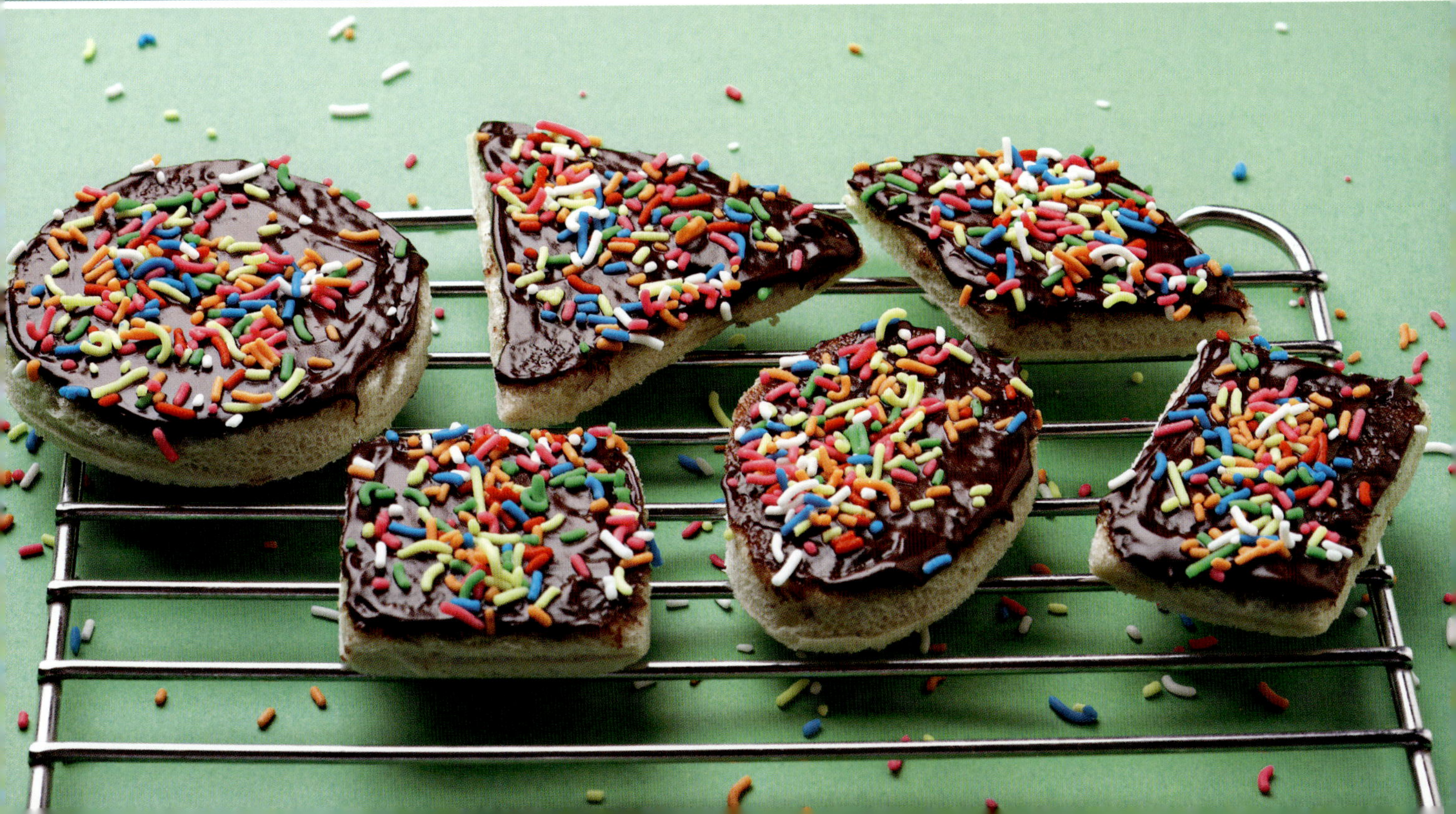

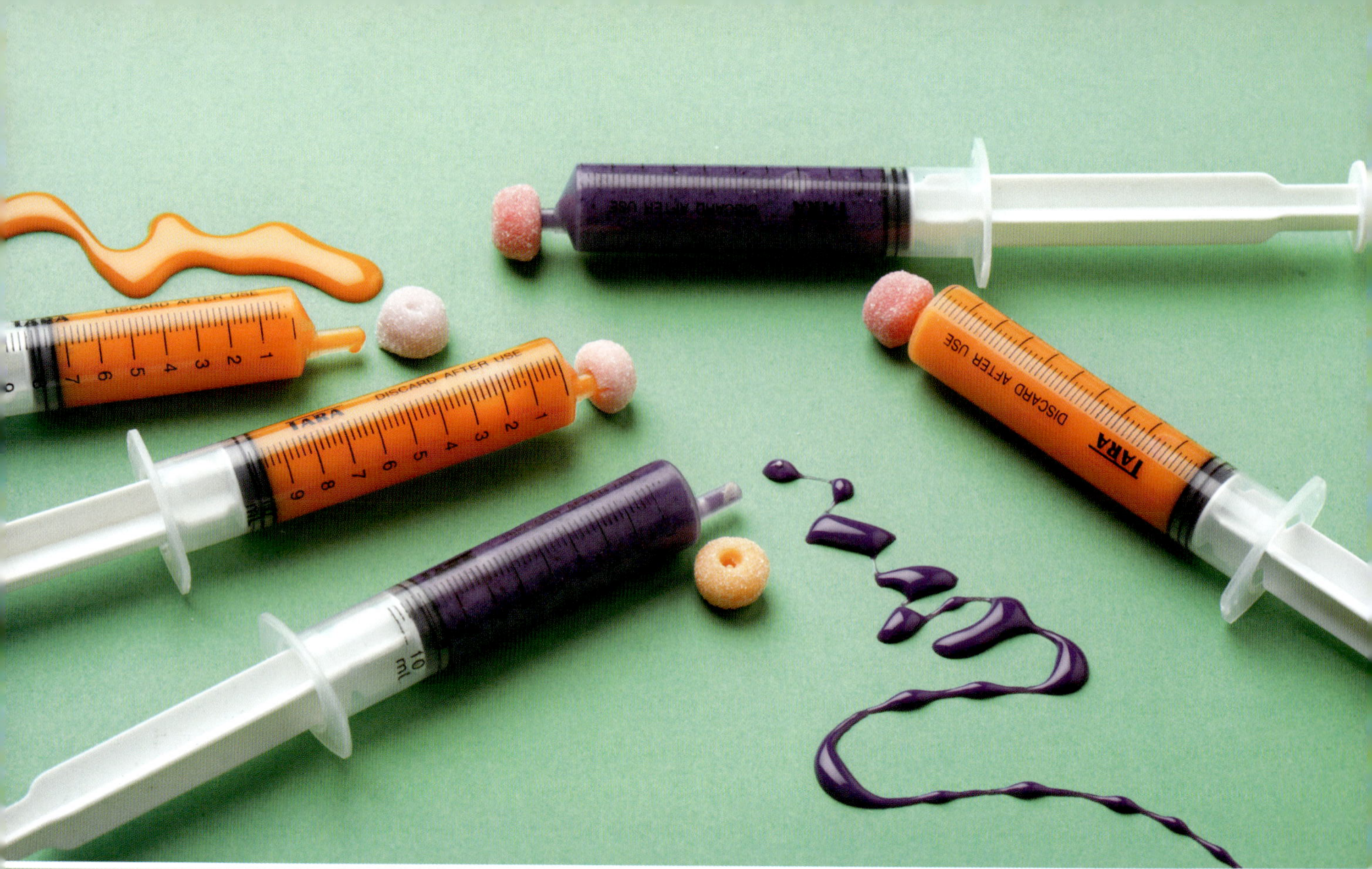
DISCARD AFTER USE
TARA

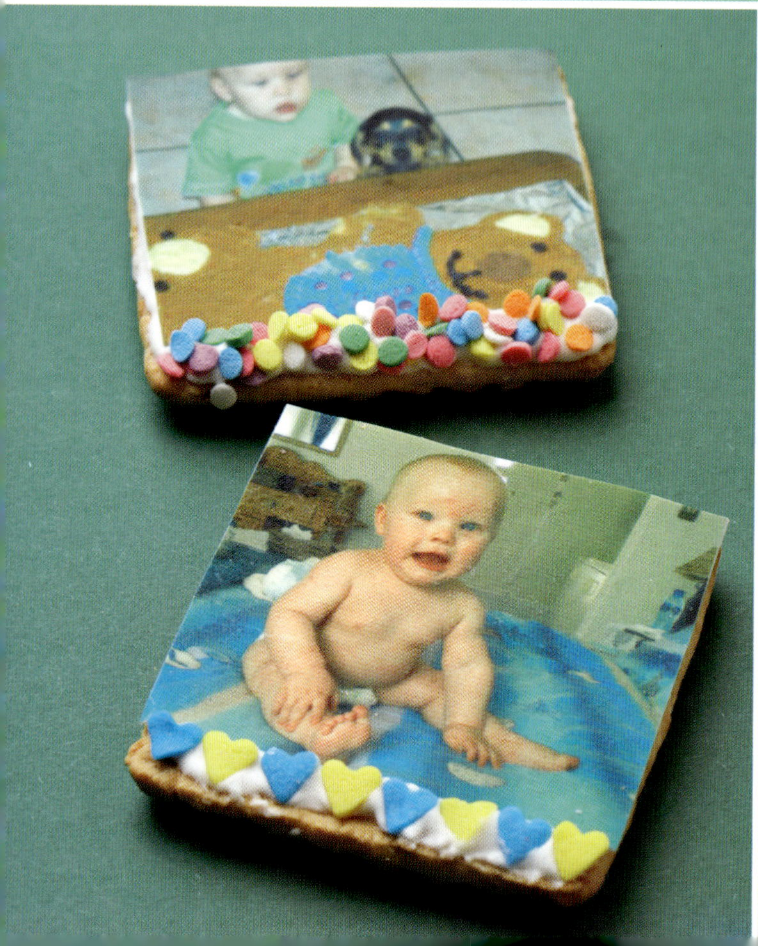

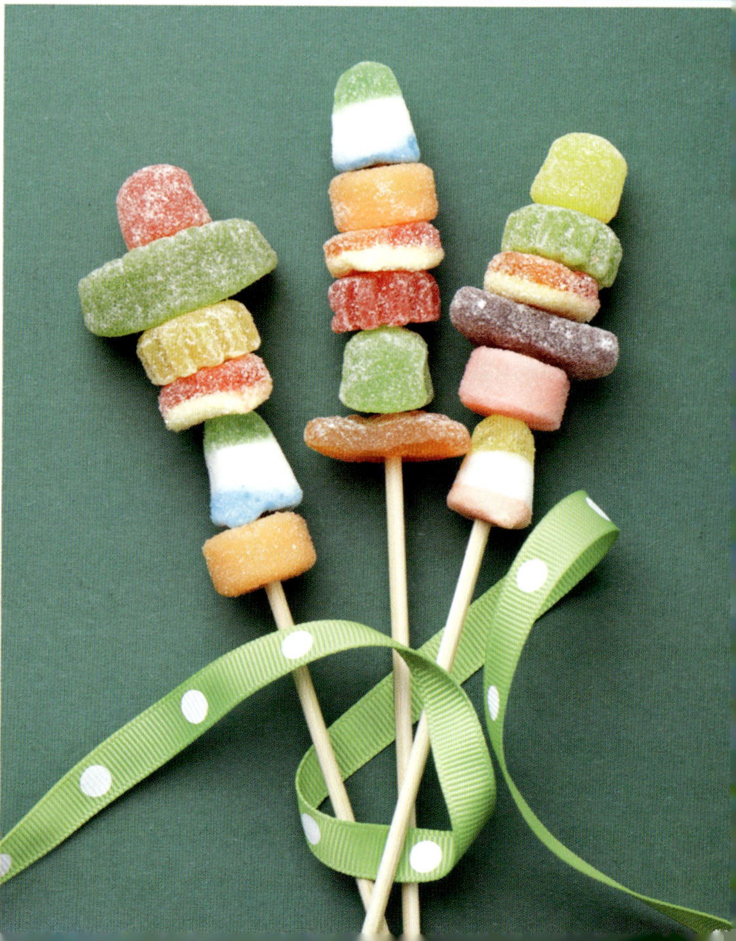

Energy injections

1 can condensed milk
food colouring in various colours
20ml plastic syringes
Jelly Tots

Divide the condensed milk into three or four small bowls, depending on the number of colours you have. Use a few drops of food colouring per bowl, stirring it through the condensed milk to achieve a uniform colour.

Fill the syringes with the coloured condensed milk and place a Jelly Tot on the tip of each syringe to stop the condensed milk from leaking out.

Tip: Coloured condensed milk can also be used as edible 'paint'.

Photo biscuits

edible icing sheets
white glacé icing (page 8)
15 Tennis biscuits
cake confetti, for decoration

Print suitable photographs onto edible icing sheets. Make sure the icing sheet is very dry before you handle it, and that your hands are clean and dry before you peel off the backing paper to cut out the pictures.

Spread a layer of glacé icing over a Tennis biscuit and position the picture on top. Decorate the edges with cake confetti.

MAKES 15

Note: Edible icing sheets are available from specialist baking shops. You should get 15 'biscuit-sized' pictures from one A4 sheet.

Jelly pops

variety of sugared jelly sweets
wooden skewers

Push wooden skewers through an assortment of different sweets.

Tip: Dip the tip of the skewer into warm water before threading it through each sweet. This prevents the skewer from becoming sticky and makes the task easier.

MISCELLANEOUS

Jelly Tot fudge

750g white chocolate, chopped
1 can condensed milk
5ml vanilla essence
375ml Jelly Tots, cut into pieces

Heat the chocolate and condensed milk in a saucepan over a low heat, stirring continuously until melted. Remove from the heat and stir in the vanilla essence and Jelly Tots pieces.

Line a 10 x 20cm baking pan with wax paper.
Pour the fudge mixture into the baking pan and place in the fridge to set.

Cut into squares.

Chocolate nests

125ml milk
60g (4T) butter
250ml sugar
60ml cocoa powder
100g milk chocolate, chopped
5ml vanilla essence
750ml rolled oats
mini chocolate eggs

Heat the milk and the butter in a medium saucepan.
When the butter has melted, add the sugar and cocoa powder, stirring until the sugar has dissolved. Simmer for about 2 minutes, then remove from the stove.

Add the chopped chocolate and the vanilla essence, stirring until the mixture is smooth. Add the oats and mix thoroughly (the mixture should be quite stiff).

Spoon the mixture into silicone cupcake cases, pressing down until the sides are covered. Leave to set.

Remove the nests from the silicone cases and fill with mini chocolate eggs.

MAKES 12

Name biscuits

basic butter biscuit mix (page 12)
royal icing in colours of your choice (page 8)
sugar decorations
pearl cake beads

Preheat the oven to 180°C.

Roll out the biscuit dough to 5mm thick. Cut out letters using cookie cutters.
(If you don't have alphabet cookie cutters, print the letters on paper, cut them out and use them as templates to cut out the dough letters.)
Bake for 12–15 minutes or until golden brown. Leave to cool.

Thicken some royal icing and place it in an icing bag fitted with a thin nozzle.
Pipe an outline along the edge of the biscuit. Leave to set.
Using thinner royal icing and a wider nozzle, fill in the letters.

Place a sugar decoration on the first and the last letter of the name, and decorate the other letters with pearl cake beads before the icing sets.

Leave overnight to set.

CHRISTINE
MARILISE

Traffic lights

10 rectangular wafer biscuits
glacé icing (page 8)
30 red Smarties or other round sweets
30 orange Smarties or other round sweets
30 green Smarties or other round sweets

Cut 5 of the wafer biscuits in half, to make 10 squares. Cut the other 5 biscuits lengthwise in two.

Using a dab of glacé icing, stick a red, orange and green sweet, in that order, onto each long wafer. Leave to set completely.

Using some more glacé icing, stand the long biscuit on top of the square biscuit. (You might need to place something behind the biscuit for support until the icing has set; a small plastic bowl will do the job.)

MAKES 10

Lego blocks

rectangular wafer biscuits
royal icing in various colours (page 8)
chocolate-coated sweets (Smarties or Astros)

Cut the wafer biscuits into different shapes.
Spread different coloured icing over the biscuits and top with matching sweets.

Note: The number of blocks you can make will depend on how you cut the wafer biscuits.

MISCELLANEOUS

Caramel cones

10 flat-bottomed ice-cream cones
variety of small sweets
1 can ready-made caramel
white butter icing (page 8)
coloured vermicelli

Fill the ice-cream cones three-quarters full with sweets.

Spoon a blob of caramel on top of the sweets.

Fill an icing bag with white butter icing and top the ice-cream cone with butter icing, swirling it to look like a soft serve.

Decorate with a swirl of caramel and a sprinkle of vermicelli.

MAKES 10 CONES

Sherbet cones

sherbet
10 ice-cream cones
20 marshmallows
sprinkles or 100's & 1000's

Pour some sherbet into the bottom of each ice-cream cone. Pour the sprinkles onto a plate or shallow bowl.

Push 2 marshmallows into the ice-cream cone.
Microwave each cone for a few seconds until the marshmallows puff up (keep an eye on the marshmallows), then remove the cone from the microwave and gently press the marshmallow into the sprinkles.

MAKES 10 CONES

MISCELLANEOUS

Index

Aeroplanes 22
Aliens and creepy crawlies 70–77
  angry aliens 76
  creepy brownies 72
  friendly aliens 76
  ghosts 72
  kreepy kebabs 75
  robots 72
  slime balls 75
  slime cups 75
  space dwarves 76
  sssnake skewers 75
aliens, angry 76
  friendly 76
Angry aliens 76
Animals 46–59
  animal cones 86–88
  bear faces 128
  bears 86
  bookworms 121
  cats 87
  chirpy chicks 97
  cowabunga 112
  cows 87
  dalmations 86
  hen and chicks 130
  hoppity bunnies 96
  Katie the cat 110
  ladybirds 110
  little lambs 97
  marshmallow bunnies 94
  marshmallow love bears 94
  monkeys 87
  Percy piglet 110
  pigs 88
  pink piglets 96
Ants 58

Baby bugs 59
Basic butter biscuits 12
Basic recipes 6–13
  basic butter biscuits 12
  butter icing 8
  chocolate Rice Krispies squares 11
  coconut ice 12
  coloured chocolate 8
  fridge brownies 12
  glacé icing 8
  lamingtons 11
  Rice Krispies squares 11
  royal icing 8
Baskets 38
Beach babes 82
Bear faces 128
Bears 86

Bee biscuits 109
biscuits, basic butter 12
  bee 109
  bundles 38
  butterfly 109
  daisies 44
  dipped wafers 38
  flower biscuits 44
  Marie 104–121
  name 138
  Oreo flowers 38
  painted 134
  photo 137
Blue boy 64
boats 31
Bookworms 121
brownies, creepy 72
  fridge 12
bugs, *see* insects
Bundles of biscuits 38
Butter icing 8
Butterflies 57
butterfly, biscuits 109
  lollies 37
  Rice Krispie 126
Butterfly biscuits 109
Butterfly lollies 37
Buzzy bees 56

Caramel cones 141
cars, chocolate 4x4 21
  F1 18
  F1 racing cones 85
  jeep with trailer 21
  sports 18
Cats 87
Chirpy chicks 97
Chocolate 4x4 21
Chocolate and marshmallow suprise 26
Chocolate hearts 126
Chocolate kebabs 100
Chocolate nests 138
Chocolate paintboxes 134
Chocolate Rice Krispies squares 10
Chocolate spoons 29
Chocolate worms 50
Chocolately bread 134
Clown faces 106
Clowns 85
Coconut ice 12
Coconut ice balls 40
Coconut ice mice 51
Coconut ice with a difference 40
Coloured chocolate 8
Colourful Krispie cups 127

Cone figures 78–91
  beach babes 82
  bears 86
  cats 87
  clowns 85
  cows 88
  dalmations 86
  F1 racing cones 85
  flower girl 80
  fly-catcher cones 89
  lady with a handbag 80
  lady with a hat 81
  monkeys 87
  one-eyed aliens 84
  pearly princess 82
  pigs 88
  rock stars 82
  spaceships 84
  volcanoes 89
Cone-arm man 67
cones, caramel 141
  sherbet 141
Cowabunga 112
Cows 88
Crabs 53
Crawly crabs 112
Crazy clown 63
Creepy brownies 72
creepy crawlies
  chocolate worms 50
  crunchy worms 128
  green frogs 48
  hairy caterpillars 59
  marshmallow worms 50
  snails 58
  ssssnake skewers 75
  Sweetie Pie snails 49
  worms 58
  see also insects
Crunchy bugs 109
Crunchy worms 128
Curious clams 106

Daisies 44
Daisy delights 115
Dalmations 86
Decorated sugar cubes 41
Dino kebabs 103
Dinosaur days 119
Dipped wafer biscuits 38
Disco dancer 69
Dragonflies 57

Energy injections 137

142 INDEX

F1 cars
F1 racing cones 85
Feeesh 112
Fireworks 116
Flipper foot 65
Flower biscuits 44
Flower girl 80
Flowers and butterflies 126
flowers 126
   daisy delights 115
   Jelly Tot 115
   mallow 115
   Oreo 37
   Rice Krispies 126
Fly-catcher cones 89
Forest log 43
Freight train 124
Fridge brownies 12
Friendly aliens 76
fudge, Jelly Tots 137
   layered chocolate 26
Fun Sweetie Pies 41
Funny faces 119

Ghosts 72
Girls 'n Guys 119
Glacé icing 8
Green frogs 48

Hairy caterpillars 59
Hats 43
Helicopters 22
Hen and chicks 130
Hoppity bunnies 96
Hot chocolate cups 37

Icing, butter 8
   glacé 8
   royal 8
insects, ants 58
   baby bugs 59
   butterflies 57
   butterfly biscuits 109
   bee biscuits 109
   buzzy bees 56
   crunchy bugs 109
   dragonflies 57
   insects 110
   ladybirds 110
   moths 59
   smiley spiders 128
   speedy beetles 56
   spiders 57
   see also Creepy crawlies

Jeep with trailer 21
Jelly kebabs 100
Jelly pops 137
Jelly Tot flowers 115

Jelly Tot fudge 138
Jolly dolly 68

Katie the cat 110
kebabs 100–103
   chocolate 100
   dino 103
   jelly 100
   kreepy 75
   marbled 103
   rainbow 103
   sherbet 100
   sprinkle 103
   twirly 100
Kreepy kebabs 75
Krispie balls 127
Krispie caramel cups 127
Krispie cupcakes 124

Lady with a handbag 80
Lady with a hat 81
Ladybirds 110
Ladybirds 59
Lamington train 16
Lamingtons 10
Layered chocolate fudge 26
Lego blocks 140
Little drummer boy 63
Little figures 60–69
   blue boy 64
   cone-arm man 67
   crazy clown 63
   disco dancer 69
   flipper foot 65
   jolly dolly 68
   little drummer boy 63
   marshmallow Maggie 62
   Miss Fizzer 65
   Mr Allsorts 64
   rocket man 68
   skeleton Sam 69
   snow ghost 66
   twista man 62
   uptown girl 66
   water bug 67
Little lambs 97
lollies, butterfly 37
   lollipop trees 40
   marshmallow love 29
   mini princess 43
Lollipop trees 40
Love bugs 29
Love treats 24–31
   chocolate and marshmallow surprise 26
   chocolate spoons 29
   layered chocolate fudge 26
   love bugs 29
   marshmallow love lollies 29
   Sweetie Pie for your darling 31

Mallow flowers 115
Mallow mermaids 54
Marbled kebabs 103
Marie biscuits 104–121
   bee biscuits 109
   bookworms 121
   butterfly biscuits 109
   clown faces 106
   cowabunga 112
   crawly crabs 112
   crunchy bugs 109
   curious clams 106
   daisy delights 115
   dinosaur days 119
   feeesh 112
   fireworks 116
   funny faces 119
   girls 'n guys 119
   Jelly Tot flowers 115
   Katie the cat 110
   ladybirds 110
   mallow flowers 115
   marshmallow sandwich 116
   Percy piglet 110
   springtime 116
   tick tock clock 121
Marshmallow bunnies 94
marshmallow kebabs 100–103
Marshmallow lollipops 98
Marshmallow love bears 94
Marshmallow love lollies 29
Marshmallow Maggie 62
Marshmallow mice 51
Marshmallow name lollies 98
Marshmallow sandwich 116
Marshmallow snails 49
Marshmallow trains 18
Marshmallow worms 50
Marshmallows 92–103
   bunnies 94
   chirpy chicks 97
   chocolate suprise 26
   flowers 116
   hoppity bunnies 96
   kebabs 100–103
   Little lambs 97
   love bears 94
   love lollies 29
   lollipops 98
   name lollies 98
   mice 51
   mini treats 37
   pink piglets 96
   rainbow mini marshmallows 98
   sandwich 116
   snails 49
   trains 18
   worms 50
mice, coconut 51

marshmallow 51
Mini marshmallow treats 37
Mini princess lollies 43
Miscellaneous 132–141
  caramel cones 141
  chocolate nests 138
  chocolate paintboxes 134
  chocolatey bread 134
  energy injections 137
  jelly pops 137
  Jelly Tot fudge 138
  lego blocks 140
  name biscuits 138
  painted biscuits 134
  photo biscuits 137
  sherbet cones 141
  traffic lights 140
Miss Fizzer 65
Mock rice cakes 126
Monkeys 87
Moths 59
Mr Allsorts 64

Name biscuits 138

Octopuses 53
One-eyed aliens 84
Oreo flowers 37

Painted biscuits 134
Peacocks 52
Pearly princess 82
Penguin on an igloo 55
Percy piglet 110
Photo biscuits 137
Pigs 88
Pink piglets 96
Princesses 34
Princesses and tea parties 32–45
  baskets 38
  bundles of biscuits 38
  butterfly lollies 37
  coconut ice balls 40
  coconut ice with a difference 40
  decorated sugar cubes 41
  dipped wafer biscuits 38
  forest log 34
  fun Sweetie Pies 41
  hats 43
  hot chocolate cups 37
  lollipop trees 40
  mini marshmallow treats 37
  mini princess lollies 43
  Oreo flowers 37

  princesses 34
  sweet bracelets 41
  tea cups 38
  Twinkies with a difference 43

Rainbow kebabs 103
Rainbow mini marshmallows 98
Rice Krispies 122–131
  bear faces 128
  chocolate hearts 126
  colourful Krispie cups 127
  crunchy worms 128
  flowers and butterflies 126
  freight train 124
  hen and chicks 130
  Krispie balls 127
  Krispie caramel cups 127
  Krispie cupcakes 124
  mock rice cakes 126
  seashore scene 124
  smiley spiders 128
  tree stumps 128
Rice Krispies flowers 126
Rice Krispies squares 11
Robots 72
Rock stars 83
Rocket man 68
Royal icing 8

Sailboats 21
sea creatures, crabs 53
  crawly crabs 112
  curious clams 106
  feeesh 112
  mallow mermaids 54
  octopuses 53
  penguin on an igloo 55
  stingrays 55
  turtles 54
Seashore scene 124
Sherbet cones 141
Sherbet kebabs 100
Skeleton Sam 69
Slime balls 75
Slime cups 75
Smiley spiders 128
Snails 58
  marshmallow 49
  Sweetie Pie 49
  Swiss roll 48
Snow ghost 66
Space dwarves 76
Spaceships 84
Speedy beetles 56

Spiders 58
Sports cars 18
spotty dogs (see Dalmations)
Springtime 116
Sprinkle kebabs 103
Ssssnake skewers 75
Stingrays 55
Sweet bracelets 41
Sweetie Pie for your darling 31
Sweetie Pie snails 49
sweetie pie, igloo 55
  for your darling 31
  fun 41
  snails 49
Swiss roll snails 48

Tea cups 38
Tick tock clock 121
Tractors 16
Traffic lights 140
trains, freight 124
  lamington 16
  marshmallow 18
Tree stumps 128
Trees 91
  lollipop 40
Turtles 54
Twinkies with a difference 43
Twirly kebabs 100
Twista man 62

Uptown girl 66

Vases 91
vehicles 18–21
Vehicles, planes and trains 14–23
  aeroplanes 22
  chocolate 4x4 21
  F1 cars 18
  helicopters 22
  jeep with trailer 21
  lamington train 16
  marshmallow trains 18
  sailboats 21
  sports cars 18
  tractors 16
Volcanoes 89
Water bug 67

Windmills 90
Worms 58
worms, 58
  chocolate 50
  marshmallow 50